We Grew Up Fast

Recollections of the Second World War
1939-1945

As told to Eleanor Clarke
by men and women of
Chorleywood

ec books

2008

We Grew Up Fast. Copyright © 2008 Eleanor Clarke
Published by ec books, 27 Solesbridge Lane, Chorleywood WD3 5SN

Typeset in Garamond

Printed in England by think-ink

A catalogue record for this book is available from the British Library

ISBN 978 0 9558696 0 0

Cover photograph Ann Turner 1942

CONTENTS

Introduction

It all started on a bus. Sitting next to Barbara, she told me about her time in the ATS. That story must be shared, I thought. I remembered that Patsy had told me about her childhood interned by the Japanese in Shanghai, and that Frank had been a prisoner-of-war in Formosa. I started asking around, and soon was hearing tales of adventure and courage, and of everyday happenings during those wartime years.

I visited my contributors in their homes, and recorded what they had to tell me. I wrote out what they had said, we met again and discussed what could be left out and what must stay in. This book is a compilation of these conversations. It is not a carefully researched historical document, neither is it a meticulously crafted essay. These are the recollections of the war years as spoken by people who lived through them, and I hope you will hear their individual voices. Photographic film was scarce during the war, some people have no pictures. All my contributors live or have lived in and around the small Hertfordshire town of Chorleywood.

I am grateful to many people for help in the preparation of this book. Jan Moore, Jo Clarke, Rachel Clarke, Iona Copley and Paul Hanson have given support and wise advice. I also thank Janet Anders, Sally Cherry, Gill Collison and Jill Leeming for proof-reading, and Stephen and Simone Binks of Robsons Estate Agency for generous sponsorship.

My especial thanks are to the men and women who have given their time and their interest in recalling their memories of the war years, and to these, my friends pictured within, I dedicate this book.

Eleanor Clarke
May 2008

Barbara Allen

When I left school, my father insisted I do shorthand typing which I hated, but I got a job at a tuberculosis clinic, clerking; I kept trying to do nursing, and joined the Red Cross.

Coventry blitz

I lived in Coventry, and was there for both the blitzes. We had three land mines near my home. On the night of the blitz I was making coffee to keep us going through the night when suddenly there was this enormous explosion, the doors were blown open, I was blown across the room, all the windows were blown out, the roof lifted and came down again. We went to a neighbour's house, she had a big hall which she had reinforced. Gas and water were cut off for the whole street, but we boarded up the windows and went on living there. After a while we would go each evening to a farm in Kenilworth where we slept on mattresses on the floor, but my father stayed at our house to keep an eye on what was going on in the road. We had a solid fuel range in the kitchen, so I was cooking for all the neighbours because there was no gas, and we had to get water from a standpipe. This went on for weeks, with the windows boarded up and the roof leaking.

On the night of the Coventry blitz, once the All Clear had sounded, a Red Cross friend and I walked to the hospital to help out.

On the way we passed Owen Owens, a big department store, and one of the huge plate glass windows fell out, which was quite scary.

Nursing in Birmingham

In January 1941, I went to the new Queen Elizabeth hospital and started nursing properly. We had the Birmingham blitz, and later became a military hospital receiving casualties from France; the hospital had been bombed and there was a great shortage of bedding. Food was pretty awful, you took in your own food, three jars of rations, one for jam, one for butter, one for sugar. We worked double shifts, eight hours on, eight hours off. When the soldiers came back from Dunkirk we received the wounded. At first it was the less severe injuries, and they wanted bacon and eggs, but later those with worse injuries arrived. We also had German prisoners of war, who were kept right away in a separate ward, and nurses were asked if they were willing to care for them; some had family who had suffered, and they could choose not to nurse the Germans. Mother had cancer and I went to care for her for a year so I got behind in nursing, but caught up later.

I was back on the wards as a Staff Nurse when Frank came in, invalided back from India. We fell in love with each other, and eventually got married. You had to do further training or go into the forces, so I went to Edgware General, which was a horror, to do midwifery. You were sometimes sent out with the ambulance to bring the mother in. One night I got to a girl who was far on in labour, she said she had no doctor as she had only just moved into the area. Everywhere was filthy, and I'd never even opened the delivery case before, but having watched deliveries in the hospital, I was able to deliver this baby, and eventually the sister of the ward arrived.

So when I had my first baby, I decided to have it at home. We had a nurse to whom we paid three guineas a week, she did absolutely everything. One evening Frank came home having called at the butcher's to see if there was any meat, and he had been given a sheep's head. This marvelous retired sister knew just what to do with it, but she did say 'Never do that to me again'. We kept chickens and ducks for eggs, the rationing was pretty grim.

Frank Allen

In 1939 I was 19 and about to go to Keble College, Oxford to read classics. I could get my BA after three terms plus five in military service. I lived south of Birmingham, my father having retired to the Lickey Hills, and in the early days of the war our area was considered safe to receive evacuees. My mother was horrified to discover she had been allocated a woman with a small rather dirty child and she didn't know where to put them. In our garden was a well built outhouse, and she decided they could live there. The woman clearly didn't think much of this, so she phoned her husband and asked him to come and get her, which he did that evening to the great relief of everyone

Call up and embarkation

I was called up into the Army in 1940 and joined the Worcestershire Regiment. We were sent to a squalid camp outside Droitwich, to buildings which had been prepared for evacuated civil servants' offices and were not intended to be residential. There was terrible weather that winter, in these little huts with inadequate sewers, so we were sent home on a fortnight's unpaid leave whilst they cleared the drains. When I passed out Class B, I was posted to the 7th Battalion Coastal Defence at Goole in Yorkshire. Next I went to train in Signals at Catterick for six weeks. Then the whole division was sent to Aldlestrop and Daylesford. The locals said 'You'll be off to India soon, they always come here first.' We spent some weeks doing training exercises all over the countryside, then were kitted out in khaki drill but still not told where we were going. We went by train to Liverpool to a marvellous passenger ship which normally ran from England to South America, it hadn't been altered so as officers we lived in great style. It was a very long voyage, out into the Atlantic in a convoy.

When we arrived in Cape Town, we heard that the lot before us had gone on to Singapore and had all been captured by the Japanese. After a year of rationing in England, here food was plentiful and there was marvellous hospitality. Walking down the street one evening, some people called out to me and invited me to join them for an evening meal and the theatre. I asked why did they ask me? They said they were so ashamed that when war broke out they weren't the first to offer to join in defence of the British Empire, so they were making amends.

India training

We were soon back on the ship making for who knew where. Past Madagascar I woke one morning to silence instead of all the noise of a convoy. It had been decided that our ship being very fast, we could sail safely on ahead and finish up in Bombay where we disembarked. The west coast of India is very beautiful but we were given really tough training, learning how to live underground or in the trees. I succumbed to anaemia and was sent on sick leave to South India, to Ootacamund in the Nilgiri Hills. It was very beautiful, and there the authorities lost track of me. I was living in the very expensive former house of a businessman, which had been requisitioned and I had a wonderful holiday playing golf for two or three months, till one of my fellow officers from Bombay turned up, also on sick leave. I had almost forgotten them; I was getting my pay sent and just living in luxury. My conscience got the better of me and I wrote to Bombay and asked ought I to do something. They wrote back and admitted they had lost track of me but would I go back to Bombay.

There the soldiers were living in tents on the seashore, on a beautiful sandy coast. We were learning to swim, had amphibious training and became the chosen instruments of Mountbatten, Commander South East Asia. He shook things up a bit. We had been in the pre-war habit of everything stopping at lunchtime for a sleep from noon till four, but Mountbatten pointed out that the Japanese would still blow us up even if it were the afternoon. We were learning to climb nets to get onto ships, it was all rather exciting. We were due to go to the Andaman Islands but the Japanese rushed though Burma and crossed into Assam, in British India, so we were sent there instead. Our train took five days to cross India, because so many people were coming the other way. Arriving in jungly country, overnight we changed from being highly mechanised troops to dependence on horseborne transport. Our transport officer found himself with 50 mules, he had never even seen one before.

4

Kohima

Mountbatten came to inspect us and as Liason Officer I was detailed to go on my motor-bike, meet him and show him where to go. As I rode along the rough road, suddenly there was a cloud of dust and his convoy with all his motor-cyclists came whirling past, knowing exactly where to go, so I tagged along at the back.

Assam was a nasty place in the war, jungly and mountainous at 7000 feet, and monsoon time was approaching. We were still doing peace-time training and when we plunged into the country on April Fool's Day 1944, no one really knew where we were. This was Kohima, once a colonial outpost and the gateway to Burma. One day there were loud explosions and we realised this was not a training exercise but the Japanese actually firing at us. I was to take a message to another Brigadier, and whilst making our way gingerly, there was a very loud explosion. My Brigadier said I'd better take cover, but I, being still in training mode, asked why? 'Those are real shells,' he said, 'from the Japanese.' The first casualty was the Roman Catholic padre, just happened to be in the way and was blown to pieces.

We realised then that we really were in the war. Kohima was a key place, and there the 14th Army became known as General Slim's Forgotten Army, and had the bloodiest fighting of the war. I was in Brigade Headquarters, a bit safer, so I never had to use my bayonet against the Japanese. We were there for weeks; the troops had a terrible time.

Japanese attack

The BBC, realising there was this huge army nobody was hearing about, sent a reporter and I was detailed to show him round. We were right opposite a mound under which lived some Japanese. We used to wheel out the gun and point it at the mound. It didn't really do anything, just blew up some soil. Then we realised the Japanese were firing back at us, so the BBC man and I took cover as best we could. The Japanese would shell for about quarter of an hour and then stop. I found a hole which someone had previously dug, it had corrugated iron and earth over the top, you could just see out, and the reporter found somewhere else. Then something happened – and I thought, I'm dead, I wonder if

I'll see Grandpa. After a minute or two my eyes opened and I realised I wasn't dead, I wasn't seeing Grandpa, but an enemy shell had made a direct hit on my hole which had collapsed around me. I couldn't move much and looking around there was a lot of blood. Beside me was a man, kneeling as I had been, absolutely motionless – because he was dead. On my other side was a soldier who moved a bit, so I tried to speak to him, but he just gave a gulp and died. I panicked a bit and started shouting 'Help, help'. A voice said 'All right, all right', it was one of the very brave stretcher-bearers, but at that moment they couldn't do anything because there was a lot of firing going on. When they got to me and dug me out I was only half-conscious, I had a fractured skull and a lot of other wounds. They took me to a field hospital which was just a bamboo building, and there a surgeon operated and lifted a bit of bone which was pressing on my brain.

Journey back to England

There I stayed till they got the services in that part of India organised. We only survived in the jungle because the Americans were dropping food and fuel by parachute. One of our brigadiers had been hit by a tin of bully beef and it broke his ribs. It took me weeks to get across India by all sorts of different transport, sailing down the Brahmaputra River towards Calcutta, then local trains stopping everywhere, ending up in Poona General hospital. That was where the badly wounded had to wait for repatriation. More and more of us were accumulating, one man waited a year with a terribly injured leg. I envied the casualties from Europe – they got sent home much more quickly.

Eventually I got a place on a New Zealand hospital ship, it was very fine but it only went as far as Suez. By now I was walking, and we were bundled out of this ship and into the Egyptian desert to a hospital in Tel el Kebir. We were there two months, still in the same condition as when we were in India but I was well enough to make a trip to Cairo. When it came to Remembrance Day 1944 I was given a bag to collect money and there were Italian prisoners of war there so I got some money from them as well, even though they were the enemy. Because we had come from India, we had to wait till all the people from Africa who had got there before us had gone on ahead. Then I got on this marvellous Dutch luxury liner at Port Said, this was its first trip across the Mediterranean and so at last to England, though all my mates were still slugging it out in Assam and Burma.

English hospital

The wounded were sent first to major hospitals with the plan that we should then be sent on to a hospital near our home. As I was in Birmingham, I could actually see my family house up on the hill. In that hospital I met Barbara, who was a Staff Nurse, so I didn't want to go anywhere else. We had got used to the very lax discipline in the military hospitals, but here Matron was like a Major-General and you had to do what she said. They had a lease-lend American brain surgeon, who decided he should operate again on my head, so he dug it all up and raised the bone a bit more. I was downgraded from A to C which meant desk duties only. By this time we were getting all the casualties from the European war. The men used to creep up to me as I lay there, all yellow, to ask what was it like in India, as they were expecting to be sent there. I told them it was horrible.

Vienna

I had a cousin who worked in the War Office and he got me a job in the Allied Commission for Austria. I was billeted in a suburb of Vienna, it was a help to the family because I brought in extra rations and they were very short of food, there was so much starvation and illness in the city. One of the first things the Commission did was to restore the tram system for the city, which went right out into the countryside. One sunny Sunday morning I had some free time, and decided to go right to the end of the line, about 20 miles into open country. I went for a little walk, then realised I needed to get back. I could see the tram station across a field and decided to make a short cut there. What I didn't realise was that I had come into the Russian zone and that this field was in fact a Russian Army transport depot. I decided to keep on walking to the barrier where there was a sentry. I tried to ask him to lift his barrier, but he didn't speak any English, so he sent for the sergeant, who was no better, so he got a junior officer who marched me to a building to his commandant. I began to get a bit nervous, nobody knew where I was and anything could happen. I had a card which said in four languages that I was a member of the Allied Commission for Austria, and this got them even more agitated and they decided to send me to the local Headquarters. There was an English lady interpreter who spoke Russian so I told her what had happened, and asked to use the telephone. I phoned my liaison officer in Vienna, told them where I was and how I had got there, that I thought I would be all right but if I didn't turn up would they come and get me. The Russian officers said they would send me to the Russian HQ in the centre of Vienna. When I asked how did I get there, they said 'On the tram'. The little soldier I had first met was detailed to take me, I made friends with him and gave him cigarettes. He knew nothing about the tramway so I decided I was in command. When we got to the stop nearest to my base I got off and he followed me to the door of our mess where it was Sunday lunchtime. When the housekeeper opened the door I asked her to give him a jolly good dinner downstairs whilst I went up to dine with my friends. We didn't know quite what to do with him, but the Russians loved forms and paperwork so we got a girl to type out a letter saying 'To the Russian Commander, received with thanks one English officer, Frank Allen', gave it to him, marched him down to the tram stop and put him back on a tram. Two days later, there came a Red Cap into my office, and said he was looking for Lieutenant Allen. So I said 'That's me'. He was most surprised as they had had a message that I had been abducted by the Russians who couldn't produce me. I always felt bad about the little Russian chap, I never found out what happened to him.

Afterwards

I was beginning to wonder what to do when I got out of uniform. There was a booklet about jobs in the Civil Service which all sounded a bit boring, but a small item said there were jobs going in the House of Commons, and to apply to the Clerk, so I did. I took the Civil Service exam, but they were so short of staff that I started working there whilst still in uniform. After a while they told me I had passed the exam and could begin working officially, and I remained as a Clerk in the House of Commons for the next 39 years.

Frank Allen died in 2007

Jo Ankers

Liverpool bombing

I was 17 years old when World War II broke out, living with my family in Liverpool and working for Cunard White Star as a telephonist, a reserved occupation. During the heavy bombing of the docks and railways, my brother was an Air Raid Warden and out most nights. One night there had been a lull in the bombing, and I went with a friend to the cinema. A raid started whilst we were in there, we could hear the bombs, but most people just stayed put even after the film ended. The management played music and sold drinks, and it was about two in the morning when it was quiet enough to come out. There was bomb damage everywhere, and I wondered how to get the four miles through the blackout to my home. I walked to the Ribble bus station, got into a bus along with a lot of other people and waited for it to start. Then a man appeared in a tin hat and called out my name – it was my brother, come to look for me! My first question was whether I was expected to ride on the back of his motorbike, which would terrify me, but after calling me an ungrateful wretch he said he had come with my boyfriend in his car.

My brother insisted that the least I could do was to become an Air Raid Warden myself, though I think this was chiefly to make up a four for card games when sitting in the ARP (Air Raid Precautions) hut waiting for action. The worst of the bombing was over by now, and when I was released from my job with Cunard, I volunteered for the WRNS. The only categories vacant were for stewards, cooks and messengers, none of which appealed much, but messenger seemed the most interesting of the three.

Call-up

I was sent to Mill Hill to be vetted for my suitability. After some days of square bashing, scrubbing, polishing and so on, I was interviewed and asked why was I applying to be a messenger, when they were crying out for qualified telephone operators! We were then enrolled and given our uniforms – and unlike the ATS and WAAF, after our initial issue, repairs and replacements had to be paid for. We were given 'chits' in lieu of clothing coupons to buy underwear, pyjamas and so on.

WRNS in Scotland

I was posted as a telephonist to the wilds of Scotland (after expressing a wish to be sent to Liverpool). I arrived at the end of a long, dark and bitterly cold journey in late December to find myself billeted in half of a large house near the edge of Loch Long – a deep water loch, being developed as a submarine base and for Beach Commando training operations. I can't remember seeing the place in daylight. To one side of the path to my office ran a steep drop to a river, and on the other there was a ghostly wood and my irreplaceable Number 8 torch battery soon ran out. Pot holes and tree roots made the journey a nightmare.

Fortunately, after a week a Wren Officer popped her head round the door and asked if anyone would like a posting to the Isle of Arran. I didn't know or care where the Isle of Arran was but I quickly volunteered.

The Isle of Arran was a small and lovely island in the Clyde, guarding the boom defence to make it a safe haven for shipping approaching the docks. I spent nearly a year there, until my next posting to a Gunnery School in Liverpool, billeted in an ancient hospital requisitioned by the Navy. A year later I was sent to a place overlooking the Mersey where the gunnery practice took place – shooting at targets called drogues, trailed by planes. We couldn't hear the telephones for the noise and were constantly being told off by callers for not answering. If you were lucky you might find a drogue shot down on the shore – they were made of bright red nylon and could be washed and made into raincoats or skirts by the nimble-fingered. My last posting was to Warrington for a few months when, mercifully, the war ended and so did my Wren career.

I have many memories of my time in the Wrens, both happy and sad. I'm glad I was able to share the camaraderie of service life and, however small a part I played, I wouldn't have missed it.

11

Frank Ashby

In 1939, I was 19, living in Watford and had been working for a year as a Civil Servant in the National Debt office in the City. I remember Chamberlain's speech on 3 September. We went into the park near my home, the air-raid siren sounded, people were dashing around, not sure what to do. There were great plans to move government offices out of London; we were given instructions to stop at home at the outbreak of war, and be ready to go to Watford Junction with suitcases. Next we were told to report to the Post Office, who didn't know what it was all about. Then the office phoned and told me to come to work as usual, our boss having refused a request to go to Lytham St Annes. I had to go and get gas masks for the family and used to do fire watching in our office, but otherwise life continued normally.

Call up

I registered for service and in April 1940 was called into the Royal Corps of Signals. I had a rail pass to Richmond, the station for Catterick, though I had been told to go to Whitby. Catterick didn't know anything about me so the next day I went back to Whitby. It took a few days for them to sort out what I was meant to be doing. Summer 1940 was very hot, we had a month's square bashing, living in boarding houses on the sea front, and later in Abbey House on top of the cliffs next to the Abbey. By day we went into the town, attending lectures on radio, telephones and so on, nights we were on the cliffs looking out for the invasion which was thought to be imminent. Then the Army decided Signals would be no good at fighting if the Germans did invade, so we were sent to Huddersfield to finish our training.

Embarkation

Having trained as an electrician in signals, I was then attached to a unit at Bakewell, doing telephone and radio repairs. We had embarkation leave, though we didn't know where we were going. After Christmas 1940, I went by train to Glasgow then onto the SS *Empress of Japan*. We were two months on the ship, and I had my twenty-first birthday moored off Freetown; we celebrated with a tin of sweets. Then to Cape Town, where we visited friends and went sight seeing. We still didn't know where we were going, though we were advised to buy strong sunglasses. Our next stop was Bombay, then on to Singapore for a month.

Malaya

By March 1941 I was driving a radio truck which carried a transmitter and receiver, four operators and me as technician and driver. We drove north for three days, to Sungei Patani, to become the 11th Indian Divisional Signals. Then a further 50 miles towards the Thai border, where we were attached to an Infantry brigade, passing signals back to Divisional HQ. I looked after the lorry and signals equipment. I had a small generator engine to charge the batteries, which was unreliable, and it was difficult to get radio signals because of the high rubber trees. Once I had to go to

Singapore by train to collect another lorry and drive it back. Then I got tropical ulcers on my leg, and was sent back to hospital at divisional HQ for three weeks, before going again to Sungei Patani.

In the summer of 1941 we knew something was brewing, and in the autumn we were moved north again. On 8 December the Japanese invaded from Thailand and along the east coast of Malaya, and we retreated. I was driving the signals truck on its own down the road, when a Japanese plane flew low and machine-gunned us. I stopped, got out and crouched behind a rubber tree. There were gouts of rubber coming out from bullet holes in the tree trunks around me. One man broke his leg jumping out of the truck. We got him to an ambulance but later he died. Through December and January we were retreating down the Malay peninsula, and I crossed the causeway into Singapore on 31 January 1942. I was driving in bright moonlight when I came suddenly into shade, the road curved and my truck ended up in a ditch, till a rescue vehicle came and towed me out. Singapore had been braced for an attack by sea, but was totally unprepared for a land invasion from the north.

Singapore

There was very little defence, no air support, a lot of ground troops, but no great sense of urgency. The battleship *Prince of Wales* and battle cruiser *Repulse* had earlier been sent out but had been sunk. In February 1942, I got malaria and ended up in a civilian hospital. On 15 February, Singapore surrendered. The Japs went round bayoneting and machine-gunning doctors and patients in the military hospital, it was just luck that I was in a civilian one. The Japanese were overwhelmed by the number of prisoners. They cordoned off the area of Changi where there had been permanent barracks in long single-storey buildings, and marched the troops the 15 miles there. As I was sick I managed to get a lift in a truck. We rapidly ran short of food.

In Changi, the Japanese wanted us to sign a form saying we wouldn't try to escape, but the officers said that this was against army regulations. The Japs then put 20,000 of us into Selerang camp, which had been built for 1,200 so it was appallingly overcrowded. I spent my time there digging latrine trenches. In the end we were given a letter from the senior British officer saying we had signed under duress and were exempted from army regulations for this. The 18th division had arrived in February, just in time to be taken prisoner. Many were from Cambridge, they set up a university and I took a maths course. I was on the anti-malarial squad, putting stuff on stagnant water. The Japanese put pressure on the Indians to be anti-British.

All was quiet through the summer of 1942, then they started moving groups of people away. My unit was put onto a Japanese cargo ship, though first we had to be fumigated with disinfectant in an enormous bath. We were put in the ship's hold on shelves, 1000 prisoners of war and 1000 Japanese soldiers going home. On this ship, a platform was fixed over the side and you had to sit on that to open your bowels; most of us had diarrhoea, and some died. The ship was built in Cleveland, which gave me some confidence.

Prison camp, Formosa

It was a hell ship, and after two or three weeks we ended up in Keelung, on the island of Formosa (now called Taiwan) in November 1942. We were taken to purpose-built wooden army barracks, with a bamboo fence around. We lived in a bunk-house, furnished with two platforms six foot wide, and a three foot table in the middle. After breakfast we did heavy navvying jobs which had no apparent use, loading dirt onto bamboo stretchers and carrying it to another place, apparently landscaping a park. We were moved to different camps around Formosa though I never understood why. I went to an agricultural camp, first diverting the course of a river, then digging. The work was very hard, we were in poor health and food was short. There was a fair amount of brutality and I was sometimes knocked about. I developed beri-beri, and was lucky that there was a British medical officer who protected me. I then got a deep vein thrombosis in my leg from immobility. We still moved round various camps, one was flooded during a typhoon and had to be evacuated. I ended up in a camp where there were many who had been sick, also a lot of officers, and here we worked in paddy fields. I went down to about six stone. When someone died, we dug a grave outside the camp. The padre wanted singing, and as the only hymn we all knew was *Silent Night* we sang this at all the funerals. It is still my least favourite carol.

We had no news, no information on the European war, though there were always stories and rumours. There was little communication with home. We had post cards, with ticked boxes to say I was well, give regards to so and so. My family had been told I was missing, then by June 1943 they got confirmation that I was a prisoner-of-war, and began getting these postcards from me. These took months to get there, and I also had official postcards from them. We had the *Nippon Times*, a paper published by Japs, which included a column 'from the Fuhrer'. There was nothing about Europe though it gave some indication of the war on the Russian front. At the final camp in April and May 1945, we were getting air attacks from American planes which were bombing a town ten miles away. I worked for a time in the library repairing books as I was unfit for physical work. One day, the camp interpreter came in and said he didn't understand why Churchill had given up as Prime Minister, and that someone called Atlee had taken over. I was the only British man there, and I knew Atlee had been leader of the opposition Labour Party. He could only be Prime Minister if there had been a general election. An American chap said if there's been a general election it means we must have won the war in Europe. Then the interpreter thought he had said too much and scuttled out, but now we knew the European war was over.

End of hostilities

Sometimes the Japs would give us treats, we didn't know why. One day in August they said we were not going to work, and we were given an extra issue of food and the luxury of peanuts. Three days later we were called onto the field and the Japanese commandant said the war was over and he hoped we would all get home safely. He wasn't a brutal man. The padre held a church service, mostly for the British. The Jap guards disappeared, and we just carried on for a few days. We heard there had been heavy bombing of Japan, but didn't know about the atom bomb. American planes dropped canisters of food and cigarettes, one canister went through the roof of our hospital and killed a man, so after that food was dropped outside. Then a few US troops arrived, and

16

we went north by overnight train to another camp near the capital. A week later we embarked onto an American destroyer, which took us out to sea to an aircraft carrier. We transferred by launch, in a rough sea, and a big American sailor grabbed me and hauled me onto the deck. They had cleared the hangar deck and laid out mattresses, with clean clothes, tooth brush and paste. We started eating a lot. At breakfast, there were eggs, we hadn't seen an egg for three years, and each man was given four of them. We sailed to Manila, to a US Army camp then to a hospital, where the doctor told me to eat what I liked. Two days later I was very sick, but from then on everything was fine. I weighed eight stone when I entered the hospital, eleven when I came out three weeks later. We then sailed in an American Liberty Ship, with bunks four high, not very comfortable. The ship broke down in mid-Pacific, the story was that the American naval engineers got drunk, and didn't notice something overheating, but the British engineers went and sorted it out and we got sailing again. We landed in San Francisco and were taken to Angel Island, an old US Army fort, where we had our first contact with the British army, and got British Army uniforms. We were not allowed into the town

Journey home

We were taken to Oakland, and put on a hospital train to Tacoma in Washington State, where we had one day free. We were for the first time in a normal town, and we had some money, though once we got into British jurisdiction, the treasury allowed us no more foreign currency. We boarded a normal Canadian train to New York, then embarked on the *Queen Mary*. An officer came on the tannoy and said 'Report to restaurant to serve food' but we said no, we'd been prisoners all those years, someone could come and serve us. Then another officer said 'Come on chaps, we've got to get this ship organised, would you come and give us a hand' so of course everyone did. There were some civilians on board who objected to the troops having free access around the ship. They complained to the Captain, who said 'They can go anywhere provided they keep off my bloody bridge.' We arrived in Southampton, and should have stayed there two days but I got a train to Waterloo, and then on to Watford. I had been able to telephone my father and he met me at the station.

Afterwards

I had leave from November 1945, was passed fit at a perfunctory medical, and was due for de-mob in May 1946. In fact I went back to my old job in March, and because the Army pay was less than the Civil Service, I got a balance of pay which was quite a lot of money. Some people were actually jealous of me.

The hardships in the camps were hard work, and lack of food and medical care. I didn't meet much brutality, though many friends died. Japanese culture is quite brutal – an officer would strike a junior if he were at fault, and he would strike the next one down and the prisoners were the bottom of the heap. Sometimes men got gloomy, gave up and died. We had a feeling that the war would end in six months, then we kept extending the six months. I read a lot, we had books sent in by the Red Cross and played Monopoly – the Shanghai version.

After I got home my mother, who had three sons safely back from the war, had a stroke in July 1946, and died within 24 hours. My brothers had left home, and my father expected me to run the house as well as going to work. Once the euphoria of being free had faded, it wasn't an easy time.

Eileen Axam

In the 1930s, I was living in Southall where my father was a coal merchant, as his father had been before him. He had four big horses to pull the carts, and my mother worked in the office. I left school in 1940 when I was 14 and worked in an ironmonger's shop in Southall. The bombing had started in London, and we had an Anderson shelter in the garden where we all went at night. There was a bomb just down our street, we thought it was in our back garden it sounded so near. During the war coal was rationed, and my father never knew when he would get deliveries. Maybe you'd get two or three trucks at once, it all had to be emptied and some ended up in our back garden. Sometimes people would climb over the fence and pinch some, so my father whitewashed the wall.

WRNS

I really wanted to join up, and when I was 17 ½ in 1943 I joined the WRNS and went to Portsmouth. I had been an only child so I thought this would be company, and I really enjoyed it. There were terrible raids in Portsmouth, we went to bed in our underclothes and when the sirens went we had to get out of our beds and lie underneath them, the floor was very hard. My job was to look after Sir Bertram Ramsey, who was an important man in the Navy. He had a butler as well, but I used to clean Sir Bertram's shoes and iron his shirts, I was shown how to iron shirts properly. He'd give me a little list to go down the shops and get things and he would give me sixpence for myself. He was lovely. I used to go down to the docks and see all the lads going off, it was awful, those poor lads, they never smiled, they never talked.

Wartime wedding

I'd met my husband before the war. He was an electrician and did all sorts of things, work of national importance so he wasn't called up, though he wanted to be. He could get down to Portsmouth by train to see me, so I wasn't interested in all the sailors there were around. We got engaged when I was 18, and were married in Southall on Boxing Day 1943. It was the same day my parents had got married. The lady across the road was a dressmaker, you could get material without coupons and she made me this lovely two-piece blue suit. The vicar said he was really pleased to see me in that, not shivering in a white frock like other brides. It was cold, very cold. At our reception there was no heating and everyone kept going into the kitchen to get warm. My mother and neighbours saved the sugar ration so I could have a cake with icing.

Wartime baby

I stayed in the WRNS till I got pregnant. My mother used to have soldiers staying in her home for a day or two when they were on leave and she would give them some home cooking. We lived in rented rooms in Southall and my daughter was born there in September 1944. My grandmother delivered her, in the front room, she used to deliver all the babies round us. We had enough food, my husband used to work all over the place, and if someone wanted to give him a tip, it was always food.

When VE-day came, we all celebrated. The news came out in the morning, and we all went out into the street in our nighties.

Birgit Baguley

Weimar childhood

In the 1930s, my parents lived in Munich where my father, Dr Karl-Theodor Lauter was engaged in post-doctoral research. Hitler seized power after the Röhm Putsch on 30 June 1934. My brother Peter was born in May 1935 and by July 1938 my mother had two daughters, Birgit and Sibylle as well. It was a terrible strain on her health but using birth control was a criminal offence. Because of the Nazis my father could not get a position as an archivist in Bavaria and he accepted an invitation from the state of Thuringia at the prestigious Goethe and Schiller Archive in Weimar.

When the war started everyone realised how quickly things had changed, with intimidation and people disappearing. You could not trust anybody. My mother found this out when, after a ladies' gathering for coffee, somebody denounced her. Because we lived in rented accommodation and she was a keen gardener, she had acquired an allotment. Some of the fruit she grew she made into jam and the rest was bottled. She mentioned this whilst drinking coffee with friends, and told them that her harvest this year was prolific and her store would last her even if the war went on longer than two years. A couple of days later some plain clothes men arrived at our door and threatened her, because even suggesting that the war could last more than a few months was a crime, as it would affect morale. Years later she told me that they only left her alone because all three of us children were hanging on her skirt.

My grandfather, a Protestant parson and director of a boarding school in Ansbach, Frankonia, criticised the arrest of a fellow parson in the Church magazine and he was promptly sacked from his position as teacher and director of the school. My grandparents lost their home overnight and came to live with us for a few months, until they bought their own home in Munich. Whilst they were staying with us he christened me.

Bavarian village

My father was called up in 1943 aged 36 and was sent to Vichy France for training. It must have been a terrible ordeal for him, being extremely short sighted and an academic. My mother recalled several occasions were he had to do extra training as punishment because the authorities loathed clever people. That was in April 1943, after Stalingrad. That summer my mother took us to Bavaria, which was her home, to a farm near the Chiemsee. The air-raids had taken their toll and we all needed to recuperate. Every night my mother had to wake us children to go to the cellar for shelter. I got so used to the raids that I woke up even when everything was quiet. Then I would lie awake for hours, and got so desperate not being able to sleep, that I actually prayed to God to make the sirens go off.

I remember my father's last visit. Was it really such a lovely hot summer? That is how I remember the time on the Bavarian farm. We were allowed to help with the hay making, soldiers on leave were ordered to help as well, but at least we were together. With the summer over, we had to go back to Weimar. I was six years old and I had to go to school. My brother was already in the third year.

Father to Russia

On 13 September 1943, my father was told to join his regiment, with orders to go to the Russian front. Whilst on the way there he wrote a letter nearly every day. They travelled across Germany, through Poland into the Ukraine. It took a month because by then troop movement was just chaos. My father's letters, written in pencil, don't reveal much. They must have been stuck for days in trains somewhere, and because every letter was censored, they didn't tell you a lot about what really was going on. What comes over is that he missed his family. He even remembered that I had started school, wanted to know how I was getting on and asked my mother if Peter should learn the violin.

The last letter my mother received from the front was posted on 14 October. Then silence. All letters addressed to my father were coming back. On 19 November at 2pm, two officials came to bring the news that my father, on his first day at the front, was on patrol and had been missing since15 October. Now the long wait started and for years we hoped, though my mother realised the chance that my father might survive in a Russian prison camp was slim.

Munich raids

So my mother at the age of 30 had the responsibility for we three children. My brother was just eight, two years older than I. She started to write everything down to show my father how she coped. What a sad Christmas we had, until my sister collected photographs of my father. A small one wearing the uniform of a private was put in the middle of the advent wreath and a very large one near the Christmas tree. 'Now we are not alone any more' she announced.

My brother was worried about our mother. He was only eight, but he had heard about a lady who lived in our street and had taken pills because her husband was missing at the Front. He tried to stop my mother taking an aspirin, until she realised what was going on in his head. She told him 'You don't really think I would ever leave you, Birgit and Sibylle all alone?' New Year 1944 was marked with more and more air-raids and we spent almost every night in the cellar. My brother's asthma grew worse and my mother took him to a clinic in the Black Forest. To travel by train during that time was very difficult, and the journey took 20 hours because you had to leave the trains during raids.

Illness

Every day we were waiting for news from my father. We had heard stories of missing people being found. We were back in the Bavarian village now, in the summer of 1944, to avoid the air-raids. After the heavy bombardment of Munich in July my grandmother joined us. In August I became desperately ill and the doctor did not recognise that I had appendicitis. He left me for days and wouldn't come, until my grandmother threatened him and I was taken to hospital. My poor mother was not allowed to see me for a nearly a week. The appendix had burst and as a result I had peritonitis. The nurses were all nuns and whenever they met me afterwards they talked about the miracle that I survived. We didn't realise at the time how lucky it was that I had been too sick to travel and go back to school in Weimar. The Russians were moving west, so we stayed in the village until the end of the war in May 1945. I vividly remember the arrival of the American army. They reached our village on 3 May. It was my brother's tenth birthday and we were all told not to go outside. I was confused seeing the adults greeting the tanks with white flags and rejoicing. We children were all frightened and hid under the tables of the hotel. No wonder, as only a few weeks before some American dive-bombers had targeted a herd of cows in the field above the village. To this day I can hear the noise the wounded animals made, and I still have problems with aeroplanes flying in formation.

Afterwards

The war was over but the hardship went on. We counted ourselves lucky because at least we were in the West. All our belongings were still in Weimar, in the Russian sector and it took a long time before my mother received any money. My father was a civil servant, but because he was only 'missing' the Russians blocked the allowances. At the end of the summer we moved to Munich and lived with my father's parents. My mother opened a shop for my grandfather selling office equipment and stationery. Munich lay in ruins and the harsh winters and lack of food took their toll. My grandmother died the following spring and my grandfather three months later. My mother always believed that he died of starvation because he would not accept any extra food. My mother knew that the rations were not enough to survive and used her contacts with the farms where we had stayed to get some extra food. Of course it was illegal, but she could not afford the black market prices in Munich. Half a pound of butter would have cost her a month's salary. I remember being hungry, but I think the cold was worse. Just to think back makes me shiver and I would rather live on simple food than in a cold house.

When my mother's brother came back from the war, and moved with his wife into my grandmother's flat, life became intolerable. My mother found a bombed-out flat, which was being repaired. There was no front door and no lavatory. My mother found both in a ruin and paid the owner, not in money, but with food. 12 eggs was the price for the lavatory. For half a year my sister and I were sent to a wonderful children's home on one of the Bavarian lakes. The owner was an English colonel and it was there I learnt my first English words. His dog was called Beauty, which we all mispronounced. We went to school in the village and by Christmas the flat was ready to move into. We still had little food, but we had our own four walls. When there was a power cut we played Red Indians and the stove which heated the main room became the camp fire.

My father never came home. The Red Cross stopped looking for him after 30 years. We children accepted eventually that he would never come back but we didn't want to think of him in a Russian Gulag. To grieve, we found a little church with a graveyard near our school. My sister and I adopted an unkempt grave and started decorating it with wild flowers. My mother never knew about it and we didn't want to tell her, because we thought it would make her sad. Years later I would watch the newsreels of the war showing the German prisoners being sent home, to look if my father was among them.

Now I am back in Bavaria and it is 2006. I climbed a mountain with my daughter and grandchildren, a mountain my father had climbed often in his youth and with my mother. This peak has a cross which doubles up as a war memorial. We climbed it on 2 August and only then I realised that we would have celebrated my father's one hundredth birthday.

Edna Baines

In 1939, I was married, living in Walkden, near Manchester, and I had one son aged three. My husband was an accountant in local government, and he was also a part-time leading fireman. We moved to Walsall in 1941, and there I started working in a day nursery for children whose mothers were working for the war effort.

Midland day nursery

We had a nursery for children from six months. As a trained nurse I was Deputy Matron and worked with the older children. We used a building belonging to the Baptists. If I were on early shift I would have to catch a bus into Walsall then another to Bloxwich, and then a walk. I had to open up the premises to be ready for the staff, and at half past seven the mothers started bringing in the children. We had two classes of 12 children, and then the babies and toddlers as well. There was a cook who did meals and drinks for them. After lunch we put palliasses onto an open verandah for the children to have a nap.

One boy came in with impetigo, and one or two caught it from him. There was a lady who told us she was desperate for a place for her children, and that she was poor but clean. But when the children arrived they had body lice and head lice. The mother drove two big dray horses for a brewery. We had a doctor who came and gave us treatment for the lice and the impetigo; it was difficult to treat then, we used bright purple Gentian Violet.

The children stayed till five o'clock, but we would often keep them till six, and sometimes the mothers didn't come till seven. When I was on an early turn, my husband would bring my son Bobby to the nursery on his way to work, but if I was in the later shift, I took him there myself.

Coventry blitz

My husband was a fireman in the Coventry blitz. The first night they dropped the explosive incendiaries he didn't see one which had landed behind him and it exploded, severely injuring his leg. He almost died, and it was six months before he could work again. For a long time he was in a plaster cast from his foot to his thigh. He went back to being a fireman as soon as he could, and when the bombers came over Coventry, he would be there on duty.

We had an Anderson shelter in the garden but it used to be running with water so I thought we would be safer inside our terraced house. I had an old-fashioned dining-room table, which we put on its side against the window to protect us from the blast; I've still got it and use it every day. I tried to get home before eight to put Bobby to bed. I would cook my husband's lunch the night before so he could heat it up when he came home for lunch the next day.

Feeding a family

I gave my ration books to a grocery wholesaler, and he would give me whatever he had. If he had any extra, he would divide it round all his customers. Sometimes he would put in a ham shank, we would eat the meat first, and then make soup with carrots and peas and the bone. You could use liquid paraffin as a substitute for fat in a cake.

Keeping hens

My husband got some orange boxes and some netting and made a hen coop. Our next door neighbour was a farmer's son, and he got us some hens, so we had eggs. When I was expecting John, I got out of bed awkwardly and fell so I had difficulty walking. Jim said he would get me some help, and a woman came with a little boy, but he threw stones in the garden and hit one of the hens. Its head was so injured you couldn't see its eye, and its beak was crossed so it couldn't peck up food. I had a hypodermic syringe left over from my mother's illness some years before, and I brought the hen in and put it on top of the wringer – we couldn't lose that hen. I used the syringe to give it food, and some whisky too which seemed to cure it.

When I took my son Bobby to the doctor soon after he was born, the doctor said he had rickets, but I said nonsense, he gets proper food, his father's legs are that shape. The doctor's surgery was next to the house we lived in; until the war maternity cases went to Stafford, but when the war came he opened a little ward and people had their babies there. This was all before the National Health, the doctor sent you the bill and you had to pay it.

I stopped working at the nursery when John was born in 1943. I learnt tailoring, and made clothes for the family, and I also learnt and did upholstery and woodwork. My husband was very good at carpentry, I still use furniture he made.

Doreen Cattermole

Training in Watford

In the 1930s we lived in Whippendell Road in Watford. My dad worked in London, in Mincing Lane. He was in the tea trade, and was also a special constable in Watford. I left school in 1939 when I was 14 and went to Pitmans secretarial college for a year, then I went to work in Bushey. There I met someone who was in the Royal Observer Corps and it sounded so interesting that when I was due for call-up at 18, I applied for that. We trained at the back of the Post Office in Market Street, Watford. This used to be the headquarters, till they moved to a new building in Cassiobury Drive. We were called 'The Eyes and Ears of the Royal Air Force'.

Royal Observer Corps

Once I'd been trained in how to do plotting, I worked at the Centre at Cassiobury. There we were in telephone contact with Posts, which were observer positions all around. The Posts were sheds, some made of wooden boards or corrugated iron, some were brick built, and there the observers looked out for aircraft and telephoned the information back to us. There was a Post in Berry Lane, Rickmansworth, on the hill where the houses are now, it was all open fields then, and another on Kings Langley Common. In the Centre, we had a long-range board on the wall, and a larger scale map on a big table, and we plotted where the planes were. Then there were tellers above us, in a gallery, and they radioed the positions to the relevant areas.

We had a uniform a bit like the WAAF. We worked eight hour shifts, you can imagine it was a nice walk from Whippendell Road right down Cassiobury Drive in the dark. On the opposite corner to our headquarters there was a Yankee camp; they were often three sheets to the wind and would whistle at me. I hated going past, and in the end I started going by the WAAF bus from Market Street.

There were the enemy aircraft coming in, and later the doodlebugs. Also our planes going out, specially the Mosquitoes from Leavesden, and Halifaxes from Handley Page at Park Street. We recorded them all, and passed on the vital information. I enjoyed the life really, then suddenly when the war ended, it was all gone.

A month later I got a job at de Havillands, that was where I met Ken and we got married.

Kenneth Cattermole

Youth in Chorleywood

My Dad was under-gardener for Lady Ela Russell at Chorleywood House and he always carried a gun. We lived in the Fishing Cottage in Chorleywood House grounds, later Lady Ela got us a council house. For a while Dad worked at The Cedars, and then he went back to Chorleywood House and we had a flat in the Lodge. He worked there till Lady Ela died. I went to school at Christ Church, and there I learnt gardening, being taught by both Mr Rupert Stacey and Mr George Stacey from The Cedars. I would have liked to work for them as they were College gardeners, but my father wouldn't let me so I went as second under-gardener to the Artists' Rest Home in Rickmansworth.

De Havillands aircraft works

Before the war came Dad started working as a storeman for de Havillands, and when I was 17 he took me along too. I didn't want to be a storeman I wanted to be a gardener, but it was war and I had to do it. When I was 18 I wanted to go into the navy but I was medically unfit, so went on working at de Havillands, at Park Royal. When I arrived the last Airspeed Oxford was just being taken to Hatfield. Then a large jig arrived, which I recognised as the jig for a wing because I'd made model aircraft in a club in Chorleywood. The foreman didn't believe me, but once we started fitting the planks of wood, the wing of a Mosquito started to take shape and he said 'You were quite right, my old son, it is a wing.' Mrs de Havilland, a nice lady, worked on the wing too, with a group of girls all in brown overalls. They were fisher girls from Southend and Grimsby. The Mosquito was made of balsa wood and plywood; it was very light and was called the Wooden Wonder.

The buildings at Leavesden were just finished when I went to work there, and they'd already got the Merlin engine. I took a look at the stores and found it was a bit of a mess but I knew my dad would sort it out. A lorry came in and the foreman wanted me to get up on it and help, then the rope broke and I fell on the concrete and got concussion and bruises. I hoped I would get the sack, but my dad said I'd got to go and be his assistant in the tool store, he was very strict.

Then the Mosquito fuselage came in on a 60 foot trailer from Aldenham where they were made, and the wings were fitted. We put the self-sealing fuel tanks under the wings, and fitted the twin engines. Then the wheels came, it took two men to move them, and everyone was working hard for the plane to be ready to fly the next day.

They pushed the plane out of the hangar, and the flight engineer tested the engines. Then an Oxford arrived with Geoffrey de Havilland, dressed all in white with a white hat and a parachute on his back. He got into the Mosquito, revved the engines and took off. He flew over Chorleywood, then came back as if he was going to land, but took off again over towards Hatfield. Then he came in again, one engine feathered, stopped, took off again, then came back with the other stopped, touched, then flew off with both engines full. Then he did a dive towards the airfield and all the girls shouted 'Pull out, pull out!' which he did. He put his hand out with his thumb up and flew off to Hatfield. That was our first Mosquito. We built a lot more, then fighter-bombers and Sea Hornets, which were a smaller version of the Mosquito and needed a shorter runway.

One day I saw a hedge moving. It was on wheels, and they had sheep and cows on wheels, all made of straw. It was to make the aerodrome look like a farm. We didn't get bombed, only the runway. After the war I worked at the de Havilland Engine factory, and it was 1959 before I managed to get out and go back to gardening.

Ken Cattermole died in 2008

Bill Cattle

Chorleywood schooldays

In the 1930s, I was a schoolboy living in the Main Lodge of Chorleywood House, where my father was caretaker for Lady Ela Russell. After Lady Ela died in 1936, she left the estate to a cousin in the Bedford family, who never came to live here, but sold the estate to Mr Batty and Mr Darvell. The original idea was to turn it into another Moor Park with a golf course, using the mansion as a club-house and building all round the edges. But Batty rather went off the idea, and Darvell's eldest son, who was to have run it, died so it was put up for sale again. The Council bought the house and so many acres of land, and Hertfordshire County Council and the London County Council joined in and bought the rest of it, early in 1939. My father stayed on as caretaker through all these changes, and I lived in the Lodge for 40 years. When my father died in 1942, my mother took on the job as caretaker till after the war when they got a resident caretaker.

Wartime at Chorleywood House

The big house was set up as a casualty clearing centre by the Red Cross. Sir Thomas Lewis was in charge; he was a London specialist and lived in Loudwater. Then there were voluntary nurses, and two ambulances were kept in the garages. There were never any real patients though, as there wasn't much bombing nearby. The Council moved some of their offices there, but meetings were held in the golf club, it was handy as there was a bar there. The stables were used for waste paper collection.

When the evacuees came to Chorleywood, they went to the Memorial Hall to be sorted. We had one for a while, but it was the phoney war, he went back and we never had another. The problem evacuees, kids that people wouldn't take into their homes, were put upstairs in the House. They had a matron and a couple of helpers to look after them. The kids weren't that bad, but people couldn't get on with them, or maybe they were covered in fleas and lice; someone got dustbins, filled them with disinfectant and scrubbed the kids. The evacuees shared our school, so half the week we were in Christ Church school buildings, and the rest of the time we would be in the Working Men's Club in Solesbridge Lane, or in a big room in The Holt, the house opposite the church which was owned by a school governor. My education was a bit disrupted, and I spent a lot of time gardening on allotments. These were everywhere – in Dog Kennel Lane, behind The Gate pub, and on the corner of Wyatts Road – those were owned by Franklin who had his builders yard where the garage is now. We used to grow potatoes and lots went off to the army. We were all Digging for Victory.

There were ornamental gates to the estate at that time. In the war they took them down for scrap metal, but no-one ever collected them and they just lay at the back of the garages for years. We wanted them to take the railings from in front of our house but they didn't. They did take the gun from the Common – after the first World War, a number of German guns were placed in public parks for children to play on, there was one on the Common, near the hairpin, at Gun Dell. That gun was phosphor bronze, quite expensive stuff. The gun in Rickmansworth was a howitzer and we were jealous because it was bigger than ours.

The summerhouse in Chorleywood House grounds was used by the WVS for sorting rivets. The factory would deliver sacks full, and the WVS sorted then into sizes. The local women used to like the smart uniforms and the commandant lived in The Readings, it was just one house then. My mother was involved in so many jobs as well as being caretaker of the house.

London job

I went to Christ Church School till I was 14. I did take the exam for Watford Technical College, but though I got good marks, they weren't high enough for me to be accepted. I left school at Christmas 1941, and went to work in London. Jack Ryman, who lived near us had a small print works to support his stationery shops. It was in Great Portland Street, with about a dozen workers. My job was arranged by Mrs Oldham, a great friend of the Rymans who knew my mother, and used to organise the nurses and the WVS in Chorleywood House. She asked what was I going to do when I left school and I said I thought I'd go for a job as a painter. She said I could do better than that, and Jack would surely find me a place, so I took an apprenticeship in his firm. I went on the train; it was very easy, almost door-to-door. We were in the basement, with a clothing factory above us. Once I was 16 I would do fire-watching, you got ten bob a night for that, well worth having as my father had died and extra money came in handy. Jack was a good bloke to work for, he doubled my wages when my father died

Chorleywood War

We had a land mine at the back of the Bakery building one Sunday lunchtime. We thought they were looking for Chenies Place which was an Army headquarters during the war, maybe they were told to look for a big white house, saw the Bakery, and let the bomb go. They missed it though. It made a big hole in the field, we had bonfires of rubbish in that hole for years and gradually it filled up. There was a stick of bombs across the Common, some of the holes are still there. One landed near our house and blew the windows in.

I used to give my father a hand on the estate when I was at school. There was a lane behind the bakery that cattle could go along and a back road into the estate from the main road, so stuff for the gardens and everything went that way. You could get right down to the river. The fields were all let during the war, mainly for grazing, Dell field was grazed with Jerseys, and they reared calves there.

Troops in Chorleywood

There had been a horticultural training centre in the old walled garden, run by Miss Young, from Rothamstead. During the war this became a training place for the Land Army. There was the permanent staff, who were local, and the students. The Army had a camp in the grounds, they put in the road by the cemetery, and used the Chapel and the Drill Hall; one was the Officers' Mess, the other the NAAFI. There were Nissen huts for the men where the new football pavilion is now. This was a transit camp, and was in use right up till D-day.

After D-day, it became a German prisoner-of-war camp till about 1947. One day I was in uniform, waiting for a bus to go to Rickmansworth and some local girls, thinking I was one of the guards, were asking whether some of the prisoners were coming out that night as they often did. The girl friends used to congregate outside waiting for them. There were some good-looking chaps, and one or two broken hearts. They used to go out jobbing gardening and farming and suchlike After the war, the huts were gradually dismantled, though there was one there till quite recently.

Supplementary rations

Food was short, but my aunt in Rickmansworth had a dozen hens, so we sometimes had eggs. Lots of people kept rabbits, we didn't because I was no good at killing them. Lady Ela insisted that everyone working on the estate had a gun, and my father used to shoot a rabbit for the pot. He was meant to be shooting the grey squirrels, Lady Ela didn't like them and there were still a few red squirrels around. She didn't have a gamekeeper, the head gardener used to shoot pheasants sometimes, but she didn't have people shooting on the estate for sport.

Call-up

I was called up in 1945, after the end of the European war. We thought we were going to the Japanese war, then that ended too. I got in with a gang, six mates together; some of the lads had serious girl friends and didn't want to be posted away for years. We kept volunteering for temporary jobs, catering corps and that, so missed Palestine, missed India and ended up in Germany, from there you could get back for leave. We went to Essen; all the Ruhr was flattened by the bombing, but it was in the factory areas, not the civilian ones. The dock in Hamburg was a heck of a mess, so were Cologne and Dortmund. The German barracks seemed pretty intact and the Black Watch took over one lot.

When I came out of the army I started back at the print works, but couldn't stand being indoors, so Jack Ryman gave me a job as a gardener. After he moved, I got a job in the Bakery Research, and that did me very well.

Sally Cherry

On 3 September 1939 I was sitting on the stairs listening to the radio announcement of war. This was followed almost immediately by the air-raid siren. I was living with my parents and elder sister Mary in Harrow, and working in the Research Laboratories of the General Electric Company in Wembley.

Civil Defence

I joined the Civil Defence and learned to drive an ambulance. This was mostly at night, driving with narrow slits for headlights. We were only practising, but the nights were long and I found it impossible to continue, as I still had to carry on with my day job.

A number of Belgian civilians who had come to this country as refugees, were sent to the Empire Pool, part of Wembley Stadium. My sister and I, with our limited schoolgirl French, went along to help in any way we could, translating their needs to those who were designating housing for them. One lady gave me letters which she hoped I could post to her son still in Belgium, but sadly they were returned undelivered.

In 1940 I married Graham at St Mary's Church in Harrow-on-the-Hill. We entered the church as the air-raid warning sirens were sounding, and came out to the All Clear. My father-in-law was a photographer but his camera broke down, so we just had one or two about this as I felt it would have been very bad taste with people dying in the blitz. We were lent an Austin Seven to spend a few day honeymooning in the Cotswolds.

Army wife

After that I went with Graham to Hereford where he was serving with his regiment, but we were billeted out in the sticks. I was very lonely during the day with nothing to do. It was a great relief when after two or three months he was posted nearer to London and I returned home to my parents. I got a job at British Oxygen in Wembley as a dispatch clerk, responsible for allocating supplies to priority customers and thoroughly enjoyed it, but it wasn't a reserved occupation so I decided to join up whilst I had a choice.

Auxiliary Territorial Service

I joined the ATS, much to the disapproval of both families. I wanted to drive, and had fond visions of doing convoy work around the country. After three weeks' basic initial training at Fulford Barracks near York, I passed as a driver and was posted to Hereford. One of my chief memories of York is that of marching to the Minster for church parade. How proud we were. Not so impressive was our experience of night patrol in deep snow armed only with a torch and a whistle.

The Hereford training consisted of driving 15- and 30-cwt trucks with crash gearboxes, a mechanics course, and instruction in aircraft recognition. At the end of all this I was told that because I had previous driving experience I was to become a staff driver which did not please me at all. My first posting was to fighter command headquarters at Bentley Priory at Stanmore, only five miles from my home. Once, three brigadiers were my passengers en route to Victoria station with not a minute to spare. Spotting an open gate at the end of Constitution Hill I drove through it, to gasps from behind me because apparently the gate was only open for the passage of the monarch. They caught their train.

I learnt I was pregnant when Graham and I were on his embarkation leave in Edinburgh, before he went to the Far East. I was discharged from the ATS after six months, and our son was born in early January 1943 in a Harrow nursing home. By this time Graham was early January 1943 in a Harrow nursing home. By this time Graham was serving in Burma with the 14th (Forgotten) Army, where his company was surrounded by Japanese, so it was three months before he knew he had a son.

Bombs in Harrow

Bombing was pretty fierce at that time and we used to take refuge in a Morrison shelter, which took up nearly the whole room, but it saved our lives when a large bomb demolished the four houses next to us. It was then that my sister Mary and I took ourselves off to Yorkshire relatives with our three children. It was not a happy situation as our aunt and uncle were childless and understandably put out by the invasion of two nieces and three lively youngsters. We stayed there a few months, but were back in Harrow by Christmas when things had calmed down. There was a lull in the bombing, and then the flying-bombs and rockets arrived. I remember walking home from the cinema with a friend when a flying-bomb's engine cut out overhead. I don't think we have ever run so fast, but the bomb came down in a recreation ground with no loss of life.

I began to feel very guilty that I was contributing nothing to the war effort. As I had been taking singing lessons for about six years, I thought I could maybe do the rounds of local camps with other amateur entertainers. I wrote to ENSA (Entertainments National Services Association) for advice and was summoned to an audition at Drury Lane Theatre. There was a large crowd of applicants for jobs – all apparently experienced 'theatricals'. I stood on the large stage (no microphones then) and sang *Habanera*, from Bizet's *Carmen*, and Noel Coward's *I'll see you again*. From the pitch-black auditorium a voice boomed out 'Would you be prepared to go to India? We need to know in half an hour.'

ENSA

I didn't have time to go home, so rang my dear parents who said 'Of course you must go', it was a golden opportunity to further what I hoped would one day be a singing career. By then Graham had been invalided out of Burma with amoebic dysentery to a Delhi Military

Hospital, so it was very tempting. Clive was two and with loving grandparents, so I accepted the six-month contract; I don't think he missed me at all.

I was allocated to a company consisting of a pianist Jimmy, a lovely ballerina who had been with the Metropolitan Ballet Company, a comedian and a comedienne, a very pretty soubrette, and me. Jimmy was somewhat erratic and once struck up with the introduction to *I'll see you again* when I was preparing to launch into *One fine day*. We had been selected by Winston Churchill to raise ENSA's flagging reputation, and the voice I had heard in the theatre was the impresario much feared in the theatrical world, Basil Dean. We rehearsed for six weeks, and were able to choose our own formal wear, which was such a treat in those days of clothing coupons and utility clothes. I bought mine at Fifth Avenue, in Regent Street, and later on these were copied for me by Chinese tailors in the bazaars we visited on our travels.

Journey to India

On VE-day we boarded a Sunderland flying boat in Poole Harbour, to fly out to India. The journey took us two and a half days; we had a brief stop in Sicily, then re-fuelling in Cairo where we landed on the Nile, and I remember being hit by the heat as the plane door opened. I was the only one in uniform (we were given honorary officer's rank, and the uniform was thick and heavy), my civilian wardrobe having been placed in the hold in error. Then on to Bahrain, where we stayed overnight as guests of the Governor, in his palace, which seemed to be the only building there. Then on to Karachi, having broken the record for that flight. The only seats aboard the aircraft were packing cases and four rather insecure bucket seats. I spent most of the time in the comfort of the galley, washing up. We were flying at such a low altitude we could see everything below us, especially the neat symmetrical fields of Egypt.

Entertainment and illness

We stayed in Karachi for a fortnight, performing in pukka theatres, stifling drill halls and occasionally in the Sind desert on the back of a truck with a piano on board. One time my false eyelashes blew away in a sandstorm, but my colleagues were all so helpful to this raw recruit, and I loved acting in the sketches. Our stage costume was practical but attractive – neat suits of different colours. We were all given honorary captaincies in case of capture, making us feel a bit fraudulent, but glad of the perks. The manager of the company received a telegram from Churchill congratulating us on our performance.

My health wasn't considered good enough to make the long train journeys, and I would generally fly. I missed the visit to Kashmir because there was no airstrip there. I had a wisdom tooth extracted by a brutal Army dentist, who after 80 minutes of tugging and several injections informed our manager that I would be fit to sing that evening. I became very ill with jaundice, and was sent to Murree, a hill station 45 miles from Rawalpindi to recover before flying to Bombay to await a ship home. Murree was enchanting, with pine woods and red soil. Every morning I had coffee on a terrace with a fantastic view of the Himalayan foothills about 80 miles away, but you felt you could put out your hand and touch them. It was a really spiritual experience.

Although I had fallen under the spell of India, I was aware of an atmosphere of unrest. One evening, a crowd gathered outside the guesthouse with much yelling, and though it soon dispersed, partition was clearly on the map even then. My husband came to visit me in Murree, and we also had a week in Delhi. I was in Bombay on VJ-day, and all the ships in the harbour were dressed overall, a magnificent and exciting sight. The parties went on for days.

Return to England

I hated the sea trip home, and it completely cured me of any wish to go cruising. Somewhere at the bottom of the Suez Canal lies a diamante bracelet which fell from my wrist when taking the air after a ship's concert. When I got back to Southampton in September, I still had some time of my contract to run, and they sent me to the Isle of Man to sing to the prisoners and internees. I didn't speak their language, but fortunately I had Italian, German and French songs in my repertoire, and they loved that.

I was still there when my husband arrived in Liverpool, so I was unable to see him for a week or two. We were demobbed about the same time, he got a job as Public Relations Officer for the Milk Marketing Board in Thames Ditton, and we resumed normal married life.

Eleanor Clarke

August 1939 saw me crossing the Atlantic in the P&O liner *Empress of Britain*, a magnificent ship. My parents were returning after 25 years as Methodist missionaries in south China, chiefly to get a proper education for we four children. It was the last peace-time crossing the *Empress* made before conversion to a troop carrier.

Herefordshire

We went by train to Ledbury, in Herefordshire, where my father had grown up and where his brother, Uncle Will, ran our grandfather's shoe shop and Auntie Kate managed to assimilate all six of us into her home. We had planned to go to Birmingham, where the Missionary Society owned some properties but children were being evacuated from Birmingham to Ledbury. My Auntie Ethel lived in Eastnor, a village two miles outside Ledbury, and she knew of an elderly couple in a larger cottage who were persuaded to take us in.

It was perfect; everything I had imagined an English cottage should be. It was sixteenth century, half timbered and thatched. There was no electricity, we had Tilley lamps and candles. There was a single cold tap in the kitchen we shared with our hosts, the Goughs, and the lavatory was a three-seater wooden bench in a hut in the garden. There were hens in the yard, and vegetables behind the house. Cooking was on a coke-fired range. Three of us children shared a big bed with a feather mattress, and my sister Barbara told us a serial story each night to get us sleepy.

Village life

We listened to Chamberlain's broadcast and fully expecting bombardment at any minute, my brother Jeremy and I ran across the field to the road and sat on a stone wall to see what would happen. The air raid siren went, then nothing. Disappointed, we went back to the cottage for dinner.

How my mother managed, I don't know. She came from a warm country, where there were servants, back to cold dark England, with ration books and a hungry family to feed, no washing machine or electrical gadgets, husband away most of the time and a war. But my memories are of a magical year. We went on walks with cousins in the Malvern Hills; there was snow, so we went tobogganing and slid on the frozen lake; Barbara had skates, but I couldn't manage them.

I joined the Brownies and we met each week in Eastnor Castle. We had a radio with a huge battery which we had to take down to the blacksmith's to be charged up. Ledbury was two miles away; Barbara cycled there each day with Cousin May to the Grammar School, my eldest brother Denis was at boarding school, Jeremy and I at the village school. This consisted of two rooms, we juniors sat in rows according to our age and I think were all taught much the same. It was a church school, so we had to learn the catechism, though as a staunch Methodist I tried, unsuccessfully, to opt out of this.

I wasn't really aware of the war at all. We occasionally heard aircraft flying over us on their way to somewhere else. There was blackout, and I remember my father quite cross that we were spotted not having blacked out a tiny back window which looked onto a steep wooded hill. We ate a lot of porage, and a lot of potatoes, which seemed quite natural to my Irish mother.

Aberystwyth

After our year at Eastnor, my father was assigned to the church at Aberystwyth, and we moved there in August 1940. At the local primary school, I think the teaching was mostly in Welsh so I went to a wonderful small private school with an inspired teacher, Miss Crawford.

Aberystwyth was already a university town, with the University College of Wales and this was enlarged to take the evacuated University College, London. We became more aware of the war, because there was a large Army training camp nearby, and we had a steady stream of visitors, unhappy soldiers and bewildered academics. Sunday tea-time was open house, and our drawing room would be full of strangers glad of Mum's scones and flap-jacks. After handing round the sandwiches, I retreated to a corner behind my father's chair, where I kept a book hidden so I could read if the conversation got boring.

Welsh childhood

I learnt to ride a bicycle, and would go off for whole days cycling with Jeremy and his friends. There was hardly any motor traffic, and the roads were safe, if very hilly. We swam in the sea off the stony beach, or in the muddy river estuary, climbed the hills behind the house and made camps in the bracken. My father grew vegetables in the garden, and we bought potatoes by the sack; we had them fried for breakfast, boiled for dinner and potato cakes for tea. I still love potatoes. Meat was scarce, but Mum made super gravy from the roasting tin; bacon she spun out through the week, with about an inch of streaky for each person each breakfast. Eggs you couldn't  get at all, and the dried eggs made a revolting yellow mess, though they were all right in cooking. Sometimes we went down to the beach and got fresh mackerel straight off a fishing boat; we tried catching shrimps in rock pools, but I couldn't bear dropping them into boiling water. We were all issued with gas masks in tin containers which came in very useful when we went blackberrying, because with the tin on its string round your neck you could use both hands for picking. We also gathered wool which the hill sheep had shed caught on barbed wire. This we took home, washed and teased out to make a wonderful warm padding for mittens.

Make do and mend

Clothes we made, as coupons went further if you bought material rather than something readymade. Things got passed down the family, and you could let in a piece of material to make a skirt longer or unpick knitted garments to make something else. At school we knitted socks and balaclava helmets for the troops, and I won a badge for making an awful lot of them.

We had living with us a German Jewish girl who had been smuggled out of Germany. Renate was a little older my sister, and she quickly learned English and adapted to our ways. Having this lovely extra sister made me feel the utter futility of war; we were supposed to hate the Germans, but I loved Renate. In church we prayed for the safe return of our troops, and I though there must be German churches, right now, praying exactly the same thing. Renate stayed with us for some years, taking a degree at UCL, till her parents managed to get out through Switzerland to America where she joined them.

We went out cycling and walked a lot, the Public Library was a marvellous treasure trove, we played card and board games, and made our own Monopoly board using Aberystwyth roads and bus stops for the stations. We went to the pictures, watching Douglas Fairbanks swashbuckling his way through history, and Mrs Miniver being very brave on the Home Front. If an air-raid siren sounded, the projectionist would put a red filter over the lamp so people could leave and go to shelters if they wanted to. Hardly anyone did, we just waited for the green filter of the All Clear.

Boarding school

In 1943, my sister and I went off to boarding-school. This I hated. It wasn't at all like the Angela Brazil books I had read. I was desperately lonely, the food was awful, and I was always hungry. We had boiled cod, dumped whole on the serving plate with lumpy parsley sauce and vegetables boiled to exhaustion. There were two big treats – dried banana custard and baked beans on toast, but these came up rarely. Any parcels from home had to be opened in front of matron, and any food was confiscated. My mother was sending me a skirt she had made, and in a letter told me to open the parcel carefully if Matron was looking. Which I did, and felt the bar of chocolate she had sewn into the hem.

Chocolate was a tremendous treat. We had a sweet ration of two ounces a week. The school would buy this in bulk, and the prefects handed it out to us on Sundays after dinner. We filled up on bread, with a scrape of margarine and jam. There were two sorts of jam, RJWP and RJWOP – red jam with pips and red jam without pips, and sometimes you could get hold of a tin of sweetened condensed milk. Bread wasn't rationed till after the war, when my father used to trade petrol coupons for bread units to feed his four teenage children.

My father had maps on the wall, and marked with pins the progress of our armies in North Africa, and later in Europe. He didn't have much admiration for Churchill, maybe because he sometimes sounded drunk – a cardinal sin in the Methodist community. Montgomery and Alexander were different, we almost worshipped them, and when our dog had puppies we called two Monty and Alex.

London

In 1944 we moved to London, to East Finchley. The blitz was over, but the buzz-bombs just beginning. The sirens would go as they approached, and we would all go down to the Morrison shelter, a reinforced iron bunker which the rest of the time served as our dining room table. We would snuggle into this with our eiderdowns, and listen. I don't remember being afraid, just excited at the novelty of being all bundled together in the middle of the night. Less predictable were the V2 rockets, which just came from nowhere. There was a huge bang just along our road one night, and our windows shook. Next day we went to look and found a house had been sliced in half, with pictures still hanging on a wall above a fireplace. The government put out a message that this damage was from an exploded gas main, but everyone knew better, and we called the rockets 'flying gas mains'.

When VE-day came in May, we had two days holiday, but at boarding school, it wasn't that exciting. Home for the summer holidays, and on Barbara's 18th birthday the atom bomb was dropped on Hiroshima. Then VJ-day, and the realisation that the war was actually over. Mum and I went into London, and joined the crowds in The Mall, cheering and singing and waving Union Jacks. Mum's relief was palpable; at last the pain and misery of occupation of our beloved China was over.

Some habits we learned during the war are still with me. I hate waste, particularly wasted food, and I am incapable of throwing away bread – it has to be toasted or made into rusks. If something is broken or wearing out, I want to mend it. I hoard shoes and clothes, you never know when they might be useful. And I still prefer baked beans to scrambled egg.

Jan Clutterbuck

Growing up in USA

My ancestors went to America from Germany as mercenaries to help the settlers defeat the English, and after Independence they were rewarded with tracts of land. I went to college in West Virginia, and on leaving in 1940, I wanted to go to Art School, but my father decided on sending me to a secretarial college. I got various jobs I didn't like in New York, in travel agencies and *Time* magazine. I had to go up 50 flights in an elevator and I told them I had appendicitis, but it was a lie, I had claustrophobia. Anyway they released me and I taught sailing instead in my home town of Greenwich.

Red Cross recruitment

In 1941 America entered the war, and there were calls for people to serve their country. A lot of my friends were getting married and I wanted to do more with my life than just that, so I enlisted in the American Red Cross. We had some training in Washington and soon after I was one of 14 girls on a troop ship with hundreds of American soldiers heading for Europe in a convoy with battleships and destroyers all round us. There were occasions when we were called up on deck because there was a threat of torpedo attack, but we were all together and that was what mattered. It took ten days to cross the Atlantic, in terrible wintry weather. We arrived in Glasgow in January 1944, and got on a train. We didn't know where we were going, all the stations names had been painted out, when I looked out of the window the only sign I could see read 'Bovril'.

Clubmobile girl

We went to the American Red Cross office in Grosvenor Square and I was assigned to duty on a Clubmobile. We came over as 'the girls back home', dispensing coffee and doughnuts to the troops. First I went to Northern Ireland, to County Down where we stayed in a marvellous hotel, the Slieve Donard. We had an enormous amount of attention, because we were the only American girls there. And we were rich, compared with the British. Our driver Jeremy was a good-looking Englishman, so elegant. He read poetry and I thought he was a Rupert Brooke. I had never met an English gentleman before. He had been wounded with the Lovett Scouts, and now had a job as a driver with the American Red Cross. There were three of us girls on the truck, whilst the soldiers were on exercises, firing at each other across no-mans-land, preparing for the invasion.

In April 1944, we came back to England, to the American air bases in Norfolk where our job was to meet the aircrews returning from the bombing raids on Germany, it was terrible. We were then reassigned to London, to wait for D-day; there were night fighters over London, and total blackout. Whilst I was there I met Jeremy again and he brought me to meet his mother and brothers at Micklefield Hall. Soon after D-day, we Clubmobile girls were sent to driving school to learn how to handle the trucks.

Normandy landing

In July 1944, we embarked for Normandy. I remember sitting on a landing craft off Omaha beach for three days before we were allowed to land on D-day+40. Just 14 girls and the rest GIs. We sat in the landing craft and played poker with invasion money. We had this special currency. I've still got loads of it tucked away somewhere. From then on, we were following the troops through France, naïve and unbattle-wise, through Belgium and on into Germany, driving the vehicles ourselves, sleeping in hotels and houses in the towns we passed though. We went though drastic death-knowing hours inside the Siegfried Line, though winter's worst in the Ardennes, and the Rhine Valley in the springtime. We came to concentration camps and their

stinking contents, a million freed Europeans straggling along the highways of Germany. Our job was to stay with the American troops, and they looked after us well. The towns we went through were emptied, you could pick up anything, and some  people did. I felt I had a purpose, we were looking after our boys. Sometimes we would go into the hospitals where the men who had been wounded came back to recover. We came through some prisoner-of-war camps, and were able to take messages from the boys to send back to their homes.

VE-day

Early in the evening of 7 May, a colonel friend whom I had met in Cannes came to visit me at First Army HQ. Colonel Johnny Johnston and I had dinner in a large hotel in the town the corps now occupied. After several quiet drinks at home we decided suddenly we should take off for Czechoslovakia, to Prague, to see the celebration there. With us went Jack Beldon, *Life* magazine correspondent, and Colonel Robert Low, a pre-war foreign correspondent, very charming and handsome. Prague, they thought, would be gay and more than usually colourful on VE-day.

I packed my camera and Johnny and I set off in the dead of night in my car, following Bob and Jack in their Mercedes. The road south to Czechoslovakia was the famous Reich Autobahn, and we reached the border in two hours. Bob knew a little hotel in Hof, and they were wide awake even at three in the morning and scrambled us some eggs.

VE morning was beautiful in that small border town. At seven o'clock, in the streets below I could hear a hundred voices singing, the shuffle of feet along the cobble-stones, and bells tolling. The sun was hot, and we had the top of the car down as we followed Bob at a fast clip trying to reach Prague, 150 miles away, by noon. Half way there we came across a division Command Post, and going inside to look at the situation map we found Prague was not yet a free city. Not discouraged a bit, we headed east again for Karlsbad, a lovely fashionable watering place. We thought we'd have lunch there then head homewards.

German surrender

Our plans however changed soon enough when passing through a small town we met a crowd of GIs gathered, cameras in hand, around the biggest hotel in town. Knowing something was up, Bob and Jack raced in whilst I stood guard over the front entrance not wanting to miss an all-time record shot. I didn't have to wait five minutes before Johnny gave me the signal at the door and out strutted a very handsome German Lieutenant-General, young and pompous. His staff, who were waiting outside in camouflaged cars, were at rigid attention. He had just finished signing a surrender.

Low and Beldon excitedly planned to follow the general back though the lines to his Control Post, adding that it wouldn't be wise for a woman to go. Johnny and I understood this, but thought we'd follow the general perhaps a mile and then turn around.

It was a wild ride through the mountains, a bit mysterious following a German general with only us behind and no escort. We came to a crest in the road overlooking a deep valley, and saw in front of us several hundred vehicles approaching in the road. Looking again, we recognised the familiar outline of our enemy. We were witnessing the mass surrender of a German army.

We were two American vehicles, that was all. The rest were Germans, driving westward, bumper to bumper, an endless line of tanks, trucks, motorcycles, ambulances and people on foot. Thousands of them, still with their Panzerfausts and P38s, their rifles and ammunition. The sick, the wounded, the dying, the women, the nurses, the snipers, the officers and generals. The degradation of an army, a sight both painful and sickening, we felt no glory here.

With one hand I snapped pictures on top of the car while we were jammed in the convoy of Germans, completely surrounded, unable to move backwards or forwards. I was the only Allied woman there, one of the only four Americans. Bob and Jack wanted to follow the General further eastwards, but we'd had enough, and headed towards a side road back though the woods. At a crossroads, set back in a clearing off the road was a German personnel carrier, completely intact, loaded with soldiers and guns mounted. There were no Americans here. We told ourselves this was VE-day, and we hoped they knew it too. We picked up speed and passed them, kicking up dust behind.

It took a long time to get back to our lines through the German columns, and I don't think Johnny and I spoke for half an hour. We drove through the warm Czechoslovakian sun quietly. With our own eyes we had seen the collapse of six years of war. It didn't make you feel victorious or smug or proud, but we both knew we had lived one of the great moments of our lives.

Afterwards

After the war I went back to New York, and wondered what to do. I was welcomed home by friends and family as a returning hero. Whilst they had all remained in domesticity I had been across the world to a war, and at last my father was proud of me. For a while I worked welcoming American troops back into the country, then in a Veterans' hospital, but it was a long time before I got back into normal life. Then in 1952 Jeremy Clutterbuck, my handsome English driver, arrived in New York and asked me to marry him. And I did.

Gerda Craven

German childhood

I was born in Germany in 1928 and lived in Stolp, near the Baltic coast. My father was an architect and civil engineer and we lived in a comfortable house. We had a car which my mother drove – quite advanced for that time, not many German women would drive. My sister was five years older than me, my brother three years older, and I adored him. We did most things as a family, in the summer making trips to the seaside, sometimes staying in a fisherman's cottage on the sea-shore. Just behind it was a lake, so we had both the sea and fresh water, and my father would go fishing. We didn't travel outside Germany. It was a long way and you could only take ten marks for foreign currency, but I did go to Berlin to visit an uncle. There was countryside all round us. In the summer we would go picnicking in the woods and gather blueberries and cranberries, and in the winter we loved to go ski-ing. The land is very flat so it was langlauf, but there are pine woods, you could go for miles and we had snow from November to March. Ski-ing through the woods everything was quiet, the only sound the thud of snow falling off a branch, and you could see animal tracks. It was quite exciting.

Onset of war

In 1939 Father ordered a new BMW car, he was very proud of it. In those days people would bring it from the factory to your home, but he said he wouldn't let any one else drive his new car. He went to Stuttgart to collect it, but on the way back, going slowly to drive the new engine in, he was caught in Berlin when the war started. It was difficult to buy petrol to get home and, when he arrived, there was a letter saying his car was to be confiscated by the military. They just took it. We had a little run about car, but even for that we could not get petrol.

When the war started, there was a lot of propaganda and talk, and boys were encouraged to join the Army. My brother wanted to anyway, especially when they were promised that, if they did, they would be given the Abitur (like School Certificate) without having to take the exam. He went to an officer training school near Berlin, then served in Russia and Norway. My father also was called up, but because his profession was useful, he was put in charge of an aerodrome ten miles away and, though he wore a uniform, he could come home every night.

Evacuees

There was no bombing near us, we had no industry, it was all agricultural, but we had to share our home with a family evacuated from the Ruhr under a government scheme. They had my bedroom and one living-room, so we lived quite separately. I was very happy to be in my beloved brother's room.

A whole school was evacuated to our school, teachers and all, so we had lessons in the morning and they had them in the afternoon one week, and the next week we changed round. This gave us lots of time to enjoy our usual games with friends, cycling in the summer and ski-ing in the winter. Then we were asked to give up our skis for the soldiers fighting in Russia, and this we did without thinking we might miss them.

Food rationing and ways round it

We were not really short of food, though everything was rationed, and you couldn't get imported stuff like oranges or coffee. We kept chickens so we had eggs, which meant we could not have any ration of eggs from the shop. You were meant to declare any other food you got. If my father went hunting and they shot a deer, your meat ration was cut by your share of the venison. Similarly, with any fish you caught, or hares you shot, but I don't think many people declared these. You could usually get fish because we were so near the sea, and the fishermen were catching them anyway. We made a vegetable garden where we had had lawn and flowers, people knew each other and would share things. We had fruit trees and would bottle fruit, and get mushrooms and berries from the woods. Mother said we must bring them back in a basket and not eat them all, so when we came back with not very many we would deny eating them, but she told us to open our mouths and, of course, our tongues were all blue. We were supposed to have a permit even for this, but no-one bothered. Clothes were rationed and if you needed a new tyre for your bicycle, you had to get a permit.

There was a Russian-born man in the town who kept racing pigeons, but when the war started he was not allowed to keep them in case he was a spy and the pigeons were carrying messages. So we bought them from him and made a cage in the garage where we kept them. They bred quite easily, so we had pigeon eggs and, when they had hatched a brood, we thought it was safe to let them out because the cage was a bit cramped, but they flew straight back to their old owner! In the end we ate them, very tasty they were too.

Propaganda

People quite liked the British, but didn't like Churchill, he was a warmonger, and on the radio, it was Churchill that was lambasted, not the British people. Propaganda was always against the East, the Russians. We didn't have children's comics like the English have. There must have been some anti-British feeling, you've got to have hatred to get people to fight, and we could see the bombers coming over. It would have been worse in the cities, somewhere like Cologne you could stand by the Cathedral and see nothing but bomb damage for miles.

We had blackout and there were very strict people who walked about and, if there was a tiny chink, they would knock on the door and you had to cover it up at once. Also there was shortage of gas and electricity, suddenly it would be cut off without warning. I suppose it was lack of coal. There were no women in the services as far as I know, but many women worked on the land. You were meant to be doing useful work or looking after your family. My sister who had trained at the Froebel Institute went to work in a kindergarten and, even as school-children, we had to go and pick up potatoes for a week in the autumn. If we weren't quick enough, they would say 'You can play the piano quickly with your fingers, so you can pick up potatoes quickly.' Women would go to the stations to meet troop trains and give them drinks or food, and take any letters.

Family sadness

In 1940 my mother died, and my father married again. My sister and I really resented her, in fact my sister got married and left home right to the other side of Germany. I kept thinking 'My real Mummy would have let me do this.' I was 13 and probably awkward anyway. I think my stepmother did her best, but it wasn't easy for me. My brother was in the tank division on the Russian front, he was wounded three times and spent a lot of time in hospital. Once when I went to visit him in a hospital near Bremen, I had to change trains at Hanover. There was an air-raid warning, so we all had to get out of the train and go to shelters. You just left your belongings on the train and hoped they would be there when you went back after the raid, and they were.

Russian advance

Towards the end of 1944 things got more difficult with the Russians advancing from the east and the Allies from the west. We dug trenches for the soldiers to use to defend us, but I don't think they were ever used. My school became a field hospital. They would recruit nurses from the local hospital and some who had retired.

In 1945 the Russians were getting nearer, and we could hear the guns. My father was ordered to organise the demolition of his aerodrome so the Russians would not be able to use it. Refugees from the Russian advance were coming through our town and told us horror stories of the occupation. My parents decided we must leave, my stepmother and I to go to her sister further west, though my father had to stay and report for duty. We waved good-bye as he got onto a lorry with other soldiers. We never saw him again.

Sea escape

We went to Gdinia on the Baltic where we were able to get a place on a ship which was meant to be going west. However, it had some munitions on board, which had to be taken east first, but we were not sure we would be able to get another boat if we got off this one, so we stayed on. The grown-ups went below into the hold, but I stayed on deck and overheard a conversation between some of the sailors. They had spotted some ships on the horizon and wondered if they might be Russian. I was so excited by this that I rushed below and passed on the news to the adults. They did not see this as the adventure I imagined and were very upset. However, the other boats did not threaten us, the ship delivered her cargo and went back to Gdinia. Then she was ordered to go east again, but this was too much for us, so we got off the boat and managed to get another ship which took us west to Swinemünde and, from there, we got a train to my aunt in Jena.

Not long after, the Americans arrived. We were all nervous and went into the air raid shelters, but these were not fighting troops, they had been in Germany some months. They treated us fairly well, no women were molested, but although we had learnt English at school, we were not fluent enough to talk to them. For some reason we had to give them our cameras, but as you couldn't get film that hardly mattered. We just wished the soldiers would go away and let us go home and have everything back to normal.

Russian occupation

Instead of which, the American generals decided they had gone too far into Germany and that the area where we lived should be in the Russian sector. So they left, and the Russians moved in overnight. There was chaos, everything collapsed, people tried to get away or bolted themselves inside their homes. Life became much worse. There were real shortages of food, we would go to the fields after the harvest and gather any ears of corn we could, bring them home and grind them in a coffee-mill to make flour for bread. It was not very nice, and I thought wouldn't it be marvellous to have fresh hot bread and real butter – that is still my favourite food today. Also we were now living in a town which had been bombed. They didn't really want us refugees any more than people do today, so there were no extras we could get as we did in the countryside. There were no eggs, just sometimes dried egg. The size of your ration was graded according to your profession. If you were a miner you got more than an office worker, as a housewife you got very little because you were not useful. So women did heavy jobs like road works and demolition of bombed houses. There weren't any men, they were still in the Army. Other countries did not want to give food to Germany, so we got no food aid. We tried through the Red Cross to get news of my father, but the Russians did not keep records of dead and captured, so we heard nothing. For years we kept hoping that he might just turn up. My brother was captured by British forces in Norway and brought to Western Germany. After his release, he trained as a civil engineer – and he had to take his Abitur, that promise was not kept! He has done well and still lives in Germany.

Afterwards

I was very unhappy at the local school. There were very few teachers, men were still in the Army and any one who had had any connections with the Nazi party was not allowed to teach. None of my family were there, but I stayed for 18 months to finish my schooling. I then went to live with my sister near Hanover. This meant crossing the border, which was not easy. I got a job as a laboratory technician and then I met my husband, an intelligence officer in the British Army. We wanted to marry, but could not as I was an 'enemy alien'. He left Intelligence and worked for Die Brücke, a sort of cultural exchange like the British Council, and we got married. We wanted to stay in Germany, but after a year that job came to an end. We came back to England, and he got a job teaching in a prep school in Heronsgate. I was desperately lonely, there was still a lot of anti-German feeling, but it got better when we moved into this house in Chorleywood where I've been ever since.

Elizabeth Cull

Yes, I was evacuated, though not to Chorleywood. I was living in East Ham in 1940, which I recall as a pleasant, leafy suburb though I believe it is not so now. A few of us had resisted all attempts at evacuation in 1939 but the Government was determined to get us out of London before the Blitz they could see coming, and in the spring of 1940 we came out of school one day to find a surprise at the gates. Alongside a brightly decorated coach a tall man on a soap box was calling us to listen. 'I've got this lovely new school in the country. Army huts! Sports field! Treks in the hills! Who's coming with me?'

Well, what child could resist? Not me, anyway.

So a week later we went, singing all the way, to find they were indeed army huts, Canadian Army huts, still smelling of new timber, nine of them on a hilltop – two girls' huts, three boys', an assembly hall, a dining room, two ablutions blocks and a schoolroom. Each of the sleeping huts had 12 double bunks, a space with tables and chairs where we had some of our lessons and a small room at each end for a teacher. They were clean and bright, and heated in the winter – to some extent – by hot water pipes running along the floor against the wall.

It was cold on that hill, and no joy on a winter morning with snow underfoot and the wind whipping it up in your face, to trudge the length of the camp to the dining room three times a day. It was good fun, that camp and I suppose I enjoyed it, but what I remember most about it now is the cold – we used to crouch on the slats in the drying room to try to get warm. And hunger – there was never enough food. I expect that's what most of us remember of the war, hunger and cold. That and being terrified when the sirens went. Even in Surrey there were bombs – one of them fell on our private sewage plant, the smell persisted for weeks.

I still have friends from those days. All in all, I wouldn't have missed it.

Charles Dee

When the war started I was 17, working as an insurance clerk in Birmingham. We lived near the Spitfire factory at Castle Bromwich, I used to watch the test flights and aerobatics of the Spitfire pilots, and I wanted to be one of them. My two younger brothers and a sister were evacuated, and my grandparents lived with us. I wanted to join up as soon as I could. My eldest brother was injured when on fire-watch during an air-raid, he was caught in the blast from a bomb and a large beam fell on him and broke his leg. He was off work for a year, and was then called up with a disability and posted to the Middle East. My parents tried to visit the evacuated children, but they had been at different schools and so went to different places in Hereford and Stroud. My sister died of kidney failure in 1941.

Joining the RAF

When I was 18 in September 1940, I joined the RAF. I was selected to be a trainee pilot, and went for ground training at Blackpool, then Babbacombe, then Aberystwyth early in 1941. This was basic and theoretical training, actual flying started in April 1941 at Anstey, near Coventry.

My first solo flight was in May 1941, in a Tiger Moth. Since the bombing of Coventry there were a lot of bomb craters around the airfield. On Friday 13 June 1941, having done about 43 hours, I landed in one of these craters, there was a cross-wind and the plane tipped over on its nose. It happened to be the chief flying instructor's favourite plane. In 1941 they were operating peace-time rules – one mistake and you're out, so I could not continue training as a pilot. I could have come out of the RAF as I was a volunteer, or I could have become a navigator, but I opted for wireless operator instead. By 1942-43, they were getting short of pilots and I could probably have rejoined as a pilot.

Wireless operator training

I did the wireless course in Blackpool, then Yatesbury in Wiltshire. In September 1942 I started flying again, in an Avro Anson as trainee wireless operator, and went to North Wales. I did well in my various tests, and was appointed as a trainer. We would go up with a trained pilot, trained wireless officer (me), four trainee navigators and four trainee wireless operators, the trainee navigators got us lost, then trainee wireless operators couldn't get a fix and I had to find where we were and tell the pilot so that we could get home. I spent several hundred hours in Ansons. Then I was offered either Skegness or Oban, I chose Oban so got sent to Skegness, for a while, then to Staverton, near Gloucester then to Aberporth on the Welsh coast, which was a grass aerodrome. We used to take trainees over the Irish Sea where there were no landmarks and they had to do dead navigation calculation. In January 1943, my aircraft got stuck in the mud of the grass aerodrome and crashed through a hedge, so we were all sent back to Staverton. The courses for navigators and wireless operators lasted about six weeks, and I did a lot of night-flying. By the end of June 1943, I had done 500 hours mostly in Ansons.

In August 1943, I went to an operational training unit near Stafford. Here we mixed with pilots, navigators, bomb-aimers and air-gunners and formed crews. We could decide amongst ourselves who would make up a crew, with the pilot leading the decisions. A full crew consisted of pilot, navigator, bomb-aimer, flight-engineer, wireless operator/air-gunner, mid-upper-gunner and rear-gunner.

Bomber Command

In October 1943, I went to a conversion unit from two-engine to four-engine aircraft. One night, there were curious cumulo-nimbus clouds and very unstable air currents, you could suddenly drop 500 feet and our plane was one of only three that got back from that training mission. In January and February 1944, I was at the Lancaster finishing school, switching from Halifax to Lancaster bombers. On 7 February 1944 I arrived at the bomber squadron outside Lincoln.

19 February 1944 was my first operation, to Leipzig, a seven and a half hour trip. The electrical release for the 4,000 pound bomb did not function, and I as wireless operator had to take up a panel from the floor and release it manually. I took a portable oxygen bottle as we were at 22,000 feet, but there was no oxygen in the bottle and I passed out. As I hadn't called back to say what I was doing, the pilot sent the flight engineer back and he found me lying on the deck, unconscious. He put the main oxygen supply connection straight into my mouth, it was of course extremely cold and when I came to, I had this copper tube stuck frozen to my lips, and in my cheek was a huge ball of frozen saliva. When asked if I had released the bomb, I said yes, as I was quite sure I had, but when we got back we found the bomb was still there. Fortunately it hadn't started its firing mechanism, or it would have blown up with us on board. It was our first operation, and had the pilot been more experienced he would have noticed that the aircraft was no lighter as it should have been on the return journey. So as not to waste anything, we were sent back to Stuttgart the next evening with the same bomb in the same plane and finally delivered it.

The bomb-aimer, who was also front gunner and second navigator, would lie flat and look for the target, sometimes there would be marker flares set down by the Pathfinders, sometimes a master bomber who would say when the bomb was to be released. As Pathfinders became more accurate, bombing became more effective.

We flew regular missions to Germany, to industrial targets, because the more anti-aircraft guns needed to defend Germany, the less artillery would be going to the Russian front. The dangers were flak, and possible collision because there would be so many planes over one target. If you were coned by the searchlights, that was it, unless you flew right down the main beam because that upset their calculations. When flak came up, you could hear it rattling against the aircraft, and could sometimes smell cordite. We had to send back weather reports, but as soon as you touched the key, the Germans were on to you, so you got the message over as quickly as possible. When not using our transmitter, we would search for and tune in to a German language message, then tune in with our engine noise which would jam the messages from their ground controller. Coming back, if there were no intruders around we would look out for the red light on top of Lincoln cathedral and know we were nearly home.

24 March 1944 was the last major Berlin raid. The Met office forecast winds of 70 mph, but our navigator was recording speeds of a 150 mph. We arrived over target early, and circled over Berlin, but on the return journey our speed was 130 mph and the wind was 150 mph, so we were in fact flying backwards and ended up being the last plane to get home. We had been coned over the Ruhr and suffered severe flak damage so had to land at an American base, which had a longer runway.

Using the main radar, the central area was called the 'fishpond'. If you saw little blips coming towards you, you would warn the gunner, 'Here's a customer for you', so he would tell the pilot to dive, as we didn't want to get into scraps with German fighters. The scanner was under the aeroplane, and once the Germans realised this they would fly above us and then come down. We didn't have fighter escort, bombers were all slower than fighters at that stage.

Quite often there would be no rest day, you would get in from a flight, debrief, then fall asleep and be ready the same evening for a briefing. We set off between six o'clock and midnight, and didn't know till the briefing where we would be going. We would ask the armourers or aircraft fitters how much petrol and what the bomb load would be, usually a 4,000 pounder plus some incendiaries and small high explosives.

Nuremberg raid

For the Nuremberg raid, we had been promised cloud cover by the Met office, but there was a full moon and it was clear all the way to the target. Condensation trails behind the planes gave a marker to the

Germans, and made it easy for them to track and shoot us down. The Pathfinders had found the weather clear, and they didn't think the planned route was right. They said the raid should be aborted, but their advice was rejected. We had very heavy losses from that raid, over 100 aircraft did not return. We got back safely, but were shot up over Norwich by an intruder. I had left open an armoured door whilst drinking a cup of coffee, then saw a line of tracer bullets coming up, which wounded the rear gunner and damaged the hydraulics to the landing gear. The pilot used the emergency air supply to lower the flaps and under-carriage, and once they were down you couldn't get them up again, so we could not go round again. When we landed, we got stuck in the mud and slid across the runway. Another pilot landed behind us (he had been told not to, but he had troubles of his own) and hit us. As soon as we landed the rear gunner leapt out of

66

the plane and ran despite his injuries, I chased after him and brought him down with a rugby tackle. I had already warned the station that we had a wounded man, and waved the torch from my Mae West so the ambulance could follow me.

Pathfinder

In April we went 'gardening', dropping sea-mines into shipping lanes from Danzig, an eight and a half hour mission. I moved to the Pathfinders, going to a training unit for five days, then to 156 squadron RAF Upwood, in Huntingdonshire. The Pathfinders were called blind sky-markers, we were the first over the target and got the warmest reception as we dropped markers to guide the bombers. On 5 June 1944, we took a 4,000 pound bomb to drop on Longues, in preparation for the D-day landings the next day. We took off at 3.00am, and could see the sea covered in ships. The following day we flew over the invasion site again, to bomb Foret de Cerisey. We continued night bombing, then daylight as well, including the flying bomb sites. We

were still going to Germany, Stuttgart and Hamburg, then back to Normandy in July, to the battle area near Falaise. The Canadian troops were in the centre, they had been told not to use markers, but they did, orange ones, the same as Pathfinders used, so our bombers thought these were targets and bombed the Canadians. Though my crew were not involved, heads had to roll and as we were near the end of our tour, we were posted away.

Once the CO brought back his bomb-load because they couldn't positively identify the aiming points, but nobody realised the firing mechanism had been started. The bomb was unloaded onto the trolley, and two men were sitting on it drinking tea from the NAAFI van which had just driven up, when the bomb exploded. There were casualties and several aircraft destroyed. Another time a Mosquito overshot the runway, hit a bomb shelter, and cartwheeled over, ending up in the house opposite to the one where I was in bed. Only one man survived the crash and fire.

We had a dog on the station called Soda (a previous one had been called Whisky) who would follow us out to the plane, barking. Once we were air-borne, he stopped and was quiet for hours until we were back in the circuit approaching the airfield, when he would start barking again. The ground crew who would sit and play cards whilst we were away would rely on him to warn them of our imminent arrival.

I was commissioned in August 1944, and moved away to officers' quarters outside the airfield. I applied to go back on a squadron, but was sent as wireless operator instructor to Wing, where in October 1944, I became a Staff operator for a Bomber Command training unit.

Far Eastern posting

From April to May 1945, I was at a training unit for Transport Command, doing cross-country flying in Wellingtons. Then we converted to Dakotas, and it was in one of these that the pilot, navigator and myself from Bomber Command, and a newly trained second pilot, flew from St Mawgan to Burma in November 1945. This took 50 hours, with 10 stops en route. There were three squadrons near Rangoon, one carried VIPs, another other troops, whilst we took coloured troops and freight. Going down the coast to Singapore, the pilot put on automatic and we all went to sleep; once a soldier looked into the cockpit and finding us all asleep, screamed in panic. We had to take off at first light because as dawn came up, mist would rise off the paddy fields and obscure vision, so we used to stop for breakfast part way down the coast in a later time zone in Penang, Kuala Lumpur or Butterworth.

When flying over isolated areas, we would drop hundredweight bags of rice. These we stacked so that when we opened the door and pushed out the first, the rest would follow. The pilot flew low, put on the klaxon for us to drop, then climbed again. The Japanese were very punctilious, and would salute us as we flew past.

A group of us had some leave, and went to Darjeeling, then on mules into high passes from where we walked. With a guide and a cook and six bearers, we went into Tibet, through 14,000 foot passes. On the way back, I drank from a mountain stream and ended up in hospital in Rangoon with an ear infection. One of the Princess Mary nurses there invited me to a dance, and sneaked a uniform in for me to wear. It was a great party with dancing and plenty to eat and drink. Next morning, when the Medical Officer came round, he took one look at me and said if I was well enough to dance all night with his girl friend, I was well enough to go straight back to my squadron.

Some airmen lit a fire to burn rubbish in a bomb-crater by the airfield, but it spread to buried ammunition dumps and the whole thing went up. We patched up one plane enough to fly home, but in New Delhi, the plane was said to be unfit to fly, so we stayed there for a fortnight. Then we flew to Aden, but the aircraft was still not fit to fly back to England, so we got a boat through Suez to Marseilles, train to Calais, boat again and back for de-mob.

When in the RAF, you never thought you would get the chop, but neither did you think about what you would do if you survived. I went on a three-month course at Wolverhampton Technical College about adjustment to civvy street, but it wasn't much practical help. It took me quite some time to get back to normal civilian life.

The painting of the Pathfinder Crew **We Guide to Strike** *is reproduced by kind permission of the artist Gil Cohen ASAA*

Eve Dee

Ambulance-driving in the blitz

I lived with my family in Birmingham, and had just started training as a nursery nurse when the war started. I took a job as secretary to the manager of a stationery and printing company. His offices were bombed and he took rooms in the Grand Hotel where I had to go and sit in his bedroom to type his letters. I also trained in Civil Defence right from the start of the war, and was part of an ambulance crew. We had a navy blue uniform and a forage-cap which we used to call a 'peekie-blinder', I had jet-black hair.

We were trained in first aid by St John Ambulance nurses. I qualified to drive the ambulance, and when it came to my turn, I just had to go a couple of miles to deliver some stuff. I drove through some huge gates and up the sweep of a drive, and they were all there waving at me, and I thought this is all right. They gave me coffee and took the deliveries and off I drove, but when I got to the gates I went smash. I was so scared they would be angry at me, but they were all laughing their heads off. They had had ten tons of tar poured onto the driveway the day before, and of course I just skidded on it. I didn't want to drive back to my depot, but they said I'd got to, and cheered me off. Back at my depot, my men were all outside with flags and cheering me in. Never again, I said, but I did go on driving for them. I was terrified driving at night, we just had little slits in the headlamps for lights.

We put out incendiary bombs with a stirrup pump. One landed in our garden, on the summer-house, but we put it out. We had a Morrison shelter in our living-room, but I was never there because I was out with the ambulance. In the daytime, I went on working as a secretary.

In the ambulance we would pick up the casualties from the blitz, both in Birmingham and Coventry. We would put bandages and splints on them, put them into the ambulance and drive them to the hospital. Once I had to go and watch the operations, and the surgeon said I could do the next one, but I didn't. The other thing I did was to go to the railway station and collect the wounded, some of them from the invasion of France, many were not too badly wounded. Then there were those from the Far East. Funnily enough one of the wounded men from India now lives just close to us, and he met his wife who was a nurse in the hospital. Charles and I had known each other since we were about eight years old. I did get dreadfully worried when Charles was off flying, but when he got leave he would come and see me. You see I wear this badge, it's a Lancaster bomber.

One time we were at my sister's for supper, and Charles must have been flying a lot because he was so tired and my sister said to him 'You're on operations aren't you?' and Charles instinctively said 'Yes', which he shouldn't have done really because it was all so secret. We didn't tell his mother though.

I felt driving that ambulance I was really doing something, and in fact I wouldn't have missed it for the world. After the war I finished my training and started a nursery school in my house, I had 23 children there, and taught them so they could read and knew their numbers by the time they started big school. Charles and I got married in 1948.

Sheila and Peter Devers

Schoolchildren in Edgware

Sheila We both lived in Edgware, though we did not know each other then. I was at the North London Collegiate, walking the mile to get there, we were young enough to enjoy good times and not be too worried about what was happening. Father was over 40, so was not called up; there were four of us children, one brother was called up right at the end of the war, and my sister worked for the BBC so was exempted. I wasn't interested in the politics, I knew we had an enemy, hated Hitler, hated Germans, we were aware of the blitz and the danger of bombing. One Sunday, Father and two of us were coming home from church by car along the Edgware Road, when a bomb fell just in front of us. The overhead trolley-bus lines had been brought down, they were all live and sizzling on the ground, and there was escaping gas from the bomb crater, it was very frightening. We got home all right, but mother had been terribly worried as she had heard the bomb and we hadn't turned up. I was sick that night but next day went to school as usual. We didn't have a lot of clothes, school uniform, also a kilt and a twin-set Mother had knitted.

Peter I was at school in Finchley, used to take buses from Edgware. When I left aged 16, I worked in an estate agency in South Kensington, mostly arranging lettings. A lot of people who had been bombed out needed to find somewhere to live. There was an enormous underground shelter at my father's works, but it was not much used, most people didn't go to air-raid shelters. At nights, the bombers used to go over, we could hear the anti-aircraft guns which felt quite near, and could see searchlights and the terrific fires. In the blackout I had a light for cycling, with a shield to deflect light down, but I didn't go out at night much. We didn't feel in any danger, and with double summer time, I usually got home in the light.

Air-raids

Sheila We were aware of the bombers going over. At school, the cloakrooms were turned into shelters, and when the siren went they

72

rang a bell, and each class went to an allotted place in the shelters so the lessons went on. We had hot lunches brought in to us and quite enjoyed the raids, especially if it was a maths class. The night-time raids were at the same time every night, eight o'clock. We had an Anderson shelter in the garden, and slept in it. Actually after the war we found out it wasn't safe, but it was quite fun, we had bunks, and I am amazed at how my mother kept us fed. We kept chickens, and gave eggs to Jewish neighbours in return for their bacon ration. We had an allotment for growing vegetables, you had to queue for everything.

There was a shortage of clothes; at 12 you get extra if you had reached a certain height or weight, I was on the borderline and had to take all my clothes off and be weighed. Nobody was fat, and there was not much illness, but I had a poisoned leg, and had to have great big M&B tablets. I never heard of people being attacked in the dark.

Youth and call-up

Peter Adolescents weren't considered different, we were kept very young and had very innocent activities. We went to the woods, took sandwiches and spent whole days mucking about and nobody worried. We didn't really have family holidays, but went with friends cycling and Youth Hostelling. I got to know the workings of my bike, replacing the chain, and mending punctures. I still can't bear waste, you had to be so careful then.

I was called up into the army when I was 18 and was sent to Scotland, tramping over Highland mountains to toughen me up. In the build up to D-day, I was sent to Worthing, training on the South Downs in a unit to repel any Germans if they landed there. There was barbed wire on the beaches, with a small patch free for swimming.

Family life

Sheila I wasn't allowed to go to the cinema because my family was religious and that was out of bounds. I did go once or twice with friends but didn't tell my parents. I read a lot, and did things with friends. My parents followed the events of the war, my father had been in World War One. You saw more of your parents then, there was much more family life and we were involved in the Red Cross, committees and so on. There were no troops around Edgware but in the build up to D-day, there were squadrons of planes going over, and many lorries on the road. Hendon aerodrome was near by.

There were gas and electricity shortages, so we had a hay-box to cook casseroles, you put it in hot and it went on cooking. We dipped eggs in isinglass to preserve them, and bottled fruit in Kilner jars.

Peter There was much more respect, you couldn't cheek your elders, if you did you were sent to your room, or caned at school. There was strong anti-German feeling then, and I am still a bit cautious about them. We all expected heavy bombing on London.

Sheila My family went to Bognor, and rented a house to be safer. Shore defences were put up, but I loved it. Mother wanted to get back to Father, who was in the ARP and fire-watching on the roof of his factory, so we went back after three months. He had a biscuit factory in Cricklewood, and he would bring back broken biscuits.

The enemy was clear, it was someone outside the country. We were taught to hate Hitler and the 'Nasties', and adored Churchill. Good and bad were clearly defined. On VE-day we went up to London, and joined the big crowd outside Buckingham Palace, it was a bit frightening, but you were swept along.

Leonard Durrant

I had all sorts of jobs in the thirties. I was married to my dearest Millie in May 1934 when I was just 18. We lived with parents and then rented rooms, I had a job in Luton making ball bearings, then Millie and I were in service but those jobs didn't last long. I'd been driving since I was 14 and got a job as driver for Guy Eden of the *Daily Express*. We got a place in Moneyhill, and I worked helping put the sewers in Maple Cross. It was very hard dirty work, but I was getting quite good money and had an open-top Austin Seven.

Royal Army Ordnance Corps

I had joined the Territorial Army in 1931, I was 15, but put my age up to get in. When the war came I was called up into the Royal Army Ordnance Corps and was sent to Woolwich barracks for training. We did square bashing and arms drill, which was damned boring. The Regimental Sergeant Major called me out, took me to his office, sat me down, pushed over a box of cigarettes and asked where had I trained? I told him in the TA, and he got me promoted to corporal and put me in the transport section. My wife couldn't afford to keep our flat on, so she sold off all our stuff for £30 and went to Oswestry to stay with her aunt. She went into a munitions factory, but after a while she developed cordite throat and had to leave, so she joined the police, still in Oswestry. One of her jobs was finding deserting soldiers, and I said this was mean.

In Woolwich the German planes came over very low making for the docks, I had a Lewis gun and stood on the top of the building firing at everything that came past. The Tate & Lyle factory was hit and went up in flames. Then I was posted to Croydon, another hotbed, we were working on First World War lorries that had seen better days. I was stationed all over as we were a mobile unit, doing exercises and maintaining the vehicles. By now I had been transferred into the Royal Electrical and Mechanical Engineers.

Air-raids

I had my first leave for ages. I was going across London to get the train from Paddington to Oswestry, when there was a raid and I had to shelter under the railway arches. I'd only just got to Oswestry and I had a call to go to Colchester. The camp I went to was empty, they had all gone abroad. I could have just gone back home, lots of people did. Anyway, I went back to Queen's Barracks, in Croydon. If I could get to sleep before the raids started at nine o'clock I could sleep through, otherwise I was awake all night. We slept in a hall which had a glass roof and was right next to the gasometer. I got in a very bad state, shaking and crying, and went to the doctor, so they shifted me to Brandon, in Suffolk. I got to the station, there was a little short stubby man, he was a captain, a Welshman, and he took my kit-bag and we walked up the road to the big hall. He said 'It's very quiet here', then I said 'Just a minute, there's a Jerry about.' He asked me how did I know, I said 'I know the sound of his aeroplane engines.' Next thing there was a rat-tat-tat and Jerry had fired on the boys playing football outside the hall. I turned round, couldn't see the Captain till I heard him say 'I'm here', and he was stuck underneath an Austin Seven. Several men were injured, luckily no one killed.

I went to Liverpool, there were raids there and I volunteered for the fire brigade, in the fire float.

Hospitals

I had to go into Mill Lane Hospital in Cambridge because I had stomach trouble. They said it was due to my bad teeth, and they took them all out. Trouble was the actual dentist hadn't arrived when they'd got me sedated, so the house doctor took them out. He showed me the little chisel and a hammer he used, my face was a right mess, all swollen up, I had to stay in a month. My wife came down and stayed with her aunt in Cambridge to be near me.

Postings around the country

I was told I had a job driving a staff car, but the hospital said I wasn't fit to be discharged so I couldn't go. It would have been driving Monty! Instead I was sent to a holding battalion in Southport. There was a sergeant there, selling First World War uniforms, he was drummed out. Then I was sent to Wimborne, a lovely unit. Our garage workshop was by the river. There was this beautiful girl, the postmaster's daughter, one of my mates came to me after we'd moved to Beaminster, told me he had married her, but had put another woman in the family way. I told him to tell the Captain, and within two hours he had been posted away, that was what they did in those days.

Then I was sent to Berkhamsted. Whilst there I hurt my back, we were doing very heavy work on American trucks and I got sent to the hospital at Ashridge, the wards were wooden huts in the grounds, the staff were in the big house. As I was getting better, there was a cricket game of patients *versus* staff, and I was instrumental in winning the match. Afterwards the matron said to me 'You are a silly boy, you were about to get your ticket, but now you've shown how fit you are you'll have to go back to your unit.' I've suffered from my back ever since.

I went to Newmarket in 1943, where I was making up bikes for the officers. My wife was living in Cambridge, and she became pregnant. We were so pleased, but she had an awful time, four days and four nights in labour, she nearly died, and there was a heavy raid on. There was a Czech doctor who said she should have a Cæsarean, the house doctor said 'No', but they tore her to pieces and killed the baby, it was 11½ pounds. There were two babies in the hospital who were to be given up for adoption, the sister showed me one and she was lovely.

77

I showed her to Millie but she said no, she wasn't interested in any discarded baby. Later that day the sister pointed out a woman who had come, and said 'She's from social services and she's going to take those babies for adoption.' My wife said 'Let me have another look at the little girl' and she held her, and saw her dimples, and she said 'She's lovely, isn't she?' and sister said that's good, and brought my wife's breast out to give the baby a feed. The milk dried up, but the baby stayed, our lovely Jackie, she's been a good daughter.

Normandy Invasion

My job was putting a sort of putty around parts of lorry engines to try to make them waterproof ready for the beach landings. On D-day+3, I went over in a landing-craft, I was so sick. I was driving a big tractor on the beaches to drag the other vehicles onto the shore. They drove the landing-craft as far as they could onto the beach, and then the vehicles drove off, and I pulled the ones that were getting stuck. I was on Sword beach for three weeks, the troops were pushing forward all the time. We followed them, intent on keeping the trucks going, one time we were so busy doing this we didn't notice that Jerry was there watching us, till they fired on us.

War's end

It was an awful time, it turned me to religion. All I could think of was my wife and that I wanted to get home. I was with the Army as far as the Rhine, then the war finished, and they called us back to England, to Woolwich. We didn't have anything much to do, so I was sent to Nottingham; a lot of men were being sent to India, but I was sent to Saffron Walden, driving old petrol lorries to the King George V docks to go to Poland. Then I was posted to Newmarket driving an officer who was looking at damaged barracks, that was a cushy job.

In 1946 I got demobbed. I went to Chorleywood for a week's holiday, then someone told me there were squatters in a camp in Chalfont St Giles, so we walked over and found these concrete and breeze-block huts, originally for the army. There was one left, and we moved in and lived there for a year, through that very bad winter. I was driving for a sand merchant, I had to pick up coal, and took some home. Then I found an old cast-iron kitchen range which had been dumped, and I brought that home too and fitted it so we had a cooker and Millie could make pies and all. Then at last we got a council flat in Chorleywood.

Olive Entwhistle

In the 1930s my father was a City of London policeman and we lived in Islington. It was a respectable area, mainly working class, and there were good schools. I went to Camden Girls' School. We lived in the flat above a shop which is now a famous restaurant – Granita's! Many of the Georgian houses around were let as rooms. My father was retired unfit early in 1940.

Chorleywood schoolgirl

My grandmother's family, the Costers, had for generations lived in Chorleywood, and for the summer holidays I always went to stay with her. She lived in a half-timbered cottage in Chorleywood Bottom, originally Younger's Farm. In the 1930s, travellers on the Metropolitan Railway used to ask at a station 'Where is the nearest Retreat?', meaning a place where they could get teas. This service Grandmother provided, so she re-named the house The Retreat. I was in Chorleywood when war was declared on 3 September and listened to the broadcast. My grandmother was dead by this time, but my grandfather, Mr Turney, was alive and living here.

Everyone expected London to be bombed heavily straight away, and as Chorleywood was a reception area, we never went back to Islington. I transferred to Watford Grammar School, where there were about five of us evacuees in my class, the Lower Vth. There were three classes in each year and they just filled the classes to 30, which was the maximum allowed. I went to school by train and bus, did my School Certificate there and left aged 16 in 1942.

Evacuees

At one point there were 14 people living in this house and I slept on the floor. You never refused anybody in the war. These were mostly people my mother knew, including an aunt and uncle. There was one stick of bombs over the common, from near the station up to Chorleywood House. A land-mine fell in Croxley Green, it brought down the church. We had an evacuated family, Mr and Mrs Wrigley and their son, John. She organised the local evacuees round here, John went up to school in London. My mother cooked for all of us. Meat we got from Higgins, there were three butchers in Chorleywood then, and two grocers, one by the railway bridge and one in Lower Road. There was a bakery on the Common at the top of Colleyland, and later Hollidays in Lower Road. We kept chickens and rabbits for eggs and meat. My grandmother had always kept chickens.

Office work

When I left school I worked for the Sun Life Insurance company who had been evacuated from London. Everyone knew the war was coming and, expecting London to be bombed to bits at once, Sun Life had bought three large houses, King John's Farm in Shepherds Lane, Myrtle in Heronsgate and Rosebank in Shire Lane. They built an enormous bunker at King John's for their records, and for the staff if ever there was a raid. There wasn't, but all the records were kept there, and that's why it was later bought by a musician who could do his recording down there without any outside noise. I had a first rate training in financial matters at Sun Life, it has stood me in good stead since. I was working at Myrtle and walked to King John's Farm for lunch, later I transferred to Rosebank.

Our evacuees stayed all through the war. Nora Saunders along the road had an evacuee, they didn't have any family of their own and they more or less adopted this boy and brought him up, he would still come to see her when he grew up, and she left her house to him. She had been a Lawrence, all that end of Chorleywood Bottom belonged to the Lawrences. Mr Batty was a millionaire and a Quaker, he owned The Cedars and gave it to the National Institute for the Blind who for many years used it as a school for blind girls. He was married twice, his first wife was Lady Violet (in her own right) everybody liked her. They had the Manor House, opposite the church, but when Violet died and he married Mary, she wanted somewhere else to live, so they bought The Court. The Little Court it was called then, Lutyens had given advice on the building of it, but he wasn't the architect. When Batty died, he left it to the National Trust, but they didn't want it so it reverted to Mary who lived there all through the war.

The buses were much better than they are now. There were farming camps, which were a sort of holiday. You were sent a list of places and you could choose where you went, the government organised it to get extra workers on the land and to give town people a holiday. I went to Bedford once, we would be weeding and harvesting. We got minimal pay and slept in tents, it was fun, we were all young.

Military Presence

There were a lot of soldiers in Chorleywood, in the camp at Chorleywood House. The first lot were the Scots Guards – a friend of mine married one of them – then a Polish regiment, then Americans. For a long time there was the glider regiment, their centre was at Moor Park, where the Arnhem raid was planned. Towards the end of the war there was a small group of Airforce men who were working on Radar, they were on the Common, near Artichoke Dell. We had some very hard winters, with heavy snow and when we went tobogganing, the aircraft boys came and tobogganed with us. There were two cinemas in Rickmansworth, the Odeon and the Picture Palace, and several in Watford. On VE-day, we went up to the Swillett Hut, and Wally Wearing was singing *White Cliffs of Dover* in a very cracked voice.

Soon after the war, the Sun Life went back to London. I was never called up because I was in a reserved occupation. When Harold and I were married in 1963, we lived in Little Chalfont, then after my father died we moved here to The Retreat in Chorleywood Bottom.

Pat Finucane

My father was in the regular army, the Royal Berkshires, so we lived in many different places. I was born in 1923 in Ranikhet in the Himalayan mountains. I was two when we left, and we lived in Germany, England, and Ismailia, then in 1936 went back to India where I was a boarder at Loretta College, Lucknow and there we stayed till Christmas 1940.

Voyage home

We left Bombay for England on the *City of Exeter*, a small cargo ship coming back via Durban where we spent a week, and Cape Town, three weeks. I was 17, and didn't realise the danger, though Father was used on the ship as gunnery-officer. We had no escort as far as Freetown, where we stayed several weeks waiting for the convoy to assemble, 78 ships, one of the largest going to Britain. If an attack warning sounded, we had to get under the tables in the dining-room. The journey took ages because we went almost to America to avoid the submarines. The warships did get a submarine, and we took survivors on board. We had a whaler in the convoy so had to go at its speed, which was slow. We came into Liverpool on 27 April 1941, four months after leaving India. We had lost all our luggage, this had been on the ship before us which had been sunk, she was the last passenger ship through the Mediterranean. Father went to the depot at Reading, where he was to be quartermaster, but the authorities thought we had been on the ship that was sunk. He was next sent to London, and then to Catterick where the family joined him.

When we arrived in England, my mother had no home, no belongings and four children. We went to the depot at Reading, where they looked after us and we had an aunt who helped out. In the summer of 1941 we all went to Catterick, and I got a job in the Post Office in Richmond. There I met Tony, his father was also stationed at Catterick. Next, Dad was posted to Lockerbie, so we all went too, renting a shooting box in Dinwoodie.

Mother was a born traveller, and we had a wonderful time. Father was only in Lockerbie a short while, and once the younger children had gone to boarding-school, mother could follow him round. She had had a very disrupted education, but a good life in India, with servants and friends. Coming back to England, she had to find somewhere for the children in the school holidays. In March 1942 I joined the WAAF. I would have been called up anyway, and Dad agreed that I shouldn't join the army.

WAAF

In the 1940s recruiting of women to the services began to change. I went to Bridgnorth, learnt marching and general duties, and I thought I would do nursing. I didn't want to do cooking or driving, but in selection they thought I would be suitable as a radio operator because they liked the way I spoke. I went to Morecambe for a further two weeks square-bashing, where I fell ill with mumps, so home for a short rest, and then to a training post at Cranwell for Radio Telephone Operator Direction Finding (RTODF). This was before  radar, and I was there for eight weeks before being posted back to Catterick aerodrome in September 1942. Tony had joined the army, and was still up there.

Catterick was a fighter station, but squadrons would come from more active stations such as Biggin Hill or Northolt, for less tough missions. In 1942 ground-to-air communication was a bit primitive. We went out to Receiver and Directional Finding stations to work the receiving apparatus, the Elevating Rotating Adcocks.

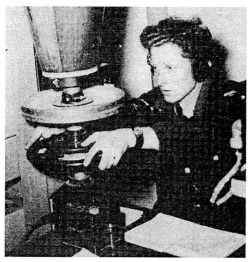

We had been trained in Morse code, but this was voice communication. We received the initial call from the planes, which we logged in a type of shorthand, and once we had established who they were, we put them through to the controller, and continued to log what was being said. The receiver stations were in bunkers in the country, and we tuned in to frequencies which the planes would use. The emergency mayday was always kept open, any aircraft could call on this and we could get a fix on its position with the Direction Finder. We had an underground operations room at the station, but when on DF or receiver stations, we could be many miles away in the middle of a field, with the rotating receivers.

Kent posting

In early 1944 I was posted to Hurn, near Bournemouth, with seven other girls, but it was a mistake, they were expecting RAF men. After working on the airfield for a short time, I was posted to Biggin Hill, then to Hawkinge, on the road from Folkestone to Canterbury. I was billeted in Maple Farm, which was a huge lovely farm, with a first aid post. There we were issued with bikes, and had to cycle to the outposts, doing RTO, from March 1944 to January 1945.

I was in Hawkinge for the invasion. We were confined to station from early 1944, whilst troops gathered secretly everywhere along the South Coast. It was very hectic, we still had shells coming over from France, our duties were severe and our life restricted. We could sometimes go on a bus to Folkestone, but if there was a warning we had to get back. Tony could write from Europe, and my father was getting over-age so was stationed in England, working with the Royal Engineers on the Mulberry Harbour. Mother was living in pubs near to him, the other children were at boarding-school, it was not easy to keep in touch. Tony came home on a short leave, and we became engaged at Christmas 1944. From early 1945 I was in Biggin Hill with a small intelligence section, doing administration, and keeping maps and briefing-rooms in order for the pilots.

Marriage

We got married in June 1945, Tony was in England on a course before going to Burma. We had to get a special licence to be married in the registry office in Salisbury on Friday, Tony returned to his course, then came back on the Saturday for the church wedding. My sister had come home from Australia, she brought material, and made me a little coat, hat, dirndl skirt and blouse. Tony's aunt did the reception, and a cousin who was a teacher in Reading got her Domestic Science department to make the cake. We had a week together. We stayed in Reading for the weekend, then to Catterick to see Tony's parents, then to Whitby for a couple of days, then to my home at Felixstowe, where I changed back into uniform. Tony went back to Europe and I to Biggin Hill.

I was demobbed in October 1945 and had a week in Whitby with Tony before he was posted to India. I spent time with his parents in Catterick; his mother had broken her back and I stayed to look after her. War matured me quickly, I had been an innocent girl, but I saw things other people didn't see, like a plane which crashed as it came in. When I came out of the air force, and was looking after Tony's mother in Catterick, it was still an army atmosphere, though I was not actually in the army. People I met seemed very insular and smug, and didn't realise what struggles we had had.

The photograph of the RDF apparatus is reproduced by kind permission of the Royal Air Force Association

Tony Finucane

I left Richmond Grammar School aged sixteen in 1938. I had got a County Major Award to go to university, but my parents couldn't afford this, so I went to work in the Post Office as a clerk. I had wanted to go into the RAF but then got called up into the army in 1942 aged 20. I had been brought up in the army, both my mother and father came from generations of Irish military.

Call up

I knew about the army before I joined up, and though I didn't want to join, I did know the ropes. I was sent to London to train in Signals, and billeted in Totteridge. There I developed appendicitis and was sent in the front of a truck to Shenley Hospital where, after quite a lot of delay, a large American surgeon decided to operate. By this time I had developed peritonitis and spent three months in hospital and convalescing. A year to the day after joining the Army, I went to the Royal Military College as an Officer Cadet. Then as an Infantry Officer I was on an exercise at the battle school in the Mourne Mountains in County Down, Northern Ireland. We were using live ammunition, when a man behind me shot me in the shoulder, so I was out of action again, in hospital in Bangor.

I then joined an active service battalion in the New Forest. We knew there was going to be an invasion, but didn't know whether it would be France or Italy. It was exciting, like looking forward to exams, but we were afraid of dying.

Normandy Invasion

I landed on D-day, having crossed in a landing-craft, I wasn't sea-sick till I saw a sailor being sick. We had seen aerial photographs and maps, and we were aiming due south, a long way from the German coastal positions. But it was agricultural country, with hedges and woods, and the German soldiers could be anywhere. I saw my first dead man, a German, there were flies buzzing round his head, and I automatically stooped and brushed them away. In Normandy, most attacks were by day, and virtually every day.

In a way it's easier as officer because you had to be responsible for your men. I can recall only one occasion when I gave a command as

a direct result of which a soldier was killed. We were in an orchard where we overran a German position. I ordered two men to silence a German machine gun, they went, and one was killed. There were many casualties as we advanced through France. After one day-long battle, German stretcher-bearers turned up with a stretcher on bicycle wheels. I got Christmas leave in 1944, came home and got engaged to Pat. On

return from leave I was crossing Belgium in a train which went very slowly, and was most crowded and uncomfortable. It came to a stop, I got out to stretch my legs in the deep snow, and found we were in a siding but that the engine had gone! We walked along the line, and came to a military establishment, the Belgian equivalent of Aldershot. There we spent the night, four to a room, and next day joined the battalion in Holland. It was bitterly cold, the Germans had destroyed the lock-gates so the canals were empty except for a layer of ice in the bottom.

Advance to Germany

When we got to the river Maas, the Germans were on the other side, shelling us. It was electric cold at night, with the stars so close you felt you could touch them. I had done a training course in explosives and mine clearance, so I led patrols down to the river through a German mine-field, with signs 'Achtung Minen'. I could hear the ice in the river crunching, but the ground was frozen so hard there was no movement in the earth to set off the mines. The day after Burns Night I was with a lot of Scots, who had terrible hangovers, being addressed by General Horrocks before a big battle. He said there was abject horror on the faces he saw before him, but to cheer us up told us the task was like shoving a telegraph pole up a flea's arse.

By February 1945 we were at the Siegfried line, this was made up of tunnels and pill-boxes and stretched from the Swiss border to Aachen. There was a lot of concrete, including anti-tank dragon's teeth, and there were attacks night and day. The Germans were fighting hard, with their backs to the Rhine. We were in the forest at Nijmegen, where there were extensive trenches and pill boxes – one even had glass windows. Goch had a big anti-tank trench round it, which was covered by machine gun fire. If you were walking you were totally vulnerable, but in a kangaroo, a tank with the top cut off, you were protected from the sides. There was a shallow escarpment going into the town, we had aerial photos and maps and knew where we were going, despite the dark of a February afternoon. On 18 February, I jumped from my tank and realised later I had broken my ankle, I felt the pain, but thought I had been shot. We went into this huge factory complex, there was firing, in the dark, and then the firing stopped, and we just took over the whole area.

Battle

We had been stuck on the edge of a wood for three or four days. During the night, a patrol had spotted a German tank which had driven into a farm building, this had collapsed around it hiding it, so it was now like a pill-box. I called for an anti-tank gun to blast this thing, and a message came from HQ that one was on its way. The anti-tank gun looked like a tank, but had a huge gun with limited traverse. When it arrived, we were trying to be quiet and I was pointing the direction where the enemy tank was, when a red head popped out of the tank – it was a boy I had known since childhood, John Macgregor. On my seventh birthday at Sunday-school, whilst waiting for the priest to arrive, red-headed John produced a gun (possibly a starting pistol, but it was a gun to me), and all the kids scattered. I cowered down behind a statue of St Anthony, whilst he fired the gun in the church. Now here he was with his huge anti-tank gun, but our shouts of recognition were drowned by the noise of the gun firing its three rounds. The policy of anti-tank weaponry was to shoot and scoot, so that's what they did, it was 22 February 1945. I never met John Macgregor again.

This was part of a very big battle lasting four weeks, from the Reichwald Forest to the Rhine. I led 32 men into the Reichwald on 8 February, and marched out with 11 on 24 February 1945.

We crossed the Rhine in landing craft, then the Elbe near Hamburg. In most of the towns between there and Minden, people had hung white sheets from their windows. The devastation of the towns was immense. Towards the end we were meeting groups of people *en masse* coming towards us to get away from the Russians.

We crossed the Elbe at the end of April in a night attack, and six officers were killed. Then the CO heard of the German surrender, and

said 'By the way Paddy, the war's over.' I set out to get hold of drinks for a party, I had a jeep, a trailer and a note to the military burgomeister that I had authority to buy three bottles of Bulgarian brandy, so I put a zero on it to make it 30. All the officers before me had signed the chit with silly names. The brewery was being guarded by a Scottish regiment, the sentry was drunk as a lord and said 'Take what you want', so I loaded the jeep and trailer with cases and cases of beer and the bottles of Bulgarian brandy.

Burma Looms Ahead

I came home and got married in June 1945. I was expecting to go to Burma in the BLA – British Liberation Army, or Burma Looms Ahead. I didn't want to be in a rifle company again, much too dangerous, preferred something a bit further back. I went on a course in England to learn chemical warfare, then back to Germany, then to a holding battalion in Pickering. I was posted to Burma, but only got as far as India where I caught dengue fever. Then the atom bomb was dropped and the war was over. We stayed in India to keep peace between Hindus and Muslims, there we were nobody's friend.

The war was my university. I came back to the Post Office, they had kept my job for me. I got promotion and began a progressive and rewarding career in telecommunications and remained with British Telecom all my working life. If I hadn't got a commission I would have probably been in the Signals and had a less dangerous war. I was never aware of any hatred of the Germans in the fighting troops, they were the enemy and we had a job to do, but that was it.

Steven Frank

Before the war, my father had a law practice in Amsterdam. We lived in a lovely modern part of the town, built at the time of the Olympic Games in the 1920s. It had a garage, central heating and an en-suite bathroom, very advanced compared to what was available at that time. I was born in 1935. My father, by then a highly respected lawyer, was a founder member of legal aid and was much involved in mental health, particularly at Het Apeldoornse Bos hospital. When the Germans invaded Holland, he realised that life would be hard for a Jew, but if you were a mentally defective Jew – and many of the patients were – you  would be marked out for 'special treatment' and he would be the only person able to speak up for them. So he felt it his duty not to hop over the North Sea to where his English wife's family would welcome him, but to remain. My mother wouldn't leave him, so we stayed.

German invasion

The Germans started to impose restrictions on Jewish people. Our radio was taken away, our telephone cut off, my father was not allowed to travel on public transport and his bike was confiscated so he had to walk to work. Unbeknown to us he had joined the Dutch Resistance, working in a complicated chain where people desperate to get out of Holland would go to his office on the pretext that they needed legal advice (by that time he was not allowed to give advice to non-Jews). They got from him false papers that would enable them to get through Belgium and France to the Alps, where they would meet a guide who would take them over the top by goat tracks, avoiding the guards and down into Switzerland and safety.

One morning in December 1942 he kissed us all goodbye as he always did, left to go to work and I never saw him again. He had been betrayed, the Gestapo raided the office and he was taken to a prison in Amersfoort where he was tortured and sent on to the transit camp at Westerbork. He arrived in terrible physical shape, was put in a cattle truck to Auschwitz and was murdered in the gas chambers on or around 21 January 1943. He was a wonderful man.

My mother had to flee from our home. I went and stayed with some people who lived not very far away, I thought just for a few days. But nothing happened to our house so we returned. There was no money coming in and we had this quite large house, so Mother turned part of it into a school for Jewish children who were no longer allowed to go to non-Jewish schools. Also she cut men's hair as they were not allowed to use non-Jewish barbers.

The Barneveld List
When my father was arrested, something quite extraordinary happened. Three of his lawyer friends, non-Jews, petitioned the Germans for clemency for my father, citing the things he had done for the community. This was an extremely dangerous thing for these men to have done, especially as they all had families. Although the Germans wouldn't release my father, they put our family on the Barneveld List, which was comprised of the upper echelons of Dutch Jewish society, and this undoubtedly saved our lives. When the Germans invaded Holland, there were 140,000 Jews living in the country, at the end of the war there were only 30,000 left alive. My grandmother, who had become estranged from her husband and had returned to Holland, was taken off to the camps, and died in the gas chambers of Auschwitz in 1942, as did her eldest daughter and her son-in-law, but their three-year-old daughter was hidden, survived, and was taken in by my mother in England after the war.

In Barneveld
In March 1943 we were told to report to the station, and went by train to Barneveld where the Germans had commandeered a castle. People were desperate to get onto this list as we had been promised we would

be kept in Holland. It got so crowded that they commandeered another house and built some barracks for the overflow. We were there for six months, the children in the barracks, my mother in the castle. There were no guards, no barbed wire, we were like a flock of sheep, safe within the group. But outside was the wilderness and if you were caught there, you would go east. We had in the group composers, musicians, professors, many professionals so we had some lessons, but there was quite a mismatch between the knowledge they had to impart and what we as small children needed.

I developed impetigo. There were no medicines of course, but a leading dermatologist advised my mother that she should take me out in the sun. Luckily it was summer, and she took me to a place near a pond in the beautiful grounds, now all overgrown, and I had to lie for an hour on my front, then an hour on my back, and in the evenings my sores were wrapped in bandages which my mother had made by tearing up sheets. The sores healed and I recovered.

Westerbork

Then one morning in September 1943 a German Army officer came in and said we had 20 minutes to prepare to leave to go to Westerbork. It was grim there. We lived in single story barracks. By each window was a table seating 14 people, between the windows were bunk beds two high, and in the centre, bunks three high. I was in the top bunk bang in the middle. There was no space between the bunks, you clambered up the edge of this huge block and walked over the others to get to your own bunk. I did have my own bunk, though. My elder brother was in with the men, my younger brother and I were with my mother. We were there at the same time as Anne Frank, though I didn't know her and we were not related. The food was pretty boring, and though we didn't starve, disease was rampant, dysentery, scarlet fever, jaundice, polio, and fleas and lice everywhere. There was no paving in the camp and we were in a sandy area, so when it was dry the wind blew the sand into everything, and when it was wet it was just mud. At the end of the barrack, a pipe took cold water into a trough. The adults were allowed one bath a week in a bath-house, which had to serve 15,000 inmates. The toilets were in another barrack, consisting of a pit over which they had put planks of wood, with perhaps 70 holes; there were no washing facilities, no toilet paper, with the dysentery you spent rather a lot of time there. I got an infestation of worms, and when I later got to England, it took nine month's treatment at Great Ormond Street Hospital to clear them.

I learnt two things in Westerbork, one was to be streetwise. I had wandered towards the perimeter wire, in a large open space beyond the huts. I looked up and saw two guards with an Alsatian dog on a lead, they let it off and it rushed up and started mauling me and the guards just laughed at this Jew-baiting. Then they called the dog off, but I had learnt that guards were bad news and that it was best to keep away from them. From then on, if I came out of the building I would stop and look all round to make sure it was safe to proceed.

The other thing that happened was that the 14 people who sat on the same table got to know each other quite well, you had your meals there, you talked, you reminisced. There were over 600 people in our barrack, and about 15,000 in the camp, but your table became your extended family. There were a couple in their sixties on our table who were absolute darlings, and would reminisce with my mother about happy times they had spent in England, and we adopted this couple as our surrogate grandparents, they were such lovely people, great Anglophiles.

RAF attack

One morning in May 1944, I had just entered the barrack when I suddenly heard this howl from the sky and a rat-tat-tat, and I looked up and saw holes in the ceiling and a terrific noise as bullets ricocheted off the metal bedsteads. I ran in panic to my table, through this hail of bullets and I didn't even get a graze. There at the table was this dear lovely old man, slumped across the table, bullet holes through him, blood pouring all over the table. It was the first time I had come face to face with death. The great tragedy was that these were British bullets from a British aircraft. After the war I found out that a reconnaissance plane had photographed this camp, in an isolated area of north-eastern Holland, just at the time they were changing the guards, when we were all confined to barracks. So the photographs showed columns of

German soldiers, and the British thought this must be some secret German army training station. Our barrack was ruined. We then went to Barrack 71, and suddenly all our little group was dispersed into this huge camp.

Tomato plants

When we were in Barneveld, we had had a small plot of land where we could grow things, and I grew some lettuces and radishes, in the shape of my initials. My elder brother insisted on trying to grow bananas, I don't know what sort of seeds they gave him. Then in Barrack 71 I met a man whose face is indelibly printed on my mind, who had managed to get hold of some tomato seeds and these he had germinated, so he had a whole row growing outside his barrack window. I would help him water them, and to pluck out the suckers as they grew. Every week the transport would leave Westerbork for the east, this was Eichmann's great project. Every week between 900 and 1,600 went on the clearly labelled trains, to Auschwitz, or Sobibor, or if you were lucky to Bergen-Belsen, and the occasional transport to Theresienstadt. You could feel the tension building up over the weekend, on Monday the list went up and on Tuesday, the transport would leave. One day this man came to me and said 'I'm afraid I've been selected to go on transport, so would you look after my tomato plants for me?' and I felt so proud that he had asked me. Today, I grow tomatoes in my greenhouse, and as I am watering them, I still feel I am doing it for him.

Theresienstadt

I wasn't aware of what was going on in the war, though there were lots of rumours. People came and people went, but the Barneveld group stayed for a year, in case there was need for hostage fodder. In September 1944, when the Allies were on the banks of the Rhine, our names went up for the transport. We were put in a closed cattle truck with four tiny slit windows, we were 39 hours in this truck with its stinking mixture of sweat, vomit, urine, and faeces. There was a barrel in the corner, but no water, no food. We arrived at Theresienstadt, the doors were pushed open, there was this great draught of cold air and I could breathe again.

My mother realising that life here would become very difficult, volunteered to work in the camp hospital laundry. Here she had access to hot water and when no-one was looking she could wash her children's clothes. She could also wash adult clothes, bartering this service for food. We did starve there, and typhus was starting to be a problem. We arrived not long after the infamous Swiss Red Cross visit, when the Germans made a propaganda film, the thinnest Jewish people having been shipped off to Poland so the Red Cross could only see more normal looking people. They were not allowed to talk to the inmates about their condition. Theresienstadt contained the Jewish intelligentsia of Europe, composers and scientists. There were many musicians, and when the Red Cross came, the Germans gave them musical instruments and scores. People were desperate to have some sort of normality in this grossly overcrowded, starving camp so they took all this with delight and open hands and put on a concert of Verdi's Requiem for the Swiss. Some musicians were constantly being taken away on the transports, so it was quite difficult to get this performance together.

Theresienstadt was initially set up as a place for older Jews, particularly any notables, professors, and men who had been awarded the Iron Cross in World War I, before they were transported to Auschwitz. It was essentially the waiting room for these other camps. Nobody knew quite what happened in Auschwitz, only that it was another camp. Some of these learned men got secret groups together to teach their previous skills, anything to get some normality into their lives. The children performed an opera, composed by a young Eastern European composer Hans Krasa. Victor Uhlman composed the opera *The Emperor of Atlantis*, a skit on Nazi Germany, but when this was discovered they shipped him off to Auschwitz where he died. His friends persuaded him to leave the manuscript behind, so it survives to this day.

We were separated from my mother, though we saw her from time to time. We played cards, chess and draughts, making our own sets. We found where the Germans left their discarded batteries, and got hold of some bulbs and wire. If you put a battery between your thighs at night, body warmth would regenerate the power enough that the next night you could wind a bit of wire round the bulb, hold it against the battery and get light. There was no electricity at night, and this little light became a magic ball, and it would transport me to Amsterdam where I was walking down the street, chatting and shopping. As the filament started to dim, people were going home, I was sitting on a bench, a bystander, watching them as they were at home, having their supper, going to bed. Then the filament would fade completely and I was back in reality, in Theresienstadt.

My elder brother was quite different from my younger brother and I – we were quite sporty and tough, he was much quieter and withdrawn and used to be bullied by some of the other boys. Once when we found him crying, we went and laid into the bullies. When the Germans came to select children for the transport, if there were a brother and sister, they would take one and leave the other, or take one of two brothers, and I can still hear the terrible screaming 'Please, let me go with her' or 'let me stay with him', but above it the coarse German shout 'Du – rausch, rausch' and kids, sobbing at this brutal prising apart. It was probably the last connection with family they had.

Treasure trove
Once in the winter of 1944-45, we managed to find our way into the attic of one of the old buildings, dating from when it was an army barrack in 1750. This was the building where my mother was, and we ran along the rafters exploring. We came across a trap-door, and prising it open we could see in the room below three lamps with metal shades dangling on wires and in the room an Aladdin's cave of treasures – coats, jackets, shoes. I rushed back and told my mother, and she came with some of her friends. They lowered themselves into the room and took some desperately needed clothes and I was allowed to take something out of the toy heap. I chose a chess set and I have it today. In retrospect, the clothes must have been taken from the prisoners who were stripped naked before they were sent to Auschwitz, to be recycled for the German Reich but by this time they were no longer used.

Hunger was never far away, you were always thinking about food. You were issued with an Essenkarte, a card which you took to the mess once a day for your one meal, and they clipped off the number so you could not join the queue again. Because my mother worked in the hospital laundry, she was entitled to extra rations, but these she stored away for us with any other food she had been able to barter for washing clothes. From time to time she would bring hot water from the laundry in an old aluminium pan (I still have it) and mix the scraps of dried bread into it making a sort of paste, then with one spoon, she would give the three of us a spoonful at a time. All round the other children, who weren't getting any were staring and I felt guilty. I still see their faces, fading away. We didn't grow, I got mumps very badly and was unconscious for two days.

Battle-front approaching

I remember the bombing of Dresden, about 90 kilometres away. I heard this tremendous frightening noise of bombing, and the great crimson glow to the north. This was February 1945 and it was very cold. One morning we children were wakened, taken to the crematorium and told to stand in a line side by side in a long cave-like tunnel. We had to stand there for a while, then a box was passed along from child to child the whole length of the tunnel, then another, and another. These boxes contained the ashes of the dead of Theresienstadt, and with true German efficiency, every box had the name and date of birth of the persons whose ashes it contained. Every now and then you would hear the sobbing of a child who found the name of mother or father on the box. The boxes were then thrown into the river to destroy the evidence before the Allies arrived.

The nearer we got to the end of the war, the worse the conditions became. The food was even less, typhus was rampant. All sorts of people were appearing in the camp, open cattle trucks arriving with transport from the East fleeing the Russians and from the West fleeing the Allies, also Russian and British prisoners of war. Many had frozen to death in the trains, my mother would go through them looking for my father. Then one day my mother was approached by some Russians who had hidden a radio and asked if she would come and listen to an English broadcast. It was Churchill who said that hostilities would cease at midnight. It was then 6.0 pm, and there was tremendous alarm, what would the Germans do in those six hours –

would we all be gassed? Theresienstadt had these new Mark III super gas chambers with maximum throughput (a refinement of the Auschwitz chambers). We had also heard they had dynamited the camp – were they going to blow us all up, shoot us all? The night passed and in the morning the Russians arrived, a motley crew, mostly Mongolians with horses and very old World War I equipment. Later came the mechanised troops, they threw us sweets and chocolates and we all grovelled in the dust for them.

Russian arrival

The Red Cross had learnt from Belsen that it was dangerous to feed us too much too soon, and at first we still had the one meal a day. They sealed the buildings one by one and decontaminated them, we were there for a month, before they started shipping people home. There were so many Dutch it took three transports. Mother did not want to go to Holland, as she feared (rightly) no-one she knew would have survived, so she asked if she could go to England. But we were in the Dutch group under the care of the Russians, and the Russians weren't speaking to the British, so she was told she would have to go to Holland and then get to England from there.

Journey to England

We were taken on the second transport to a holding camp at Falkenau and there my mother, protesting she did not want to go to Holland, was finally allowed to join an ambulance truck with wounded soldiers being repatriated to France. It was going via Pilsen, which was under American control. We arrived at Pilsen at night, it was dark and we were put in a huge barrack like an aircraft hangar all lit up, there was wailing and crying. In the morning we were taken with the French to the airfield, and when we got there, the Americans said 'Sorry, only the French', and told my mother to go back to the camp. 'I am not going back' she said 'I've been in one of those camps for two and a half years and I am not going back now.' She was five foot tall, tiny from starvation and she insisted on seeing the Camp Commander. Eventually he came and said that RAF Transport Command flew in each week with stores and flew back empty. One was due that afternoon, he would ask. In the meantime he allowed our family to be billeted in an old barrack outside the camp.

The British pilots were reluctant to help but did interview my mother. They said they would think about it and give her an answer when they next returned a couple of days later. On returning, they agreed to take her and us children out of Pilsen. The flight was going to Paris, and on board were some journalists. One was a very tall Swede with a big coat and a trilby hat, and he advised my mother that if she were told to go to the British Embassy, not to do so.

So she pretended she couldn't get through on the phone, and persuaded the two RAF pilots take us on to Croydon, where they opened the door of the aircraft to let us out, and then the plane took off again. So there we were, my mother and we three boys just standing in the middle of this vast airfield. Another plane came in with a lot of British people who had been interned in France. We just joined in with them and the whole crowd of us were taken to London to a centre for Displaced Persons. There was a policeman there who took pity on us boys and taught us our first English words, the days of the week, and then gave us each sixpence. That was a memorable act of kindness.

Family re-union

After my mother had been de-briefed, she was allowed to ring her father at work, only to be told by his secretary that he had just gone home, she could try again in the morning. Next day he arrived by coach, and when he got out there was a long straight road and my grandfather standing there. My mother rushed to him, we three stood back at first, then we all embraced. We went to his flat where we all stayed.

I was very small – when I had to go to hospital to have my tonsils out, they put me in a cot because they thought I was three. I was nearly ten, and I spoke only Dutch. We rented a house in Albany Street and I went to the London County Council primary school in Princes Road, which was lit by gas mantles. I had to learn how to behave at school. I didn't know the most basic things, like what plus and minus meant, and I was too frightened to ask. When I arrived I was called

Dutchy, then after six months I could speak English but couldn't disguise my small size, so I became Nipper.

We were like animals with no scruples, we were really little horrors. The first birthday I had there in July, I had two presents, one a Jewish prayer shawl, and one a football. My younger brother and I were playing football with some other kids in Regents Park, when my mother came and called us in for supper, and the other boys took our football. They were twice our size, but the two of us laid into them and they fled, petrified of us, leaving the football behind.

Having had no education between the ages of five and ten, I was missing the fundamental building blocks of learning. I had to learn how to learn, so I was nearly always bottom of the class, failed all my O-levels, re-took them, and managed to get two. I studied hard in the summer before I was called up for National Service, and again whilst I was working as a laboratory technician, got my A-levels, enrolled as an external student into London University and got an Honours Degree in Chemistry.

Bryan Hedley

Chorleywood childhood

My family lived in Lower Road, Chorleywood, and my father was a plumber. When the war started he had to go to Newcastle to work in the shipyards there, and we joined him for the holidays in 1940. We moved into Capel Hamlets, my sister was born in that house, my Gran delivered her. Only the lower end of the road had been built, beyond that it was fields. Where the vicarage is now was a dell, there were chickens in the fields and huts, we would make camps there.

I went to Stag Lane School, there were about 30 in a class and three classes. There were three rooms but there was a partition so the big one could be divided to make another room and the toilets were outside. The teachers were three ladies, they seemed very old to us. We started school aged five, stayed at Stag Lane till we were ten then went to Shepherds School at Mill End till 14.

Evacuees

In 1940 evacuees came to Chorleywood. They were all lined up in the golf club car park on the Common and local families went up there to pick them. The girls were always picked first, there was a family of four girls who came from Chiswick High Road two came to us, Betty and Eileen, and two to my aunt's. They were full of lice so my Gran sat them on the table and scrubbed them with Lysol. Mr Barnes was in charge of getting them sorted, it was like a slave market, there were a few left at the end who were more or less forced onto people. They used to go home sometimes to visit and my mum would have put them in decent clothes but they would come back in rags, maybe their parents kept the clothes. They used to do odd things, if we'd managed to get some apples, they'd take a bite out of one and then put it back. They had their school at The Holt, opposite Christ Church School, and after school they might start scrapping with the locals, but on the whole we got on fine. I went with a girl called Anita to pinch some leeks from the allotments, we ate them and were very sick. When they were 14, they went back to London to work.

One girl, Carol, stayed with my Gran right through the war, and we had a lady and her grandson Michael. She came from Stoke Newington, and she could get hold of anything, we don't quite know how. When we went to London with her, we would get a bus from Baker Street, and we always looked out for a black man who was sweeping the roads. In 1943 he was the only one we ever saw. We had to stay outside the house till she came out with loads of food.

A friend of hers used to make clothes in his factory in the East End. One day we were up there, a bomb had dropped and made a hole in the road so you couldn't get past, but he said 'You come with me, boy' and we clambered down and though the hole. They had a restaurant and because of the bomb there was no electricity, but they made meat-balls, marvellous they were, great big ones. We were up in London when the first V2 rocket landed.

Air-raids in Chorleywood

There was a stick of bombs across the Common, we could see them from Capel Road. The plane had been chased away from London and just wanted to be rid of the bombs. There were lots of shelters, two in the playing fields at the Swillett, two at Stag Lane school, two on the Common – they are still there – two in Capell Way and an unfinished one at Hubbards Court, two at Christ Church school; then there was a siren at the Memorial Hall and one at the Swillett. We spent quite a lot of time in the shelters at school, I always blame that for my bad spelling. We saw doodlebugs, one landed at Mill End on the electrical substation and put out all the electricity in the area. A lady in Mill End was killed by the blast from a bomb, I was at school with her daughter.

A German plane came down in Bottom Wood in Heronsgate. We went there after school and picked up bits of perspex and made rings out of them. There were troops, in tents on the Common and huts in Chorleywood House grounds. We used to go up there and play cards with the soldiers, there were a lot of Scots from the Gorbals. We spent whole days on the Common, Mum didn't worry. Once a doodlebug stopped over us, my Mum was having her hair done and I was playing in the alleyway, it came down in Amersham. I remember all the planes, hundreds of them going over for the massive raids on Germany.

Schoolboys

There was a retired schoolmaster who couldn't see very well and when he played golf we used to caddy for him. Sometimes we'd tell him his ball had gone this way when we knew it had gone that and we'd pinch the ball and sell it. Once we tried to sell one back to him, but he recognised it as a North British ball and knew he was the only player who used that ball. He didn't mind though.

On Saturday mornings we would take a four-wheeled trolley along Main Way to the woods at the end, where they were cutting the trees for the war effort. We'd go and collect wood for our fires and on the way back we had to queue at the shop to get potatoes and all that. Cheshire's, from Rickmansworth used to come round and we'd buy groceries from them. The Wearings at the Swillett had hens, and we would go round and get 'the order for Gran' but we weren't meant to know what it was. Mr and Mrs Walker had a small-holding near the Blind School and they got a piece of land on Lower Road, dug it up and grew vegetables. They had a hut at the back and sold stuff from there. Later they opened a shop, which became a supermarket and is now owned by Budgens.

War's end

At the end of the war, we had a big bonfire by the Old Shepherd pub, built up with gorse. We pinched a 50 gallon drum of oil from the airmen on the Common and rolled it down to the bonfire and were just about to put it on the fire when an airman arrived and told us off. The he said he hadn't got the heart to take it back, so he helped us get it up to the top and poured it all over the stack. There were three bonfires, one at the Memorial Hall, one by the Black Horse and one at the Shepherd, and there was great rivalry. But I wasn't allowed to stay after nine o'clock.

Arthur Toates was the local policeman, he would clip us round the ear if he caught us, but never did any more. Once we were sitting by the railway eating rhubarb we had pinched from the allotments and he caught us. Another time we had been birds-nesting, we came out of Woodside Road and saw Arthur coming towards us pushing his bike, so we dropped the eggs into the grass, all except Alan who kept his in his pockets. 'Been birds nesting have you?' asked Arthur, 'No Mr Toates' we all said, so he banged all our pockets and the eggs broke in Alan's pockets and went all down his legs.

On the railway bridge by the Old Shepherd, there's a line of blue bricks on the railway side which sticks out a bit. When a train was coming, we would climb over with our arms over the parapet and our feet on the blue brick in all the smoke and steam. One time Jack was doing this when we saw Mr Toates coming so we called to him to get back; he scrambled over and was just by the fence when Mr Toates arrived and asked Jack what was he doing. 'Looking for my golf ball, Mr Toates' 'What, on that blue brick?'

The war didn't really affect us kids much, it was just something that happened.

Derek Jennings

I was 12 when World War II started, living in Barnet and a pupil at the Queen Elizabeth Boys' Grammar School. When Chamberlain made his wireless broadcast telling us that we were now at war, the sirens sounded, Air Raid Wardens came down our road blowing their whistles and we all stayed indoors with our gasmasks beside us. But nothing happened, and it being a Sunday we were expected at my grandmother's for supper, so off we went, carrying our masks.

Schoolboy in Barnet

Everywhere was blacked out. Wardens patrolled the streets to check for offenders who could then be fined. Vehicles had headlight hoods which gave out a tiny light focused a few feet to the front. Windows of houses, shops, offices, trains and buses, all had criss-crossed sticky tape to prevent flying glass from bomb blasts. All important buildings, including schools, had sand bag protections in front of ground floor windows and doors. At school this meant that the lower floor classrooms had no natural light.

In the summer of 1940 during the Battle of Britain we watched dog fights over Barnet, especially when the Duxford Wing, commanded by Douglas Bader, came into action. There were vapour trails from the combating aircraft and the sound of machine-gun fire.

Air Raids

From 1940, there were regular air-raids, initially by day, but after the Battle of Britain they changed to night bombing raids which went on for months on end. My cousin Ann was staying with us, her mother thinking that the healthy air of Barnet was good for her despite the bombing! She and I slept on the floor in the cupboard under the stairs while my father, if he wasn't out with the Home Guard and my mother kept watch in the front porch. Quite a number of landmines landed in Barnet, they could be picked out by searchlights as they drifted down by parachute. The other fear was to hear the whistling of falling incendiary bombs, small but extremely combustible and needing immediate dousing. Houses and other buildings were equipped with stirrup pumps and buckets of water and sand.

Barnet was quite badly bombed, our windows and front door were blown out more than once. The fields around were pitted with deep bomb craters in which we searched for bomb fragments. Some were filled in quite quickly but others remained till the war was over.

The night of the great fire raid on London, the sky was lit up in shades of red and orange. We walked to the end of Wood Street where we could see the flames rising into the sky on the horizon. It was a frightening sight and my father was very concerned about their offices and factory. The factory was not damaged but the offices were.

About a mile away a battery of anti-aircraft guns would open up firing with terrific noise. Showers of shrapnel fell to the ground, which friends and I would go out to collect the next morning. Mobile Bofors guns would stop nearby, firing smaller shells but more rapidly. As the blitz progressed, people took to sleeping on the floor, under their beds rather than under the stairs.

There were other military units nearby. Half a mile over the fields a decoy dummy airfield was set up, with canvas covered mock Spitfires and lit up at night. This was to distract German bombers away from proper targets, resulting in Barnet getting more than its share of bombs. A wireless transmitting station was built in nearby Arkley. During its construction my friend John Miller and I were very suspicious of what was going on and reported it to our local policeman, who was highly amused and assured us they were not German spies.

In the summer holidays of 1940 schools were kept open as it was thought children would be safer at school during air raids where there were primitive air raid shelters available, and lessons were on interesting and topical subjects. Open trenches had been dug, and when the sirens sounded, the whole school filed in an orderly manner across the field behind the school buildings and clambered down into these ditches. Gradually concrete sides and covers were added, and some primitive lighting. We spent hours in them; initially we amused ourselves playing cards but after a time lessons were held. Later in the war, when there was a raid we merely moved into the school ground floor corridors.

Virtually everything was rationed. We got a few extra eggs from my uncle's farm at Hertford but offers of black market meat from a butcher were turned down. Due to Father's business connections we were never short of shirts or pyjamas and could get plenty of blackout fabric. We grew vegetables, and my grandmother kept chickens. Spam was just about all right but got terribly monotonous even when fried up as fritters; snoek was some unrecognisable fish, and there were dried eggs and soya bean flour. When there were fresh eggs to spare they were pickled in isinglass.

Fire watching

We did fire watching at school one night a fortnight, alternating one hour awake with two hours asleep on the hard floor of a classroom. Compensation was a really slap-up supper from the school kitchen! The idea was quickly to tackle incendiary bombs with stirrup pumps or sand to prevent them setting a building on fire before the Fire Brigade arrived. We would practice climbing over the steep slopes of the school roof, reasonably safe as it had a two-foot high parapet.

Farm work

In 1943 and 1944 I helped the war effort by doing farm work. During term time the school organised days out for gangs of us boys to go to farms – in the spring thinning out and hoeing enormous fields, in the winter picking potatoes, both tedious and back aching but we did get paid a bit. The summer holidays I spent on my uncle's farm near Hertford.

There at Swallow Grove Farm it was far more interesting, albeit hard work, getting in the wheat and barley harvest. The corn was cut by a binder drawn by a tractor and I set up shocks of wheat sheaves for drying out, also killing a few rabbits to supplement our meat ration. I was in charge of a huge Percheron horse and a cart laden with sheaves of wheat to take back to the farm for stacking, till a threshing machine came later in the autumn. I was up by six each

morning to bring in one of the riding horses (an ex Royal Artillery horse), harness her up in the milk float and take the churns down to the dairy depot in Hertford, over a mile away. Then it was cleaning out, grooming, watering and harnessing up one of the three Percherons which would be my horse for the day. From time to time I would ride the horses bare-back down to the blacksmith in Hertford, for shoeing.

My uncle was taken very ill in 1944 so at 17, in addition to working on the farm, I was given the responsibility of supervising the farm workers, and for this I received my first substantial earnings. I would have liked to have become my uncle's apprentice and make a career of farming, but sadly he died later in the year.

Air Training Corps

At school I joined the Air Training Corps. I learned rifle drill, aircraft recognition, Morse code, air navigation, map reading and rifle shooting. I was not very good at Morse but quite passable at navigation, and was proud to be one of the best shots in the .22 bore rifle team which won several competitions. On occasion we would go on a parade through Barnet, with other sections of the local military. There would be a band, and parades finished in the local cinema where some visiting dignitary made a boring speech.

We went to RAF Kidlington, near Oxford, for a week to get flying experience in Air Speed Oxfords and Avro Ansons, kitted out with a parachute, sitting in the flight deck and being allowed to take the aircraft controls for short periods. The most interesting flight was with a new pilot who was being taught low level flying and navigation over Oxfordshire. We also trained in bomber aircraft gun-turret simulators.

Home Guard

I had experience with the Home Guard in a machine-gun platoon which my father commanded. I learned about the American Browning gun, how to strip and reassemble it, how to aim and to set on fixed firing lines. I learned a lot more about map reading, landscape recognition, how to describe and indicate a particular feature or target and judge distance.

The platoon HQ was in the hall of the Arkley Working Men's Club. On occasions we took the machine guns onto Ridge Hill, between Barnet and St. Albans, where there was a wonderful view for practising setting gun sights and target indication. During the height of the invasion threat, this area had been part of the outer defence of London. But when the platoon had to spend nights guarding Hadley Wood railway tunnel, to prevent any last ditch German sabotage attempts, I wasn't allowed to go! I still have the silver cup presented to Father when the platoon won 'The Best Machine Gun Team' competition.

VE-day was celebrated in May with parties and bonfires but VJ celebrations were a little less spontaneous – perhaps due to the awesomeness of the atomic bomb devastation in Japan. I was rather miffed that I wouldn't see any active service, but it was a great relief for my mother who stopped worrying about me having to fight in the jungle. Though of course I was called up in September 1945, and served three years in the Army in Northern Ireland, India and Libya.

Elsie Johnston

German childhood

I was born in north-eastern Germany in 1925, in an area which is now Poland. My father drove delivery carts, they used horses of course, there was only one car in the town and it belonged to the people who owned the cinema. One day when he was collecting a load from the station, something frightened the horses, they took off and my father injured his back. He was ill for a long time and never really got strong again. I had two brothers, the older one was in the Navy, he was posted to Norway. I went to school in the town, there was no talk about Nazi Socialism. We had the Hitler Youth, it was like the Scouts here and I joined. There were Jewish people living in the town, they owned nearly all the shops except the baker's and the butcher's. We all went to school together, there was no anti-Jewish feeling and none of them were taken away.

Child care job

I left school when I was 13, my mother wasn't very well so I helped to run the house. When the war broke out, I had to find a job and I worked in a shoe shop. Food was rationed, but we had relatives who were farmers, one would kill a pig and we all had some. After my mother died, I had to go to the Labour Exchange in the nearest big town for another job. The Gauleiter who ran it, he was a Nazi, I suppose, but it wasn't a term we used at all. He offered me a job helping his wife to look after his children, so I did that, living with the family. They had another girl doing the cooking and cleaning.

As the war went on, there was news that the Russians were coming, and this family took me with them to an aunt who lived near the Dutch border. We went in a big truck with a lot of other people who were leaving. The family rented a house, but there was nothing much for me to do, so I got a job working in the launderette and had a room above it to live in.

Au pair in England

When the war ended, I saw in the newspaper that they wanted German girls to work in England. I got a form and filled it in and so I came to England. There was a sort of agency, and we had the choice did we want to be au pair, or work in the country. I chose au pair, and went to work in a doctor's family in Luton. There were quite a few of us German girls working there and we would meet up for coffee in Marks and Spencer's café, or go to the cinema on our half day. There was no trouble with visas, though you had to show you were reliable and clean as clean

Then I met my husband who was an electrician on the Vauxhall site, and we got married. I moved to this house in Chorleywood in 1954, and I've been here ever since.

Beatrice Macgillivray

When war broke out in Europe in 1939 I was 10,000 miles away in Vina del Mar, Chile and on that bright Sunday morning was watching a men's hockey match between the British and German teams. Later my relatives in England wrote to say how lucky we were to be in Chile away from the awful bombing, but we wanted to do our bit. My brother Archie volunteered to join the RAF in 1942 and I went with him planning to join the WRNS. Later my sisters came, Audrey to the WAAF, then June to the ATS, also Colin, whom I was later to marry.

Journey to England

We travelled by train to Buenos Aires where we had a splendid week with parties and night club visits. We boarded the *Moreton Bay* at dead of night and sailed for Montevideo. Here we were entertained by the British Consul till we sailed, again at midnight and proceeded zig-zagging across the Atlantic to Freetown. We were in constant danger of U-boats, and at all times had to have our life-jackets with us. Everyone was given a job, so most mornings I did secretarial work for the captain and chief officer. I learnt that a nearby ship had been torpedoed and some of the crew and passengers had managed to escape in life boats. Another lifeboat had been found floating in the Atlantic, with starved and dehydrated corpses.

One evening as we were sitting in the blacked-out wardroom having a pre-dinner drink, the ship gave a terrific lurch and the already dim lights went off. When they came on again, the Captain and Chief Officer were nowhere to be seen – they had rushed off to the bridge and later told me that we had narrowly escaped a torpedo.

As we approached Freetown a plane flew towards us, and all guns were aimed at it till, at the very last moment, it identified itself as British. The Captain was furious that we women had stayed on deck whilst the plane approached, because had it been an enemy aircraft it would have straddled the deck with bullets.

At Freetown we joined a convoy to England. As the biggest ship we had to take the Commodore, but could only go at the speed of the slowest. Then the Admiralty signalled us to proceed to England on our own, which meant that the Commodore had to be lowered on to a boat with his staff and taken to the next biggest ship. We had corvettes circling round us, as we were a sitting target for enemy torpedoes

London

We arrived at Liverpool the day after a heavy air-raid. As our luggage was being unloaded, a sling broke and my brother's entire belongings, including my father's gold signet ring, fell into the Mersey. Next day we went to London by train to enlist. I was told that the WRNS were not recruiting at that time and that I should enter either the WAAF or ATS. I said I would wait till I could join the WRNS. We volunteers from South America had the use of a house in Hyde Park Crescent, to be called South America House where we could stay, and have meals. One of my uncles, whom I had not met before, invited me to lunch at his club, Whites. I sailed gaily in, not being aware that women were not allowed in that men's holy of holies. I was accosted by the doorman who politely informed me I should remain in the hall whilst he called my uncle.

Special Operations Executive

Waiting until call up, I had to find some war work to do. I was offered a secretarial post in the Ministry of Information, but then a friend took me with her to be interviewed for a different, highly secret job with

Special Operations Executive, then known as the Inter-Services Research Bureau, situated in Baker Street, at Sherlock Holmes' address. There I became secretary to Lord Glenconner in the Balkan Section. We were dropping supplies to General Mikhailovich – until we heard that he was also getting supplies from Hitler, so we switched to Tito.

The work was fascinating, so it was a difficult decision when my call-up came. I was doing far more interesting work than I ever could in the WRNS, but all my relatives in Chile and England were wondering why I was not in uniform. I was not able to explain, so eventually I packed up my civvies and joined up.

WRNS

A Wren Officer friend warned me that during the first fortnight I would be allotted menial tasks that I should grin and bear with good grace. I met many new companions and off-duty my previous social life continued, meeting friends at the Overseas Club, going to dinners, dancing, being taken to the Café Royal and night clubs. We were young, and there was always the feeling that life might be short, so we tended to enjoy every moment.

My first posting was as a secretary with the Royal Navy Liaison Division on the staff of General Eisenhower in St. James' Square. We were preparing for the invasion of North Africa, so the work was extremely secret. The night the troops landed, I was on duty. We were all excited, if apprehensive and relieved when the operation was a success.

After the invasion of North Africa, I was allocated a new job, as secretary to Commander Bett, who was organising St.Mark's College in King's Road to become a college for trainee engineer officers. We had to convert the abandoned premises into suitable classrooms and living quarters. Apart from the Captain and myself there was a small group of naval officers on the permanent staff, and being the only female I had my meals with the officers.

During my free time I continued to meet my friends. The WVS often joined us for a chat or a meal, and other Wrens arrived, including one officer. This posed a problem as officers and other ranks were meant to eat separately, but I had always had my meals with them. Then

I was told to report to Greenwich College to attend a pre-Officers Training Course.

Officer training at Greenwich

This was hectic, a constant rush between lectures, meals in the famous Painted Hall, drill, more lectures, then drill again. Social activities were organised for us, such as entertaining naval officers, and I imagine we were being watched to see how we would cope.

On Sundays we could invite visitors to lunch in the Painted Hall; my sister Audrey came and Colin, who was working in the War Office. I had a happy time at Greenwich, meeting old friends and new, including making up a dance party where my partner was Bill Simpson, a very badly scarred and injured fighter pilot and the author of 'One Of Our Pilots is Safe'. I saw plays and films, and fortunately the London air-raids did not damage the buildings at Greenwich.

HMS *Haig*

I was posted to HMS *Haig* in Rye, Sussex, a newly established naval holding depot, prior to the invasion of Europe. My boss was a retired Captain who was rather sceptical about women in the Royal Navy, but then I heard him talking proudly to the Duchess of Bedford about 'my Wrens'. I occasionally went up to London for the weekend, staying at South America House and meeting friends. During our spare time in Rye we played tennis and hockey, went for walks, dances, and concerts given by ENSA (Entertainments National Services Association). We were invited on board some of the ships and met officers from the Norwegian and Dutch navies as well as our own.

Doodlebugs

One night as my colleague Eleanor and I were late to bed after a party, I heard a strange noise in the sky, as if one of our aircraft was coming back on one engine. From my window I saw a plane on fire making for the coast. I presumed the pilot was trying to reach land before bailing out, but it chugged over us on its way north, and I pictured him unable to unstrap himself. I got back to bed feeling very sad, then a few minutes later I heard a similar noise and jumped out of bed to see the same sight again, like a cross of Lorraine, on fire, coming across the Channel. I realised then that it must be Hitler's secret weapon that we had heard about, but when we two Wrens mentioned this to the naval officers the next day they thought we were imagining things. Two days later these pilotless planes started coming over in great numbers. They had noisy engines, and when the sound ceased it meant that they were about to land, so one would have to dive for cover rapidly, as I did once when walking in the countryside. That doodlebug made a great crater and broke windows in Rye.

When the invasion took place it was a fantastic sight. We watched from high-up Rye the thousands of ships crossing the Channel. We had a special church service to pray for all those taking part. So many did not return, and it was heart-breaking reading the casualty lists in the newspapers day after day.

Wedding day

Colin and I were married at his local church, St Mary Abbot's, Kensington, on Trafalgar Day, 21 October 1944. An ex-Ambassador to Chile, Sir Charles Bentinck, who had been ordained after leaving the diplomatic corps officiated, and my dear Aunt Elena gave the reception at her flat in South Kensington. The officers of HMS *Haig* had tried to persuade me to get married in Rye and have the reception in our wardroom, but my aunt flatly refused.

But what to wear? As Colin was not in uniform, he wanted me not to wear mine, though this would have been far easier for me as I had no civilian coupons. Friends and relations gave me some, but I still didn't have enough to buy a dress. Eventually I persuaded Harrods to sell me a coat and skirt, and a smart blouse, and a friend made me a hat.

The day before the wedding I went up to London to stay with friends. Arriving in the evening, I found they were out, and their elderly very deaf aunt did not hear my knocking, so I had to sit on the doorstep until they arrived home, very much later.

My aunt had limited the numbers because her shared flat was not large, and I felt particularly sad that all the officers who came up to London from Rye and sang so well during the service, could not be invited to the reception. We had a cake which looked splendid, all white and elaborately decorated, but when you came to cut it, you lifted the white off – it was cardboard.

Admiralty post

Our honeymoon was spent near Torquay, and whilst there I received a signal informing me that I was being posted to the Admiralty in London and I had been granted permission to sleep out. I was very pleased, but then found it was quite hard because up to then, everything had been done for me, cooking, cleaning, laundry. I was starting on a new and demanding job at the Admiralty and when I got home in the evening, exhausted, I had to do all the housework. A blind patch developed in my eye which was very frightening. I saw the Medical Officer and two eye specialists who discovered that the nerve in my eye was at fault and told me I must stop work and rest immediately. This my Captain was scathing about as I had just had a fortnight's holiday for my honeymoon. I was very relieved when my eyesight became normal again, and I could resume work

Attached to the Admiralty was Churchill's Citadel, which was just like a fortress. In the plotting room, maps all over the walls showed where our ships were and I felt immensely proud to be a part of such an important establishment.

Then victory in Europe! I joined the crowds in Trafalgar Square and was caught up with a group doing the *Lambeth Walk* and the *Hokey Cokey* down the Mall to Buckingham Palace, where the King and Queen and Churchill stood on the balcony. Of course we were still at war with Japan, and the Admiralty was engaged in planning the invasion of that country.

I used sometimes to walk from the Admiralty, up Whitehall to the National Gallery's lunchtime concerts. Walking back one day, the news came through that Japan had surrendered. When the official celebration took place, my Captain and I invited naval friends to our window over Horse Guards Parade to watch the procession.

I carried on working at the Admiralty until October 1945 when I discovered that I was to have a child, and I was de mobbed. John was born on 29 April at midnight. In 1995, this baby, now a tall six-footer, was standing next to me in front of Buckingham Palace on the fiftieth anniversary of VE Day, on the spot where Colin, his father, had stood 50 years previously.

Barbara Marke

At the end of the summer term of 1939, my school friends all said goodbye to me and wished me well for Bedford College, where I was to fulfil a long held ambition to train as a Physical Education teacher. Then at four o'clock on an August morning the phone rang, it was father's adjutant from the Territorial Army telling him all Territorials were to be called up. Father had seen action and been decorated in the First World War, so he just said to me 'Make me a cup of tea and polish my buttons. Don't go to Bedford, stay here and look after your mother and your little brother. Go down to the works and see that it all keeps going.' He went away and we never saw him for eight months.

Running the family business

I stayed at home in the small Cheshire town of Sandbach, running my home and my father's central heating business. I learnt to type and did the invoices. I had to come home at lunchtime to make sure my mother had her meal – she had had a breakdown following the birth of my brother five years before, spent two years in hospital having various treatments, and hadn't really recovered. I had to blackout the whole house, and organise gas masks. All my friends had joined up, though sometimes they came home on leave.

Friends' call-up

All the boys in that year from the grammar school joined the Cheshire regiment and went to France. At first nothing happened, but once things started, nearly all those boys were killed including nine men who had sat on my family sofa. One chap, Basil, volunteered to be a Spitfire pilot, though he admitted he was scared stiff. Later Basil had to bale out with his friend who was badly wounded. Before he died he said to Basil 'Go back and see my wife and give her my watch.' Basil went to see her, fell in love and later married her. I wrote to eight men, who had all been at school together, and told them news of home. One, a vet, went to Burma where he was having to remove the vocal cords from hundreds of mules because they made such a noise going into battle. I sent him *Punch*

When Basil was training, he would bring a car full of pilots home to Sandbach every Thursday night and we would go to the pub. Some pilots went to Narvik, they had to fly low over a road where Germans were walking and had to pepper them with machine-gun fire. One came home and took me to the cinema; he told me he had killed 40 Germans. He was not proud of it, but sad.

We all thought the war would soon be over but when France capitulated it was a terrible blow. Father's brother now ran the business, and I was running the house. After two years my father was demobbed, and said I could go to college for a year because we knew I would be called up when I was 21.

College at Edinburgh

My father said I might get married some time, so I should learn how to run a home and cook. So I went to college in Edinburgh to do a year's course in domestic science. We students didn't take it very seriously, living in a hostel and having an awfully good time. I shared a room with a girl from Dundee, whose father had jute mills near Glamis, and at weekends we sometimes went to her home at Kirriemuir. Hitler didn't drop any bombs on Edinburgh because he wanted it intact for after the war, but planes came over Edinburgh to bomb Glasgow. We spent every night in the cellars for a week, 40 of us. Edinburgh was full of sailors, with warships in the Firth there were parties on board, and sailors coming up into the town to enjoy themselves. Great fun, but all transitory. A group of us put on a lavish production of Ivor Novello's *The Dancing Years* and I danced on stage every night for a week with a trainee vet, we did the *Leap Year Waltz*.

Call up

Then I got my call up papers. I went first to a camp near Warrington, in the grounds of a stately home. There were masses of Nissen huts filled with girls from the Liverpool area, some never having left home before. In my hut was a girl called Pearl, who offered to sleep in the bunk above me. We were unpacking before supper when the door was flung open, the police came in and asked 'Are there any prostitutes here?' Pearl said 'Yes I am', and there were four others. They were told there had been a mistake in the paper work, they shouldn't have been called up. The police said they had a van outside and would take the girls back to Liverpool. So she said 'Nice knowing you', and went.

I was only 15 miles from home, so I used to hitch hike back. You were told never to go in a car with a man on his own and never a black man. You came out of camp and stood at the crossroads, the lorry drivers stopped, got out and helped you in – with an ATS skirt that was quite difficult. One lorry was carrying scent for Pears soap, and our uniform carried that scent for days after. The drivers were awfully good and I never had any trouble.

I was asked to help in the de-lousing of the new recruits, and I said I didn't know what I was looking for. They said 'Come and see this, with black hair it's more obvious' and it was crawling. Poor girls had the stuff on their heads for an hour during lunch and everyone could see who had it.

Girls were there for five weeks initial training, then were posted all over Britain, and my job was arranging these postings. Faith Brooks, the actress, was one – the press heard she was there and wanted a photo of her marching. She happened to have a huge boil on the side of her face so the officer said 'We'll wheel round so you photograph her good side'. I think she got a job in ENSA (Entertainments National Services Association).

In order to teach us that gas masks were essential they had a hut with a male sergeant in charge and gas burning. You had to stay in with

the gas for two or three minutes, and I got into such a state because I had had asthma as a child and I was hammering on the sergeant's chest and shouting 'Let me out, let me out'. There was a window and I wanted to break the glass. I came out, collapsed against a tree feeling absolutely terrible and was sent to my hut.

A girl went AWOL (Absent Without Leave), her name was Smith, EM, with an address in Liverpool. I went with an officer to apprehend her; we took bully beef sandwiches as we would be away all day. We found her at her mother's house, handcuffed her and took her back to Lime Street station. The platform was heaving with troops, so we took the cuffs off. I asked if she would like a sandwich, and when she said 'Yes' I gave her the bully beef sandwich, which she flung in the officer's face and made off into the crowd. We couldn't get her. We had to report a lost prisoner, which was a serious offence. Later, another officer went to get her again, and this time she escaped by crawling under a lavatory partition.

Hampshire

After a year, the training centre closed down overnight, and the 50 girls in my company had to be posted by the next morning. I knew them a bit, and tried hard to get them posted to somewhere they would like. I then had to post myself, to a camp in Hampshire where they were training railway construction workers. They had brought diesel trains from Canada which were to go to Italy in pieces, where soldiers would have to put them together again.

We were preparing for the invasion of France, with vast concentrations of troops and vehicles in the south of England. It was a huge camp and included a group of Jamaican recruits in check trousers and straw hats. We were in the depths of the country, and not allowed

124

to use trains or buses, so I didn't get home for eight months. But we had bicycles, and cycled to pubs, there were dances in the camp, a camp cinema where I saw *Casablanca*, ENSA entertainment and even a visit from Noel Coward.

My officer knew I wanted to do Physical Training and she had a letter asking for a volunteer to go on a PT course. So I went for three weeks very intensive training at Aldershot. After training all day, I would lay on my bed with my feet above my head for 20 minutes till I felt renewed, and then went out dancing. It was the darkest part of the war, but we had such fun – most of the time. Each evening, the whole sky was full of Lancaster bombers going to Germany, then next morning fewer came limping back.

York

I was posted to York, and issued with khaki bicycle, pump and bell, and a brown tracksuit which got baggy at the knees. My job was to take PT classes for groups of girls in army offices. They hated going outside in the cold, ties off, suspenders undone and stockings rolled down, to play team games and go running. I had to cycle to the classes all round York, with a ball and hoops, and I got to know the policemen. If it was raining I would cancel, and go into a coffee shop. Monday mornings we were at Bishopsthorpe, home of the Archbishop of York, where I took a class on his front lawn.

The girls hated the PT runs, and said they had the curse, so couldn't do them. But I kept a register and told them they had said that last week. The NAAFI was very good, and the Salvation Army had a place where you would be welcomed with sardines or beans on toast, a wonderful sanctuary. But when the Salvation Army came to the NAAFI on Sunday to play hymns, people walked out.

My friend from Liverpool and I had a weekend pass, so we went to the Pickford's removal depot and asked if a van was going across the Pennines. We were told 'Come to the yard at ten tonight, and get into the van with the furniture.' There was a grand piano in the van, and when we stopped at a pub on top of the Pennines, I played my one tune, *The Leap Year Waltz*, over and over. We got to Manchester, then another lift to get home. We had to be back in camp next day by 23.59.

A girl from Congleton was getting married, and she had no cake, so we went to the cooks and asked if they could make her one. We hitch-hiked with the cake to Congleton, to her cottage near the mill. Her father said he couldn't come to the wedding as he was filthy and had nothing to wear, but we persuaded him to scrub down in the kitchen sink, and he went. The bride wore her uniform. The reception was in a hall next to the Methodist chapel, there were sandwiches on trestle tables. When it came to the best man's speech, he stood up, said ' 'Ere's to 'em', and sat down.

We were billeted in old infantry barracks, and next to us were Cavalry barracks, where I met my future husband Terence at a NAAFI dance. The officers in training ran out of beer at their end of the hall, and one, who was a friend of mine, asked me if I would get them a beer from my end, which I did. Then the friend said to Terence 'Old chap, I do think you should have a dance with her, after all she has been decent enough to get us a beer' which he did. Then he took me to an Eileen Joyce concert at the Empire theatre, and we got to know each other. We would go to dances in uniform, the men danced beautifully in their big boots. Make up was scarce, but we were told by an officer 'You must wear make-up, you can't see yourselves but we have to look at you, so keep your hair off your collar, powder your nose, and use a little lipstick because khaki is such an unfortunate colour.'

One day Terence and I cycled to a pub for a drink, and left the bikes outside. When we came out, my bike was gone. I got back to camp and had to report the loss of the bike. I was put on a charge, and marched in front of the officer. 'You are charged with the loss of one Army bicycle, pump and bell. Do you agree with that?' so I said 'Yes' and the punishment was to scrub the sergeants' mess every night at seven o'clock for a week. At the end of the week the police came and said they had found the bicycle in the river. An RAF chap had missed his last bus, pinched my bicycle, rode back to his camp and then threw the bike into the river.

When the war ended, we celebrated, doing the conga through the streets of York on VE night. Terence had to go to Italy for a year, and I stayed in the ATS till I was de-mobbed in 1946. The war shaped my life, I can tackle anything, and get on with anyone.

Jean Nash

In 1939, I was six years old, living with my father who was an RAF officer, my mother, my brother five years older than me, and Nanny who had become a dear family friend. We had moved about a lot, but that summer father was posted to run the Cambridge University Air Training Corps, and after 11 years of married life in quarters, my parents bought and furnished their first home there. We moved in early August, and three weeks later, war broke out. My father told me this, and seemed sad he would not be back with Sopwith Camels over France, as he had been in World War One. I, however was very excited, and rushed to the big bay window expecting to see a circle of men with claymores and spears coming down the road in the rain. I was hugely disappointed.

Dog-fight over Fife

My father was immediately posted back to the Air Ministry. He sent Nanny and me north to my grandmother in Burntisland, Fife, whilst my brother went back to boarding school, and Mother stayed with Father. My cousin Christopher joined us, his father also having been hastily posted in the Marines. On 16 October, Christopher's birthday, Granny arranged a small party and we two children and two grown-ups were sent for a walk so she could prepare. I remember walking down to the town, when there was a strange noise and people were running. We wondered what it was, but went on down to the harbour where we saw an amazing sight – lots of aircraft, doing a sort of sky dance – it was wonderful, they wheeled and dived and zoomed around the sky. Having lived on Air Force stations, I 'knew it all', and told the others they were practicing, and why. But privately I thought my father had arranged it all as a special display for Christopher's birthday, and was deeply jealous.

When we got back through the deserted town, my grandmother was faint with worry, for we had been right under the first air-raid and dog fight of the war. German bombers had tried to bomb the Forth Bridge and the Rosyth dockyards, and had been driven off by fighters from 603 Squadron. I still thought it had all been arranged by my father.

Nanny taught me mostly, service children were not allowed in local schools, but in Spring 1940 we formed a school in a Brownie hut with other service children aged between five and ten. We were taught by a lovely lady who took us, from knowing nothing to spelling words like 'maximum' and 'minimum'. It was a wonderful basic schooling.

To the Highlands

The first summer of the war, we took a house in Stanmore to be near my father. We lived in a cul de sac where there were other children and had a great time. Then I was sent to Scotland again. Granny, having given up her house to the Red Cross, had moved to the village of Newtownmore in the Highlands. I knew the village well, we had been there with Mother and Granny before. I used to bicycle to school, the village itself was flat, but was surrounded by mountains. That winter, 1940-41, it was bitterly cold. There was a big highland river, which froze absolutely solid so you could walk on it, all the boulders were covered with ice and you could slide down them. Nanny got para-typhoid, from eating a cake that had come from Inverness, and we were immediately put into complete quarantine. A girl, Mary, who came from the village to the house to help in the mornings was not even allowed to go home, where her dishes were still in the sink and my grandmother had to come and toss food over the fence to us. We were in quarantine for about three weeks, it was bitterly cold, but lovely. We were all given injections, and none of us got the illness. I couldn't go to school, but my friends came and waved through the fence.

I was a very active child, in the summers constantly bowling cricket balls to my brother. I bicycled, climbed, ran, walked, played. I read a lot, my family were all good readers. Someone gave me 'Swallows and Amazons' for Christmas, and after that I just waited for the next volume to come. We played board games, Nanny was a marvellous person, I loved her very dearly.

Then suddenly in April 1941, my father was posted to South Africa. Mother decided we would all go, and we had two weeks to get ready. She gave away everything we had except for bits of luggage for the journey, I even had to give up my bicycle. Nanny said she would come with us. The day before we had to get the train to go to Liverpool for the boat, Granny and the aunts came round and there were lots of tears because they thought that with the attacks on the convoys, they might never see us again. But I was just excited. Next morning the taxi came to take us to the station, and then a telegram arrived to say it was all off, we were not going. We had given everything away. Mother said to my brother Michael and me, 'We'll go round to Granny's house' which was by the golf course, and from which she could see the train and had promised to wave to us. So at ten past ten she waved at the train, and then Michael turned up at the door and said we weren't going. I was really cross, because wee Willie down the road had my bicycle and Mother said we couldn't go and ask for it back. Our luggage sailed to South Africa – I don't remember if we got it back.

Stranraer

Instead we went to Stranraer, a port and bomber training station in south-west Scotland where my father was Commanding Officer, and we were there 18 months. We were the only civilians living in the station, and I went to the local service family school, in a church. The Padre was an expert ventriloquist and conjuror, and then there was Eric, who had drawn cartoons for Beano and Dandy. He spent hours doing Eggo the Ostrich, Keyhole Kate and Korky the Cat for me, but I was not allowed to keep any. There were some Polish airmen there, I was told they would be sad because they were away from their families, but I enjoyed going to see them, I think I reminded them of families back home.

Then my father was posted to Cheng Tu, in south-west China which was still held by the Chinese Nationalists. His journey out was dangerous, going via Cape Town in convoy, then on to India. He was one of a small group of RAF men sent to help to train their Air Force. He did not enjoy this, the Chinese would not answer questions in case they were wrong in which case they would lose face. Father just wanted to be back home with us, and kept applying for a return posting.

Montrose Academy

We went to live in Montrose and there I started at a proper school, the Montrose Academy. I had been really well educated at the little schools, with ex-headmistresses who were glad to be teaching again and I had no problems settling in to a normal school. I loved it there. We lived three miles out in the country and I had to bicycle to get to the bus for school. There was wonderful countryside around, sea and sand and rocks and exciting things to do. I would go out with a 'piece' – a sandwich – and be out all day and mother never worried, though there were all sorts of dangers with the sea and tides. I just ran wild, it was great. I was never lonely, never bored. We lived near a farm, so we were never short of milk and eggs. Mother and Nanny used to save up their jam and butter for when my brother came home from school, Nanny was a wonderful cook, so I grew up loving mince and Brussels sprouts and rice pudding. In October we had three weeks off school for tattie-

130

howking, picking the potato crop. This was great fun at first, but became really hard work.

We used to get letters from my father, flown out by the Americans over the Himalayas to India. I suppose he was safer there, though he was pretty miserable. He arrived home two days before VE-day. We had been told he would be coming, and went to meet the train at eight o'clock that morning. I expected him to look just as he had when he went away, but he was much changed, had put on weight, and his face was very drawn. My mother had got a lobster from the local fisherman as a celebration, but when I learnt it had to be boiled, I threw a terrific tantrum and spoilt everyone's day. We had scrambled eggs instead.

Two days later my father told me the war in Europe was over. He was posted to Lossiemouth, and later to Banff where I visited him, but I stayed in Montrose with Nanny where I was well settled at school, and would soon be going to boarding school anyway. Boarding school was very strange, it was girls only and very strict after my free and easy life, and though I missed my freedom, I enjoyed it, being by nature a happy person. I was so lucky to have my father home and safe.

Ray Newell

Art student to Artillery-man

When the war the war started I was studying at Hornsey School of Art in north London. During my fourth year I took my final painting exams, and also registered in the Services. I joined the Royal Artillery and trained as surveyor-cum-specialist in a Medium Regiment on Salisbury Plain. At the end of 1940 I was posted to Watford in the Second Mountain Regiment (Pack Artillery) though the only mountain we could find was Mount Vernon in Northwood. We were told that as 'specialist surveyors' we would have to ride horseback. We started theoretical training and were informed that we would get our horses when we arrived overseas. We would also be introduced to our guns – the 'screw gun' of the nineteenth century's Afghan wars. This was a little howitzer which could be taken apart and transported on numerous mules, then reassembled to fire a 13-pound shell a few thousand yards. As we had trained on heavier field artillery and the modern 25-pounder field gun, we weren't over impressed, especially when we heard the latest German mortars would easily outgun us.

Palestine

By March 1941 I was learning to ride up and down the mountains in Palestine. It was quite exciting, although we never did see any example of the Screw Gun. In June I celebrated my 21st birthday with tepid lemonade, and our unit was disbanded to replace casualties in the campaigns in Greece and Crete. I joined the 64th Medium Regiment, and was instead sent to Syria to fight the Vichy French. They must have heard I was coming, for as we crossed the frontier, they surrendered and we became the Army of Occupation. We wandered round Damascus and Beirut, up into the mountains and to Baalbeck. Then I fell ill  with diphtheria, and was hospitalised in Jerusalem where I spent months flat on my back, very bored.

Western Desert

The regiment had gone to North Africa, into the Western Desert, and I rejoined them just after Christmas 1941. We took over defence positions on the Libyan border, and stayed there until the Germans attacked after capturing Tobruk. They surrounded us, but we managed to break out and dug in again at Mersa Matruh. Meanwhile the Eighth Army had reached El Alamein. We attempted to rejoin them, but our truck got shelled and set on fire by a German tank. After running round the desert all night we were eventually captured by another armoured column of the Afrika Korps. This was June 1942. They took us back to Bardia, gave us a meal and then with profuse apologies handed us over to the Italians. I had never put much credence in reports of antagonism between the Axis powers until I met it. The Germans really despised the Italians, who hated them in return.

Benghazi prison camp

The Italians treated us terribly. We were nearly six months in the prison camp at Benghazi. There was nothing there, just a stretch of desert enclosed by barbed wire. For each three men they gave us two groundsheets which you could clip together to make a sort of tent, no blankets, no water laid on, just a tank, no sanitary arrangements at all until we dug some pits in the desert. I had a tiny notebook, the size of a pocket diary and in this and on any scraps of paper I could find, I made drawings. I dared not let the Italian guards see them so I carried them

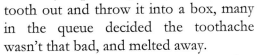

in my boot. By the time I'd done six months, they were pretty tatty. I sketched the dentist at work, extractions only, no anaesthetic of course. To start with there was a queue of men waiting outside the tent but when they watched the Italian dentist just put his pliers in, wrench the

tooth out and throw it into a box, many in the queue decided the toothache wasn't that bad, and melted away.

We were supposed to get one hot meal a day, but we only got 60 in the six months we were there. Otherwise you got a couple of tasteless Italian biscuits or sometimes some British bully beef. I drew a sketch of us thinking about a table laden with food and a bottle of wine. I was 11 stone when I went into that camp, and less than seven when I came out. One man in ten died. Sometimes they would bring in a de-lousing machine which they lit and it made fumes, you were meant to put your clothes in but if you did you couldn't wear them when they came out. There was an RAF raid on Benghazi harbour when they hit a boat full of armaments. It made the most gorgeous explosion and of course we all cheered like mad, but we didn't get any rations for two days. You got very depressed, and that's when I started drawing. People asked for portraits of themselves, we had all grown beards because there was nothing to shave with, and no water anyway. They used to pay me, maybe two cigarettes. I saved up cigarettes and traded them for a second hand toothbrush. A group of us produced a newspaper *The Benghazi Forum* with my drawings and written contributions, using any scrap of paper we could find.

Italian prisoner of war camps

Then came the German defeat at Alamein, and the Italians were told to ship us out of Africa because they didn't want prisoners-of-war to be rescued by the British Army. The bombing had cut the road from Benghazi to Tripoli, so they sent us by sea and then on to Italy. The camp was at Tuturano, near Brindisi and there we sometimes got Red Cross parcels. We were in tents to start with but there's a note in my diary 'Moved into huts for the first time in months', there was even a washing place. We used to hear about the progress of the war from new prisoners coming into the camp, and our Newspaper Set produced the *Tuturano Times*.

As the Allies advanced, we were moved from Tuturano to an old jam factory at Fermo, inland from Ancona. The Newspaper Set kept together, and we produced the *70 Times*. The Italian guards saw some of my drawings of fellow prisoners, and the medical officer, a handsome man with a fine face, asked me to draw his portrait. I was given a room next to the officers' mess, and here I could spend the whole day. The Italians found me drawing materials and, best of all, I got some of the proper decent food they were serving to their officers. I spun out the completion of the portrait for as long as I could. Then the dentist asked me to draw him. He was very different, with fair hair, a pale complexion and protuberant eyes. As is my wont, I drew him as near life-like as I could, but he was not pleased. He said he wanted his face to look more like the doctor's, so I did another portrait, less accurate but more flattering, and this he liked. But when he showed them to his mother, she had no time for the second portrait, preferring the original.

These officers were royalist sympathisers, and wanted a portrait of King Victor Emmanuel to hang on the wall. They gave me a book which contained an illustration of the king, and from this I did a larger crayoned portrait, and mounted it on cardboard for them. All the time I was working, there was an Italian guard in the room, and he was in charge of the book. One day I opened it at another page, and there was a picture of Mussolini which had been defaced and made into a cartoon, using my coloured pencils. I was terrified that the officers would see this and think I had done it – I suppose it had been the guard. Mercifully, no one seemed to notice. One day I glanced at that guard, he had crossed his legs with one foot on the other knee, and I saw that though the top of his boot looked normal, it had no sole, he was in fact walking barefoot.

Italian surrender

Then came the memorable day in September 1943 when the Italians surrendered. We heard cries of 'Finito guerra!', the guards tossed their rifles over the fence and with shouts of 'Andiamo a casa' off they went, and the camp was suddenly open. The senior British officer took charge, he told us the Allies had landed in Genoa and in Venice, and we would be rescued any minute, so everyone was to stay in the camp. He kept telling us 'Don't panic'. My diary says 'Italians surrendered, produced two-page edition, up till 4am'. There was a British guard posted at the gate, and no one was to leave without permission. We did go out of the camp for a walk some days, in organised groups of 20 or so.

German PoW camp

On 17 September a group of Germans arrived. We hid under the weighbridge for a few hours, with the Germans lobbing hand grenades into the compound till we gave up. We were put into trains, 40 men to a truck, with a bucket of water and no sanitation. We had taken all the Red Cross parcels from the stores, and after four days we arrived at Innsbruck, and were allowed out to relieve ourselves. On 29 September we arrived at Jacobsthal concentration camp, there were starving Russians in the next compound in striped night-shirts. We were in huts with multi-storey bunks, bugs, fleas, lice and rats. It was the first time we had met rats, because in Africa if there were any animals they would have been eaten. On 16 October, we were marched four miles to Stalag 4B Muhlberg. Here there were 20,000 men, 200 per wooden hut, with a concrete wash-house for every two huts which had a trough with cold water running from 7.0am till 5.0pm, jolly cold water it was.

Our newspaper group formed an office in one corner of the hut. It was all hand-written, we stuck pieces of paper onto a board, and one of the men used to take it round the huts. We had radios – unofficially of course. There was a central chimney in the hut, you lit a fire under a hot plate and the smoke went up the chimney, that was the heating system. To start with there were two men on each level of the three tiered bunk, but then there was the Battle  of the Bulge and a lot of Americans were brought in, an extra 100 in each hut, so we were three men in each bunk.

Formation of Art Class

I started an Art Class, and was given all the art material that came in from the Red Cross which I divided up between ourselves, the theatre group, and the newspaper creators but of course I could keep some back for the Art Class. Ours was a transit camp, and international law states that an officer or non-commissioned officer (NCO) prisoner doesn't have to work, but a private is more or less slave labour. Though he isn't supposed to do any war work, our men were getting shoved into mines or arms factories. You could be 'promoted in the field', so I set myself up as a bombardier and promoted a lot of the men to be NCOs, so they could stay working on our newspaper. My largest art class was 25, and some of them carried on afterwards; for one man I wrote in his report 'should be able to make a living by art' and he did. He went to New Zealand and sent me copies of some of his work. There was another man who wasn't quite so skilled, but he was good at drawing animals. After demob he worked as a gardener, then he started to draw people's pets, and it went on from that and he made quite a go of it.

Sanitation consisted of emptying latrines into a truck we called the Bombay Belle, it had a long wooden drum, and was drawn out of the camp by two oxen. There were a couple of Russians who used to take this out, and they would do a lot of trading with the local farms, maybe taking a tin of coffee and bringing back some white bread. I never fancied using their services, they would go out with a truck and empty all the sewage, then what did they bring the food back in?

I did several portraits, including one of an American sergeant who was captured in Italy. He kept himself immaculate, and got very cross when anyone called him a Yankee 'I'm not a goddam Yank, I'm a Southern gentleman'. He was a great character. Another man, half Mexican, arrived who had a big, bushy beard. Coming into our camp, you had to pass the Indian Sikh compound (they were kept separate from us because there were attempts being made to persuade them to join the Japanese against the British). As this man walked past their compound they called out to him, thinking he must be a Sikh, and they threw over to him a small round close-fitting red cap. He decided the hat was a good luck talisman, and nothing would induce him to take it off. By the end of the year, it was absolutely black. Another man was a hypnotist who used to have a stage act, and he would hypnotise anyone who needed minor surgery as there was a shortage of anaesthetic.

Liberation

Our camp was very close to the place where the Russians and the British met. The Germans were moving their army from the east away from the Russians, and from the west away from the Allies. The Russians got to us first, on 23 April 1945. They pulled down some of the wire and told us to live off the land. Then the Americans came and said would we like to write home, took our letters and went away again. There was some dispute between Churchill, Roosevelt and Stalin about what to do with the Ukrainians, who had been helping the Germans and didn't want to return to Stalin. It was agreed that they should be given refugee status, and all prisoners-of-war were to be repatriated. We were sent to a town called Riesa where we had to find our own food and accommodation. The German civilians welcomed us into their homes because that made it less likely that the Russians would interfere with them; they were scared stiff of the Russians, especially the Mongolians. Muhlberg remained as a de-Nazification centre for a while, later it was pulled down and now there is a beautiful beech wood there.

We stayed in Riesa for several weeks. Then one day we were told to parade in the main square at 5.30am ready to embark. A band played excerpts from the 'Maid of the Mountain' and there were lots of farewell speeches. After an hour or two, some trucks came in with a load of Russian prisoners who got off, and the trucks being American, they filled up with American soldiers and drove away. All day long the trucks came and went, collecting more ex-prisoners whilst we waited in the drizzle. It was 10.30 that evening when we got on, and were driven to Halle, into what had been a German airforce camp, now an American one. They fed us right royally, and the next day they flew us in Dakotas to Brussels. That gave us a chance to see what had happened to Germany, village after village completely flattened. Just a pile of rubble, connected by more rubble to another pile. We spent a night in Brussels, then got onto a Halifax bomber; we were only allowed one army pack, so I emptied mine and filled it with my sketches. It was very heavy, and not knowing how I was going to pass it up to the airman, I swung it to and fro as I walked, then swung it up to him; he caught it in one hand and promptly fell out of the plane. 'What you got in here, the Crown Jewels?' 'No, only bits of paper.'

We flew into Thame, quite smartly dressed by now, with clean shirts. We were put into a nearby camp, and the WVS were there to greet us with a cup of English tea. Whilst we were sitting enjoying this, an Air Force man came in with a big drum and attached to it a hose. He told me to stand up, stuck the hose up my trouser leg and released a great jet of white DDT powder which blew up into my hair and all over the place. As I had been free of lice and bugs for at least two years, I really didn't think it was necessary, and all this powder was everywhere, in my hair, in the tea. We were then issued with uniform and put into barracks, and they took the phone numbers of our next of kin. We couldn't understand why we couldn't just go home, but it had happened that men had gone home and found it bombed and empty.

I had a medical inspection, and went home for three months leave on double rations before being called back. Initially it was to go to the Far East, then to the Army of Occupation in Germany, but then it was decided not to send ex-POWs back to Germany. Instead they made us into a Formation College, and anyone who had any training was made an instructor in whatever trade they had. The colonel asked me to do a drawing of him, and then asked could I teach drawing. I said I could so they made me a Sergeant Art Instructor and I continued as this till September 1946. After de-mob, I got a grant to go back to Hornsey School of Art. Having finished my course, I taught there for a while, then in a grammar school. I did not enjoy this, so I resigned, and became a commercial artist.

The drawings were done by Ray Newell during his imprisonment.

Ruth Osborne

I was born in 1927, when my family was living in Berlin. When Hitler came to power in 1933, my father realised the threat to us as Jews. He did not wish to bring up his children under such a regime, so we left Germany for Belgium. Over the next six months before my father himself left, he posted money from the Berlin bank, in different letterboxes, to a Poste Restante address in Belgium where my mother and we two children were living.

Ealing

My father, an ophthalmologist, was one of a group of German doctors who in the 1930s were invited to come and practice in England, provided they re-took their MB exams. He passed his after a year at Edinburgh University, and we settled in Ealing. It took some three years before any patients ventured to see this foreign doctor and we had to live on his savings. Because of the depression in the thirties prices were low, my brother and I could go to good schools, my parents bought a house and we became British citizens.

Oxford

The summer of 1939 was lovely and we were on holiday in sleepy Somerset when we heard on the wireless Chamberlain's declaration of war. Everyone thought London would be bombed straight away, so my mother, brother and I went to Wolvercote, near Oxford where my father visited us at weekends. Before the war, we avoided speaking German as we wanted to improve our English and during it we feared we might be taken for spies if we were heard. Our name had been anglicised from Lipschütz to Lytton because my father had enjoyed the novels of Bulwer Lytton as a boy. We were unaware of the aristocratic lineage of the name!

Journey to the New World

Throughout the war my father worked in Moorfields Eye Hospital, and remained living in Ealing. He would visit us in Oxford, where my brother went to the Dragon School, and I to Oxford High. In May 1940, part of the British Expeditionary Force rescued from Dunkirk camped in Cowley Meadows, opposite our house. The invasion of Britain seemed imminent, so my father, wishing to save his family from the Gestapo, sent us to the United States where he had deposited some savings with friends. At that time you were not permitted to take any money out of England. To get a visa we had to have a medical, which involved my stripping down to my shoes and socks, humiliating for a girl of nearly 13.

The day the Battle of Britain began, 15 August 1940, my mother, brother and I left Liverpool Street station for an unknown port. We arrived in Glasgow and saw the Clyde teeming with ships from the Royal Navy. We boarded the SS *Duchess of York*, a Canadian Pacific liner, manned by cheerful Scots mariners, which took ten days zig-zagging across the Atlantic. We were protected by a convoy, as a previous ship with 500 unaccompanied children had been sunk. For the adults, the journey was nerve-racking, but for us children it was an exciting adventure, and once we had got over the initial sea-sickness, we enjoyed being allowed anything on the dining-room menu, a change from the austerity of rationing.

We arrived in Halifax, Nova Scotia and went by train to Montreal and then to New York. It made me aware of the immensity of the New World, prairie land and forests, lakes and mountains. Then, magically, we saw New York at night, ablaze with lights, after a year of total blackout at home. We failed to meet our friends because my mother had said we were arriving at eight o'clock, and they, working on a 24-hour clock, presumed this meant eight in the morning. At least we could make ourselves understood, and found accommodation.

New York

I went first to the local American primary school. My class teacher was a Republican isolationist, who was furious with me for wearing a Roosevelt button during the presidential elections. She quoted the Monroe Doctrine warning against foreign entanglement, but Roosevelt was supporting Churchill and sending lease-lend supplies to Britain.

The English Speaking Union took the British children under its wing, and arranged a free place for me in the Garden Country Day School, where I was happy and made friends. We were now living in Jackson Heights, which, unbeknown to us, was a restricted area, where Negroes and Jews were not allowed. A girl school-mate could not believe that I was Jewish, but when I convinced her, she shook hands with me. We had a scheme for getting money to help the British war effort, selling pencils with Churchill's motto 'We shall not flag or fail'. One boy from a German family background bought up my bundle of pencils and burnt them. The headmaster knew of my background, but wanted me there to educate the others!

We were now living in a three-roomed apartment. My brother had gone to boarding school, but my mother and I were in one bedroom, and the other was occupied by a mother and two children. Everything was shared, so there was no privacy. The news was full of dire reports of London burning, we were short of money, my mother was worried about her parents trapped in Germany and she desperately missed being able to turn to my father who had previously made all the decisions. Communication with England was by letter in mail boats, which was slow and often didn't arrive at all.

I had turned into an American teenager and wanted to be just like the others. My English clothes seemed ridiculous, we didn't have school uniform so I raided my mother's wardrobe. My mother had all but succeeded in getting sponsors for her parents to come to the States when the Japanese attack on Pearl Harbor brought America into the war. In 1942, my grandparents were deported to Theresienstadt where my grandfather died in May 1944, my grandmother perished in Auschwitz.

My brother, a good chorister, was serving at the altar of his school, and would have become an Episcopalian had my mother not intervened. Poor Alfred, he left Germany before he could speak, lived for six months in Belgium, a year in Scotland, and five months in Germany before we came to England, and then on to America, no wonder he suffered some confusion.

In June 1943, my mother took the opportunity to return to England to look after my father. My brother remained at boarding school and holidayed with good friends, and I went to summer school in Greenwich, Connecticut, the richest town per capita in the States, where people lived in baronial style in Disney-like fantasy castles. There I was tutored by an inspiring Cambridge graduate who formerly taught at St Pauls Girls School. I was offered a place at Radcliffe College, but as I was still under 16, it was decided to place me in Pembroke College, Brown University where I was under the kindly care of a house-mother. Throughout my stay in  America, I received the most generous hospitality. I went to a marvellous summer camp in Maine, and made friends with whom I am still in touch. A distinguished violin teacher lent me a beautiful violin and gave me two lessons a week, one at half price and the other free.

Back to London

In May 1944, it became possible to sail for home, and I went in the *Mauretania*. I had dreamt of this moment and so had my parents. My mother prepared a welcoming meal for me which I ate heartily, not realising that it was a whole week's rations. My cabin trunks had to be transported in wheelbarrows from the station and looked excessive by wartime standards. My friends admired my American clothes, but my mother frowned on my college gear of rolled up jeans, loose shirts, Sloppy Joe sweaters and dirty saddle shoes. To my chagrin, I had to return to wearing school uniform as my headmistress considered the first year of an American college to be the equivalent of the Lower Sixth form. Home life became turbulent. My parents tried to re-shape me into the obedient child I had once been, but I felt irredeemably emancipated and missed the free and easy American way of life.

Added to which, the V1 and V2 bombardment was on, and we slept in our cramped coal cellar at night. Though people were weary after five years of war, I confess that I was glad to share in what Britain had endured. At school I worked hard for my Higher School Certificate, taking time off on VE day to join the crowds surging from Piccadilly Circus to Buckingham Palace to celebrate. We were in a state of euphoria, there was no rowdy behaviour, everyone was simply happy.

When Hiroshima finally ended hostilities, I was on holiday in the Lake District, nervously awaiting my exam results, and unaware of what an impact the bomb would have on all our lives. The following year I went up to Cambridge, where I read English and played the violin in the University Orchestra.

Beryl Pepper

When I left school, I started work in the financial department of the John Dickinson paper mill at Apsley. I used to cycle down the hill from Felden where my family lived. My brother was already in the Navy, and when the war started I wanted to go into the forces, but my father wouldn't sign the forms which I needed as I was under age.

Joining up

As soon as I was 17 ½ I joined up, on 29 May 1942 and went to York, where I had four weeks of drilling, gas mask training and having to do PT in our knickers. I volunteered to go into ack-ack (anti-aircraft) because my friend was in it. We had lots of tests, especially for our eyes. On 26 June I went to Devizes for ack-ack training, going by train from York, picking up girls all the way. For eight weeks we had classes learning how to use the very primitive radar. There were Americans there, they were gentlemen, used to bring us candy. We then split up to go to different batteries. I went to Tile Hill, Coventry.

Aircraft tracking

I arrived a week after the raids. Coventry was devastated, a big department store reduced to an eight-foot heap of rubble, but there was no more German bombing. By now I was on a Mark Two battery, and was Number One in a team of four girls, three working the receiver and one the transmitter, tracking in-coming planes and passing on the information to the gunners. I went to many different places as the batteries moved around a lot. Having been trained, I could go to any battery as they were all the same. We didn't get much time off, maybe one half day and one evening in the week. One time we went to the pictures, we missed the beginning and we missed the end because we had to get back. At this 492 Battery, Grimsdyke, we lived in Nissen huts. Now it is being made into a heritage centre.

There wasn't much enemy aircraft going overhead at this time. Next I went to Bude on a secret course, to learn a new American type of more advanced radar. All they told us was the lay out and the drill, they had a very early computer. I was posted to Dovercourt near Ipswich when the flying bombs were coming over. We worked a 24-hour shift, one day on, one off, sometimes we were doing domestic work, cleaning and cooking. I couldn't quite get home and back in the day. You only had your uniform, no other clothes. Some places you just did GL (gun-laying), others you had to do domestic jobs as well. One time we went to a park with an underground map room, to observe the WAAFs there, plotting the course of planes, during a raid on Torquay.

We were constantly moving, I worked at 35 different sites, and the experience made me self-reliant. My mother saw me off at Kings Cross when I joined up, but that was the only time I let her.

I was at Dovercourt when the war ended. VE-day was a Tuesday so we didn't have much money, payday being Friday. We went to a pub, the Bird in Hand, and had one drink then went back to camp and had a bonfire. Most of the men were older so weren't being sent out to the East.

Demob preparations

The battery went to Bristol to be split up. Whilst I was there, I was summoned to the Sergeant Major one Sunday afternoon. He told me there were some blokes leaving and he wanted me to do the paper work. There was a thick book on what we had to do before they could get demobbed; I must have done the job well as I was given same job again later. Next I was sent to Liverpool. We were in a territorial hut, the woman in charge was a university lady; there were various activities on offer and you put your name down for everything, otherwise you'd be given routine work to do. She taught us to row on the lake, we went on the Mersey, visited the Sunlight Soap works, and were the first to go into the dockyard.

Then I was sent to an FVPE (Fighting Vehicle Proving Establishment) in Surrey, where we tried out all sorts of vehicles. The men did the test-driving, I did the paperwork, and I stayed there till I was demobbed.

On the whole, I enjoyed the experience, I had good comrades, and I've kept up with several of them. I came back to the same job at Dickinsons. They had kept jobs open, but only for those who had been called up; I had volunteered, but I still got my job back. I found the wages book hadn't been touched since I left that Christmas, so I had to start it up all over again.

Cora Portillo

Oxford student

When the war started, I was at Oxford reading Spanish and French. My parents wanted their three daughters to be well educated, my two sisters both got their LRAM (Licentiate of the Royal Academy of Music), one on the violin, the other on piano. They stayed in London, and their fate would have been to teach music to children, but when the war came, Dorothy got a job in the admiralty, and Margery joined the BBC Arabic section, where she remained all her working life.

At Oxford there were not many women doing Spanish. War didn't make much difference to academic work, but once it started we no longer had the good food and the maids to do our rooms because women were called up. We bicycled everywhere.

Because of the Spanish Civil War, I could not go to Spain to practice the language so my tutor advised me to visit the Basque children's colony at Aston, near Oxford.

Spanish Children's Colonies

In 1937, the Spanish Civil War had reached the Basque country in Northern Spain. Bilbao and its surroundings were devastated by the Nationalist attacks carried out with the help of the German Condor Legion, which in a bombing raid annihilated the ancient city of Guernica on 26 April. There was no warning, the raid lasted three hours, fleeing civilians were machine-gunned as they ran and farmsteads in the surrounding hills were set on fire by incendiary bombs.

Civilians were hastily evacuated from the area, by boat or over the mountains. Other European countries agreed to take children, and 'colonies' were founded to care for them. Some 4000 children came to Britain and Ireland. There was no government money for them, it was all done by volunteers and the children themselves gave concerts to raise funds.

Meeting Luis

I would take the bus to the colony to help out, and it was there I met Luis. He had studied law at the University of Salamanca, and became Professor of Law. He was the eldest of ten children, and of his six brothers, two like him were left wing, and the rest were pro Franco – one was in Franco's Army. In the Spanish war, Luis said he wouldn't shoot as he might shoot a brother. So he carried guns up into the mountains but he had heart and kidney problems, was invalided out, worked in the legal department of the Republican movement and became their Minister of Justice. His parents were very religious and his father was the village doctor.

In 1937 when the Spanish war collapsed Luis escaped over the Pyrenees and through France to England. Many of his colleagues were kept in concentration camps in France where the regime was quite brutal, especially where they had Senegalese guards. But some English MPs stood guarantor for intellectuals to come to England and here he got a job teaching in one of the children's colonies.

In 1939 the Spanish war ended with Franco in power but the European war was threatening. Franco demanded 'Give us back our children' and a committee was set up in London to decide which children it would be safe to return. Many of them would be children of left wing parents, often the fathers were in prison and the mothers living hand to mouth. Some children even had letters from home saying 'Don't come back.'

Luis was in Oxford with many other Spanish intellectuals and when in 1940 the last of the Spanish children went back and our colony closed, these men were supported by local academics. Luis stayed with one who had a wife and two children, also two other Spaniards, and he felt he should move out. He got a room for five shillings a week, and peeled potatoes for 11 hours a day in a local café. I would smuggle him into college to have a bath, and with my friends kept watch on the stairs to see no one tried to enter! It was a very cold winter and he also swept snow to earn money. When his English was fluent enough, he got a job in Reuters translating Churchill's speeches.

When we were doing our finals at Oxford in the summer of 1940, we wondered what were we doing it for, because a German invasion was expected at any time. I remember the Oral exam, there were only two women and many men, and the professor said 'Shall we do the ladies first?' I was chatting away and I could see the faces of the other students who hadn't had as much practice as I did. I got a First because I spoke so well – I had my Spanish fiancé by then, a very good idea that was.

After my degree I didn't want to go home, because by now Luis and I planned to be married and I feared my parents wouldn't like that. When I told them, they said 'Let us see him.' It was a very tense meeting as there was so much against him, he was foreign, Catholic, had no money and wore shabby clothes, but he was an intellectual, a Professor no less and he shared my father's love of Wagner! Luis' mother was very upset that Luis was going to marry a Protestant, she thought Protestant churches didn't have crosses

Move to London

After my graduation we moved to London, where Luis had found other Spanish refugees living in a big flat, rented for them by a rich young man who had known them in the colony. This man was a relative of Tolstoy and a Communist, and though the Republicans didn't really like Communists this amazing young man sympathised with the Spanish plight and paid the rent. Then the blitz started, quite suddenly in

September 1940. We used to go to Gloucester Road tube station to shelter at night. It was a very hot September, and we were glad when the first train came at 5am, bringing a rush of fresh air. We slept on the platform on what turned out to be a very valuable hearth-rug belonging to our landlord. From the underground we heard the bombs falling, and one morning went back to our flat and found a big piece of glass sticking into my bed where I would have been sleeping. We had to leave that house, but found a tiny flat in Woburn Square with concrete floors so you could sleep in the basement.

Wedding

We decided to get married in June 1941. As a Protestant, I could not marry before the main altar, but a Basque priest and another from Westminster Cathedral married us in the Crypt. I had made some cakes with butter from friends in America, but no eggs and we were to have these with my sisters and friends in the Basque Delegation. Luis and I first had to go to register me as an alien, and this took so long that all the food had gone by the time we got back. We went, hungry, by train to a remote Oxfordshire farm (the last two miles across fields on foot) where we had our honeymoon, and it was the next day before we had a proper meal. It was a good one though, with bacon, eggs and sausages.

As an alien I had to show my card wherever I went. Luis used to write poetry when he travelled in trains, and once he went past his stop, got out many stations later and had to walk back. He should have been indoors by seven and the police found him, but he explained and they took him home. If Franco had declared war, Luis would have been an enemy alien.

I got a job in the postal service in London, then heard of a better paid post in the Foreign Office. My boss there, who had been a prominent citizen in Argentina, criticised the Spanish I spoke because it wasn't like Argentinean Spanish. I would get a bus to work, there were plenty of buses. Sometimes we went to the country to record in Spanish a magazine about what was going on, for overseas readers and listeners. The BBC had a recording station in the grounds of a house belonging to the BBC's director of music. One night I had to stay there, I could hear the bombing and wished I could have been with Luis in London. I heard the sound of a bomber overhead just as I was coming into the room carrying two plates of milk pudding. I had to get down on the floor and I managed to slide down with my hands outstretched so the rice pudding remained intact and not spilt. You had great respect for food during the war.

Birth of sons

I became pregnant, was very ill with kidney trouble, and in the Elizabeth Garrett Anderson hospital for two months. I needed a blood transfusion, and this Luis gave me as amazingly he was the same blood group.

In July 1942 my first son was born. Just afterwards, there was an air-raid practice in the hospital, and the babies were put on a shelf all wrapped in blankets, even though it was so hot. We moved to Carshalton, to an upstairs flat with a garden, then to a house in Wallington, where my second son was born in Sept 1943. Then the doodlebugs started. The Air Ministry had learnt to deflect them from central London, so we got them in Surrey. Evacuation was planned but I decided to go home to my parents in Scotland. My sisters saw us off at Kings Cross which was packed, the boys had to be handed to me through the train window and the pram was left behind. We were with my parents for some weeks, but I felt we were becoming a burden and moved to Devon to a friend's empty attic. We moved again, and again, and eventually got back home, where all the windows had been blown out and were covered in black paper. We did have many moves, but we had very few possessions, just a typewriter and a few clothes. I was frightened for the children and worried when away from Luis, but felt we would be lucky.

The worst time was the bitterly cold winter of 1946, when you couldn't get coal. My new baby had been born in April 1946, then the others got first measles, then whooping cough and gave it to the baby who didn't cough, but died of pneumonia in April 1947. It was 1953 before I got my British nationality back.

Joan Pott

Before the war I lived with my parents, three elder brothers and a younger sister in Kennington, in south-east London. Children left school at 14 years old then, unless they were considered good enough to attend grammar school. All the schools were closed and evacuated out of London in 1939, but as I was just 14 and without a place at grammar school, I was counted as grown up.

Outbreak of war

That Sunday morning when Mr Chamberlain made the announcement on the radio that 'We are now at war', we all expected to be bombed at once. We had the Anderson shelter in the back garden, and it did protect us during the heavy raids. Dad tried to make it pretty by growing nasturtiums over its roof.

My three brothers were 'called to the colours' and my mother and seven year old sister were evacuated to Buckfastleigh in Devon. Dad and I stayed in our house, which was shattered by bombs three times. Twice I was dug out of the debris. Once was when the factory caught it, and the ARP (Air Raid Precautions) man, checking to see how many of us were serious enough to warrant hospital treatment, was glad to get my assurance that I wasn't too shaken. He gave me a lit cigarette, tapped my shoulder, said 'All right mate' and went on, which was as much as we expected in that situation.

Factory telephonist, London blitz

As there was no chance of further education, I went to work in the offices of a boot and shoe factory in Southwark Bridge Road, sorting and filing invoices. Quite soon I became Assistant Telephonist as well. My wages were 12/6 per week, less fourpence National Insurance, and 10/- for board and lodging at home. I would go to work by tram (if it was running), otherwise walk. One day after a night's bombing, as I walked through the Elephant and Castle crossroads it was blazing, firemen were trying to save the warehouses and factories, the heat was terrible. When the docks were bombed the fire was so intense you could read a newspaper in the street at midnight, and the noise of it all was frightening. Dad and I brought down all the furniture from the bedrooms and packed it into the front parlour. We could then fight fire bombs should they fall on the roof, using the stirrup pump which was kept on the landing with buckets of water.

Dunkirk was a terrible day, but we were all so very proud of the way the ordinary men and women who could sail a boat risked their all to rescue our stranded soldiers waiting on the French coast. It made us even more determined to fight the Nazis when they came to invade us as we were sure they would. We worshipped Mr Churchill, he was our 'Bulldog' and we knew he would make the right decisions. Even my Dad, who was an out and out Socialist, being a newspaper printer, was proud to have been able to shake his hand as he passed him in Fleet Street on his way to a meeting. He even talked about it which was unusual for Dad, he was a very private sort of man.

Another wonderful time was after the Battle of Britain, we were all full of admiration for our young RAF fighter pilots. We started to get some good news after that, forces in North Africa seemed to gain instead of lose, there weren't so many losses of convoys in the Mediterranean, and we didn't have the air-raids night after night.

Whilst the bombing was on, you still went about your normal life, going to work, queuing for rations and so on. Everyone who could gave blood every two months. You helped each other out – if you heard there were sausages off ration at the butcher's, you would tell your neighbour before rushing down to the shop. If you were out and you heard the whine of a falling bomb, you immediately went flat on your face on the ground. Once this happened in a busy street and I was so cross that I had made holes in my precious stockings and my smart little hat had been knocked sideways. Then a gentleman behind me helped me to my feet, raised his bowler hat, said 'Good morning, madam' and walked on. One day, walking to work early in the morning there was an old lady sweeping the doorstep of her house after a raid; she said 'I'm Hitler's bloody house maid now'. Another time my friend Maureen and I were on a train coming home from work in Woolwich and there were several soldiers in our compartment. A raid had started and as the bombs got closer, the soldiers shouted to us to get down on the floor and they stood with their backs to the train windows to protect us from any shattered glass.

Move to Surrey

About 1941 Dad decided we had had enough of living rough, without gas or electricity most of the time and water in short supply. We had to light a fire in the open kitchen grate to boil water for tea or a wash, let alone clothes washing. The whole area was getting to be a bit of a shambles, and we slept in the Anderson shelter, fully dressed. The house roof was holey, the windows were boarded up, the doors wouldn't close properly. Though we didn't fear looting, it wasn't difficult to get into the house. So we went by the Northern Line train to Morden to see what the local estate agents could offer in rented accommodation. Dad found us a place we could have for 25/- a week and by being just that bit outside London we missed being under the air-raids and could sleep either in a Morrison indoor shelter or in our beds. We could travel into London to work, but I was delighted when the factory moved to Kingston, just a bus ride away.

Encounter on a bus

It was on that bus route, the 213, that I met my future husband, because of an air raid. The bus I was on got caught in a bomb blast, enough to shatter the windows and make the bus unroadworthy, so passengers had to leave and await the next. I managed to get on, and walking along the gangway looking for a seat, I felt a hand on my elbow. I glanced down to find a young man I had noticed on previous

156

journeys smiling and saying 'Come and sit here.' I learnt he was a structural engineer working in an office just outside Kingston, and after that we got friendly.

I always knitted on my journeys, and if I was lucky I could buy silk yarn without clothing coupons which I made up into cami-knickers. My new friend was very interested to know what I was making but he didn't learn the truth for a long time after. We dated, went walking or to the pictures until he went into the Navy in 1942. He went to Scotland first and when he came home on embarkation leave, he asked me to wait for him. He thought to be engaged was better than being married in case he left me a widow. My family (my mother and sister came back home once we had moved out of London) approved, they really liked Robert and he gave me an engagement ring. Then he went out east on overseas posting. I didn't really expect him to come back and marry me, not with all the lovely Wrens he would meet. I used to write to him every day, and he did to me, we got to 1,500 and something letters. It was only three ha'pence for a forces letter and I numbered each one on the outside so Robert knew which to read first because the letters arrived in batches. I got his letters and even presents, including a box made out of a tortoise from Ceylon. I wore his ring all the time, with a leather fingerstall to protect it when I was at work.

Motorcycle works

Once we were settled in Cheam, Dad said I had to get some qualification to get a decent job, so I went to night school for a secretarial course. I wasn't much good at shorthand, typing was a bit better but I found I loved figures, so I switched to accountancy. I passed two or three exams before I was called up. I had dreams of joining the WRNS (with that lovely three-cornered hat to wear), and maybe go and find Robert. But when I went for my interview at the Labour Exchange I was greatly disappointed by being told 'We don't need any more in the Forces, but as you are good at figures, we will send you to a training college at Croydon aerodrome. You can brush up on algebra and logarithms, learn tool drawings and so on.' I was there for 16 weeks, and came fourth in the final exam. The first two girls went to work at Faireys Aviation, and Maureen and I, third and fourth, went to the AJS Motorcycle works, next to the Royal Arsenal in Woolwich. We were employed by the Ministry of Supply as inspectors. Our team was of three men testing and approving the whole bikes, and it was a wonderful sight to see the dispatch riders take them out of the yard, perhaps 30 or 40 at a time, thanks to our efforts. We three girls, Marjorie, Maureen and myself did the spare parts, making sure they were correct, packed in grease so that when the crates were delivered to troops in Africa, Italy and later France and Germany the spare parts would be serviceable.

Court Martial

During this time I had the uncomfortable experience of being court marshalled. I had a batch of brake pads, but the surfaces were all greasy so they would have been useless. I said I was not prepared to put my name to this batch as fit for service and argued with my immediate supervisor who told me not to make such a fuss. I stood my ground and he called a more senior man who agreed with me and I thought that was the end of it. But a bit later I got a letter summoning me to appear before a board, with my two supervisors. We had to go to a hall where there was a long table with lots of military men with red tabs on their shoulders and I had to stand in front of them and put my case. They listened and then we went away and heard nothing except that the matter would go no further.

Being in the factory with all the women working at the benches, eating in the canteen, sharing memories of the raids, listening to *Music while you work* and singing above the noise of the machines was an experience I shall never forget. We were a family really, cheerfully fighting the same cause. On the concrete columns that held up the roof we chalked up as high as we could reach the dates each of us thought would be the date for the invasion of Europe. You put a penny into the kitty to have your date put up, and when 6 June proved to be the one, everyone went mad and the lucky winner got all the pennies!

Factory work

We worked 12 hours a day, and for that we earned eight to nine pounds a week, less income tax and National Insurance. We had meals there, which helped with the rationing, so we were fit. Sometimes I would get a lift on the back of a motorbike if there was someone going my way home, otherwise it was a train to London Bridge, then the tube to Morden. As we had to be at the factory at 7.30am, that meant leaving home at 5.30 and I didn't get home till late. We would get one Saturday afternoon off a fortnight and the next week we had a whole Sunday. No summer holidays of course. Very occasionally Maureen and I would go up to the West End on our half Saturday and queue for tickets to a concert or the ballet; we got seats in the 'gods', the upper gallery, for a shilling each.

The doodlebugs that replaced the ordinary air-raids were a constant nuisance as they came at any time to any place. The first one I saw coming to earth I cheered because I thought it was an enemy plane being shot down. Once during the heavy raids I had seen this, and the pilot had parachuted out. The whole street was filled with women, carving knives at the ready, rushing to try and reach him before the police got there!

I remember well the evening the 1000 American bombers passed over our garden on their way to Germany. I sat on the coal bunker, and all the neighbourhood cheered at the magnificent sight, as we had suffered so much from German bombers. Afterwards when we learnt what had been done to Dresden, we were not so happy, after all they were ordinary people like us.

Two of my brothers failed to survive the war, but my brother Jack, one up from me, got injured in Africa. He managed with his gammy leg, had a happy marriage and two sons, and lived till he was 84.

Victory days

When VE-day came it was marvellous, no more blackout, no more carrying gas masks everywhere, no more deaths in London. But Robert was still in the Far East and we were getting news of the awful treatment of the Japanese prisoners of war. Robert was in Ceylon as a Lieutenant Commander, Fleet Air Arm, building aerodromes. He was worried about us, he thought we were having a tougher time than he was – he even had his own elephant. But I was worried he might find a beautiful Wren to share a tropical beach with, especially after hearing that they marked their football goal posts with girls' knickers!

Then came the news of the atom bomb, and we were pleased because this must mean the end of the war. VJ-day came, and then – a cablegram that Robert was on his way home. I found out the name of his home-coming ship and I dressed myself up and went to Waterloo where the boat trains came in. I saw both boat trains arrive, and he wasn't on either. Disappointed I went back home and went to bed. Very early the next morning I was woken by a ring on the doorbell, and I went down in my dressing gown with my hair unbrushed, expecting a telegram – but no, there was Robert! I was so surprised, I shut the door on him, after four years he had to see me at my very worst. He didn't seem to notice, so I let my Dad entertain him whilst I made amends to my appearance, and then we went to his parents to celebrate his return.

I'd been discharged from the Ministry of Supply by this time, and was working in the Post Office Savings Bank offices in Epsom. We were married on 31 August 1946 in Cheam Village church, there were eight of us married that day and it was four o'clock by the time it was our turn. I had a white dress, but didn't have enough clothing coupons to get a long petticoat and it shows in the wedding photographs. We paid five shillings a head for our guests at the reception in the café of the local cinema. People queuing for the picture gave a cheer as we alighted from the wedding car.

We lived for eight years with Robert's parents till we were able to find a house. We came to Chorleywood in 1955, where we lived happily till Robert died, aged 70, in 1991. And I am still here.

Sheila Regis

Evacuee

On 2 Sept 1939 I was on a train with gas mask and label, travelling from Haberdashers School in Acton and ending up in Dorchester. We were taken to a hall where local people came and looked at us to choose who to have. I was billeted with the bank manager. Our school used Dorchester Grammar School for lessons in mornings, and they worked in the afternoons. I don't recall much work being done, it was not a very happy time. I got terribly homesick, became quite unwell, and went back home after Christmas.

At home I was not aware of hardship, food was simple but we were never hungry. We sometimes had holidays in Yorkshire. Our parents were not worried when as children we would go out with a picnic on a bike, all day long over the moors. Trains were better, there were little local stations at Skipton and Ilkley.

I went to another school which I hated, did my School Certificate, and went to Pitmans college in Ealing for a year. This was during the London blitz, we had an Anderson shelter in the garden and a Morrison in the dining room.

London secretary

The Pitmans training was good, but the job I got as a secretary in Queen Anne's Gate was a bit boring for a 17-year old, as was life in the blackout. At the end of Queen Anne's Gate was the WRNS enlisting depot, and life in the Service looked tempting, I had read so much about other countries as a child and had always wanted to see the world, so I went along and said I wanted to join. I was too young, but having got my school certificate was in my favour. The day after my 18th birthday (early 1944) I went along again to join up. I was told I must be prepared to be a cook or a steward, and I said anything, I didn't mind as long as I could join. In a month my papers came by post, telling me to go to the training depot at Mill Hill. I was very excited, I wanted to move on.

WRNS enlistment

In the line for signing on, I got chatting to two girls, and we stayed friends all though WRNS and after. We were kitted out at Mill Hill; we had to be up at five, scrubbing floors or washing up, it was hard work and I lost a lot of weight. My two friends and I went to Rochester, stayed in the Deanery and worked at Chatham barracks; there was a lot of marching and drilling Next we went to the Base Fleet Mail Office in London, then the doodle bugs started.

Clothes were rationed, but it didn't matter that much. I was keen on tennis, and made tennis dresses out of sheets. You could get wool, so I did a lot of knitting. Curtain fabric was not rationed so we used to buy remnants to make long skirts.

Topography in Oxford

After London, we moved to Oxford to be trained in topography. Still with my same two friends and another joining us, we lived in the Wrenery in North Oxford, and worked in the New Bodleian Library. The Admiralty put out a request on the radio asking the public for any post-cards or holiday snaps of Northern France. Our job was to sort and categorise these pictures, then the top brass came in and asked for photos of particular spots. We didn't know what it was all about, and all photos were eventually sent back to the people who had sent them. Although we didn't realise it until after the war, this was planning for D-day. We were having a wonderful time and were very wrapped up in University social activities. At weekends we hitch hiked everywhere, in lorries to Burford or Stratford, all around.

We were invited to colleges, had tea in college rooms, had musical evenings, went to the cinema, were fascinated by the buildings. When it came to the May Balls, one friend had relatives in America who sent her dresses. We were all much the same shape, so she lent them around and I borrowed a green net dress. That Christmas it was snowy, and we went for long tramps over Boars Hill. It was a wonderful year, if a strange place for the Navy, as we couldn't have been further from the sea. We were not allowed more than ten miles from the base at weekend, but one friend's mother lived in Princes Risborough, and we would cycle over for a lovely roast beef lunch, by a log fire. In the Wrenery, there were six bunks to a room, the only heat a coal fire downstairs, nothing in our bedrooms so we used to go to bed in our clothes. Mice appeared because we kept food in a cupboard, a girl who was a farmer's daughter had a mouse trap and we kept a tally of mice caught.

Overseas posting

A notice went up about postings overseas, would people sign if interested – which we did with great glee, and were posted to Ceylon. We had two weeks pre-embarkation training at Crosby Hall in London, with lectures at night, and during the day we went to Peter Jones to buy clothes for the tropics. There was very little available but we managed to get one evening dress each. They wanted secretaries to go in advance of map-readers, and I was one of three who went ahead by air. None of us had flown before. We left from Brize Norton, took a day to get to Malta where we stayed a night, then another day to Cairo, where we stayed in a desert RAF station and had a day wandering round the city.

We re-fuelled in Basra, then on to Colombo, had two days there, then by train to Kandy, Mountbatten's South East Asia Command Headquarters.

Kandy

I stayed in Kandy a year, and had a wonderful time. My job was mostly secretarial, concerning the Far East war. I typed out lists of Japanese atrocities, and filed photographs of Singapore and Shanghai. Kandy was the base for Dutch, American, and British forces, who would come there between operations in the Japanese war. Our work huts were in the beautiful Botanical Gardens, we used to walk there through these magnificent palm trees, and in the evenings there were fire-flies. We live in big bashas, straw huts where 20 of us slept on hard wooden bunks with straw palliasses. There were dances, for which we received formal invitations often accompanied by an orchid.

We witnessed the Perahera, when Buddha's tooth is paraded once every four years. There was a fantastic parade through the streets of Kandy every evening for a week, we would catch a jeep down to watch it. The final elephant was supposed to carry Buddha's tooth in a casket, surrounded by fire dancers. The freedom we were given was immense, we had to be in by 10.0pm but up till then could go off anywhere we liked with anyone we liked.

The father of one of the naval students in Oxford was a tea planter, so we went to his estate in the hills and had a lovely time. It was a wonderful climate and we went around the island by train, to Nuwara Elya, Dambulla, Sigyria. I've never been back, and friends who have been said there are so many tourists and newly built hotels everywhere it is not the same. We could go to Colombo by train for weekends, staying in the YWCA and swimming from beautiful beaches.

I got malaria followed by pneumonia, and was in hospital for six weeks, so ill that the Admiralty told my parents that I was on the danger list. Penicillin was just being tried out, and I had the injections which saved my life. I went on convalescent leave to a Wren holiday bungalow in the hills, recovered and went back to work.

War's end

VE-day came, then VJ-day, then in early December we were sent back on a troop ship. It was crowded, with three-tier bunks, and we were home by Christmas. I was demobbed in February, from Oxford. It was a terrible anticlimax after Ceylon. I got demob clothes, and dockets to buy civvies, met up with old friends, and came back down to earth. Food was still short, Mother had a big hall bench and whenever any extra was available she would buy it and store it. I got a job in an advertising agency, played tennis, and met my husband. When he came to our house, he would always look in Mother's bench to see what exciting tins she had there!

I was an only child, and always envied big families. Joining the WRNS was like going to boarding school, I made close friends who became my family. We kept in touch, and became god-mothers to each other's daughters, then after all our husbands had died in their 60s, we have been on holidays together.

Joan Roberts

Raids on Cardiff

I was 22 when the war started, living in a house on top of a hill in Cardiff where my father was a Baptist minister. The raids on the docks were heavy and a friend of my father's who ran a nursing agency suggested I should become a nurse, as it was the only way to be helpful. So I started in Cardiff, cycling to work round roundabouts which were often slippery with rain. One morning the bombing had stopped, but there was this dreadful noise and there was a plane just skimming the rooftops. I thought it must be one of ours but when I looked up there was this ghastly swastika and it was so low I could see the face of the rear-gunner and he had his gun aimed at me. He looked at me, and then moved the gun away. He could so easily have pressed that trigger.

We had a Morrison shelter in the study. During the bombing of the docks, we would all get in there, including my great-aunt Emily who was staying with us. She had a cat who always sat on her lap. When the doodlebugs came, you listened till you heard the engine cut out, and then you knew the bomb would fall. But Aunt Emily's cat purred so loudly we didn't hear this one, it fell nearby, the blast blew out the windows and shook all the books off the study shelves. We weren't hurt, and the cat was fine.

During raids, my father as Air Raid Warden had to go off to the docks, and often my half-sister and I would just sit under the stairs.

You carried on life much as usual. One morning early as I was waiting at the bus stop, one of our gunners got an enemy plane just overhead. I was in the bus-shelter which was shattered with great chunks of shrapnel, still hot. Another morning cycling to work there were men from the navy who stopped me. I protested and said that was my way to the hospital but they said 'Just have a look' and there in the middle of the roundabout was an unexploded land mine.

A family of ship owners that we knew in Cardiff had two sons. The younger, Llewellyn, and I were very good friends. Before he went off to the war he gave me a book of Rupert Brooke's poems, and inside he wrote 'Joan, wait for me'. He became a liaison officer in the Balkans, and in getting a secret message through to the resistance, he was killed. Later his brother was killed in the attack on the bridge at Arnhem. That poor mother, both her sons dead.

River Emergency Service

I went to London to train at Guy's Hospital. It had been bombed and part of it was evacuated to Orpington. We used to go to the Borough Market, most people were in uniform of some kind. We were so near the Thames that I applied to join the River Emergency Service,  though I couldn't swim. We used a paddle steamer called the *Essex Queen* which had been to Dunkirk. We had eight beds on board and one medic and could go down river to the estuary, wherever we were needed. A friend and I got so tired of the constant motion of the ship, we were given two days leave, with strict instructions to be back on time. Hurrying to do this, we could see the ship moored in the river, but there was no way to get to her. Two young boys said they would take us out in their little rowing boat. We were going very quickly because of the tide and as we were swept past the ship the captain leaned over and pulled me in by my hair and the cook pulled in the two boys. The captain was furious, and when I asked why, he said 'Look', and I saw the rowing boat being drawn into the paddles where it splintered. One day when we were called to a mine, we were lent a little speedboat by Mr Smith, the man who started making potato crisps, it was a lovely ride, and fortunately there were no casualties.

When the doodlebugs started, I was working in a hospital in Uxbridge. When you went to the pictures there would be a message on the screen saying 'Doodlebug Overhead' but there wasn't much you could do. Once on the train going to Uxbridge, I was with a doctor who was always making up songs, and I challenged him to write one before we got to our destination. This is what he wrote:

> An Alperton girl whom I met
> Travelled nude on the tube for a bet.
> This glorious surprise
> Did so gladden the eyes
> Of the war-weary men on the Met.

RAF nurse in India

Both my brothers were in the Royal Army Medical Corps, and I went for an interview for the Princess Mary's RAF Nursing Service. I was selected and posted to Calcutta, going through the Suez Canal. We were stopped in Aden when I was summoned by the tannoy to the captain's cabin, and there was my half-sister's husband, who was adjutant for traffic to the East. He told me that my brother Harold was on one of the other smaller ships going to India. As soon as we left Aden, the Japs started bombing, and every morning a signal would come to my cabin to tell me my brother's ship was still all right. After we landed we only had the briefest meeting before I went to Calcutta and he went to Bangalore.

Wedding in Karachi

My fiancé Iain had just qualified as a doctor and managed to get a job as ship's surgeon on a boat coming to India. He sent me a cable to meet him at Karachi to get married. I went by seaplane, and in it were a lot of Japanese prisoners of war, many of whom were very sick. At the end of the flight we stopped on a dark brown river, and I saw a rowing boat below us. Two men said 'Jump and we'll catch you' but it was only with a helping shove from behind that I became airborne – and my bag fell into the river. I called out that this contained my wedding dress so one of the men leapt overboard and swam furiously to get it from the filthy brown water. The dress was stained but not too badly, and later the Embassy provided beautiful flowers which we made into a bouquet to cover the stain. There were very few at my wedding but they were so good, and I still have a beautiful ivory box one of them gave me. The day after our wedding Iain had to go back on his ship to England and I went back to Calcutta.

Cholera

In Calcutta the officers used to go to a hostel where they could have a couple of nights' rest. One day they tried to open a door to get in but it wouldn't open, so they asked why was it locked and I said it wasn't. I went in another way, only to find it was crammed full of victims who had died of cholera. Another day I bought a beautiful ice cream but a Military Policeman saw me, put his hand on my shoulder and said 'Do you realise what you've got there? That is the source of the cholera.'

In the Princess Mary RAF Nursing service, we had never learnt drill and marching. This was an embarrassment recently when at the Royal Albert Hall Service of Remembrance I had to march across the auditorium in front of all those people.

Hilary Sagovsky

I was born in 1923 in Liverpool, and went to boarding-school in North Wales. I think my parents struggled to pay the fees so I left in 1939 after taking School Certificate. When war was declared we were caravanning in the Lake District. I remember that on the way home we had to stop in Kendal and buy yards of blackout material ready to meet the new regulations. That year I did my Higher School Certificate working on my own at home with some private coaching.

Newspaper reporter

I had always wanted to write professionally so I took a chance, plucked up courage and walked into the newspaper offices of the Waterloo and Crosby Herald. I asked the editor if I might be allowed to contribute the odd paragraph and I could hardly believe my ears when he said I could take over the back page. I guess he was short-staffed because some of his reporters had already been called up. Whatever the reason, I was bowled over by my luck and came out walking on clouds. To a young and innocent teenager, working on a newspaper seemed a very special calling. I suppose I had seen too many films where the reporters wore green eye-shades and yelled instructions to 'hold the front page' but I soon discovered that the stories I was covering were not, by any stretch of the imagination, world events. I was sent to the Town Hall to write up the Mayor's tea parties and once a week I had to try and find something amusing to say about tea dances in the church hall. This being wartime, the number of girls often exceeded the number of lads

170

on leave. The alternative to an afternoon of wall-flowering was to do what Joyce Grenfell was later to describe as 'dancing bust to bust'.

My parents' home was in the little village of Hightown, half way between Liverpool and Southport. There was a clear view at that time right across the fields towards Bootle and the docks and during the blitz you could see the line of fire that was Liverpool. The damage was extensive but we heard stories of kids from the back streets who would tackle the fires with stirrup pumps and saved valuable timber yards from going up in flames.

After a year on the paper I wanted to join up as a number of my friends had done. So once I was 18, I went into Liverpool and signed up for the Women's Auxiliary Air Force. If I hadn't been to boarding school I would have found it hard to meet the challenges of communal living. I was billeted with a social mix that included girls from the slums, and in retrospect I can see that it was no bad thing for me to be shaken out of the presuppositions of a moderately privileged life. Certainly nothing had prepared me for the indignity of having my hair combed for nits, but that was part of the process of being initiated into the Air Force

WAAF

My first posting was to the workhouse in Leighton Buzzard. From there I was sent to Morecambe for initial training. I recall endless marches along the front in my grey lisle stockings, which always seemed to be a bit damp. I remember frequently crossing the road to avoid having to salute an officer. I was very shy of the top ranks, the women commissioned officers could be daunting to a new recruit. My next posting was to Preston where I was trained in plotting – mapping the flight paths and strengths of incoming enemy aircraft. We worked at a big table and above us was a gallery with senior officers. The information was fed to us over headphones from observation posts and Fighter Command.

In our free time there were dances on the station and occasionally the much prized '48s' – short home leaves. At this time I had a number of different boy-friends of assorted nationalities. Most men look good in uniform, and my parents must have had a few shocks about these short-term escorts.

It's hard to recall the predominant emotions of those years. All feelings, both joy and grief, were intensified. The bombing, both in London and Liverpool, was extremely scary but mercifully intermittent. I was to feel grateful at a later time for the issue of tin hats when we were fire-watching on a roof in Piccadilly. At intervals there might be a smatter of shrapnel, but I don't think I was ever in extreme danger, unlike my cousins who were fighting in Europe.

Military hospital

I had begun to be seriously concerned about backache which made the angle at which we worked, leaning over a plotting table, extremely painful and I was packed off to a military hospital. The Services had taken over a mental institution at Winwick, outside Warrington, a gloomy Victorian building which still housed some very disturbed patients.

We presented a mixed bag of medical conditions. There was a girl of 18 in my ward who had worked in a munitions factory and had been blinded by an explosion. Her hands and arms were pock-marked with scars. The nurses, many of whom were young themselves with no experience of serious war wounds, treated this traumatised girl with a jokiness that was doubtless well meant but added to her shock and confusion.

Invalided out

Eventually I 'got my ticket', was invalided out of the Air Force and had to go home for a year's orthopaedic treatment. But my stay in Winwick was to bring me unlooked-for blessing. I met there a soldier who before the war had worked in the film business. After call-up, he had been part of a searchlight battery team, and had cut his thumb very deeply. The wound had become infected and the surgeons were debating the possibility of amputation, but mercifully that didn't happen. He was wonderfully unselfish in his concern for me and when he discovered that my ideas for Civvy Street did not include going back to the newspaper, he offered to try and get me an interview as a scriptwriter in the documentary business. He was as good as his word and arranged an introduction to Edgar Anstey, a respected figure and a delightful man.

Anstey's advice was to go away and write a film script. I spent a lot of time in the Liverpool public library trying to master technical terms. The subject I chose was the use of the special skills that refugee aliens had brought into this country. There were, for example, a number of precision engineers whose knowledge would be valuable in the war effort. I sent off the script and nearly had beginner's luck. The Ministry of Information were interested and came close to producing it but eventually backed out because the subject was politically too sensitive. A distinction had to be drawn between the Germans and Austrians who had come over here to seek asylum and those who were part of the enemy Axis forces.

London and the film industry

However the MoI passed on the script to a small documentary company in Shaftesbury Avenue, and they liked it well enough to offer me a job. So there I was, working in the film business, in London which was to me totally unknown territory. I found digs in Lancaster Gate in a house with a cellar – a welcome refuge during the bombing. This could be frightening, but I guess you developed a certain fatalism; if the bomb hadn't got your name on it you would be getting up as usual next morning and going to work, probably scrunching though broken glass on the way.

Some of the scripts I wrote were explicitly related to the war effort. I was commissioned to write an Army training film 'Driving Instructions for Combined Operations' when I had not yet learnt to drive a car. I did my own research with the aid of a military supervisor who would feed me the technical stuff. Once when I went to Great Yarmouth to a military camp, they were a bit surprised when they found it was a woman doing this job. Having the Christian name Hilary helped as they didn't know what they were getting till I was there and then they had to make the best of it.

The company I was working for didn't have its own studio, we would either be shooting on location or hiring studio space and facilities. When the editor had made his rough cut, we would have a preliminary viewing in a small theatre and I would read my commentary over the visuals. We rarely worked with synchronised sound because of the expense.

One day I had a letter from a man called Sagovsky, a Russian of whom I had heard. I knew he was an editor of feature films and he was offering me a job in his cutting room. I wrote and refused because I was well aware of my lack of technical knowledge. Remarkably, he wrote again and said he would keep the job open for me. I was so sure he would sack me when he discovered the depths of my technical ignorance (the gulf between documentary and features was a wide one) that I expected to last about a week.

That is not what happened, as you may have surmised from my Russian surname. To quote Jane Eyre, 'Reader, I married him.' Surely it was a God-directed decision. Sadly, a number of wartime marriages came unstuck in the turbulent years that followed the end of hostilities, but I never had cause for one moment's regret. How can one express adequate thankfulness for all the years of a long and wonderfully rewarding partnership.

Mona Satterthwaite

From Wales to Buckinghamshire

I was brought up in Wales and spoke Welsh till I came to England when I was 17 in 1933. We did learn English at school, so I knew a bit, but Welsh was my natural language. My mother had come to a job in Chalfont St Giles, and I came to live with her. I used to go to the local Baptist church, where I met a lady who was supervisor of the telephone exchange in Gerrards Cross and she offered me a job. I had to learn all those English place names, it was a terrific strain but I loved it in the end. I remember the Chamberlain broadcast and I just didn't believe it. There can't be a war, never, that's stupid. I wasn't called up because I was in the Post Office, though I longed to be.

Telephone operator

I got a flat in Amersham, living on my own. You got moved everywhere to work, Windsor, Gerrards Cross, Slough, and I went by bicycle. When the war came, I was on duty one night in Chalfont St Giles, there was only me on the switchboard. I could hear the sound of the German planes flying over and then there was a strange noise. I went to the window to check and there was a mass of flares coming down into the village pond. It was beautiful, no one was hurt, but the whole switchboard came alive. In those days, a little flap came down on switchboard when someone telephoned in, uncovering a hole into which I would plug in the line. That night it was flap flap flap, all the little flaps came down as everyone was wanting to telephone to see if relatives were all right, and there was only me to deal with them.

One night I was cycling home to Amersham when I heard a German plane, going woow, woow, woow just over me. So I turned off the light on the bike because I thought he was following me, but he was still there so I got off my bike and hid in the ditch and still the noise went on. He dropped a bomb outside Amersham, I don't know what he was aiming for.

Marriage

There were a lot of dances those days and a lot of lovely men about; there was an army camp near Amersham, and all of us girls used to go to the dances. I had one good dress for the dances, I made my own underwear and darned my stockings. At one of these dances in 1941 I met my husband. I had won a dozen eggs in a raffle and he carried them home for me. After we'd known each other three months, we got married. Our wedding was in Chesham Bois, the Post-master gave me away and we went to the Mill Stream pub for a meal afterwards. I had a lovely two-piece suit, sadly not a white one, and by this time my husband was an officer. That night we went to Portsmouth by train because he had to go abroad the  next day. There was another officer there whose name was Ernest Simpson, such a good looking man, he was the ex-husband of Wallis Simpson who married the Prince of Wales. He gave us a dinner that night and made a lovely speech. I couldn't believe it, he gave the waiter a ten pound tip! I was earning one pound five shillings a week then, and that was good money.

My new husband and I had one night together and then had to get up really early in the morning. I remember hearing his boots going clump, clump, clump, down the street, and I never saw him for four and a half years. He served in India and Burma.

PO Engineer for Bomber Command

I went back to my job, and trained as a Post Office engineer. We went to Cambridge for training, there were lots of Americans there swarming round, they would give you anything. Of course I didn't go to bed with them, I was married. Then I went to work for Bomber Command in Winslow where I had digs in the High Street. One night, a hot, hot August night, I was sleeping with nothing on and a Lancaster bomber was coming back, flying very low. It crashed into the other side of the street, flattened the pub and all the houses, they were all in flames. I got dressed quickly, my landlady was in great shock she took all her jewels across the road to where they had a dug-out shelter. They took the bodies to the church, it was devastating.

My job was to work the teleprinters and put them right if they went wrong. All the aerodromes had their own teleprinters so I went everywhere. It was a lovely job. I was still employed by the Post Office but attached to Bomber Command, and I used to sit on a stile to watch them go in the Lancasters, all these lovely young men. The bombing went on right to the end of the war. Then it was VE-day and I rushed up to London for the day. I came back on the train to Aylesbury, and a man kissed me and it went on for ever and ever. Never found out who he was.

My husband didn't get home till 1946 and he went back to his job in Whitbreads Brewery; we lived in a flat owned by the brewery in West Hampstead. Our children were born there and then my husband wanted better schools for them, so we came to Chorleywood.

Lola Sledmere

Family life in Java

In the 1930s we lived in Java where my father was an importer of textiles. My mother had asthma so we lived half way up a mountain next to a tea plantation where the climate is absolutely heavenly. My father only came back home to this house at the weekends. It was a bit lonely for us children, just me and my two brothers, one older and one younger, and my Granny who came from Vienna.

It was a very free life, we had a big garden and could go anywhere, visiting other villages, playing in the river. We children spoke Malay fluently, also Dutch to our parents and German to Granny, so now I have a very odd accent. There were no other Dutch families near, we didn't meet other children until we went to school, a Dutch Catholic primary school 20 minutes drive away.

Mother was a trained concert pianist. As a young woman in Vienna she would play for parties, though she was not quite good enough for the stage. She met my father when she was on a cruise to get over a love affair and he was on his way back to the colonies where he had gone when his family had lost most of their money. She went to live in the jungle, but she was quite happy and her mother came to live with them. She didn't have to do any housework because, like everyone else, we had servants. She learned to do first aid, and as there were no local doctors, she would dress wounds or sores though she wouldn't change a baby's nappy. We had a really lovely childhood, though a bit lonely.

War begins

I wasn't aware of any anxiety, though now I realize there had been movements for freedom among the Javanese population. I was nine when the war started, and  we could see from our house the bombardment of the town below. Three other families came from the towns to live with us, in empty bungalows. It was a wonderful time for us because there were more children. In March 1942, four months after Pearl Harbor, the Japanese invaded. They didn't intern us at first because they had no camps ready, but we knew it would come.

When the Japs came, they closed all the schools and at first we thought this was great. Then we got bored so little groups got together and organised some teaching. The Japanese soldiers had the right to enter any house to ask for a bath and tea and this they did, usually in groups of three or four. They would come and walk around in their funny underpants; the bathroom was outside the house, they would have a bath, then sit down and ask for tea. They weren't allowed to ask for meals or take any possessions, but one might pick up a child to put on his lap. My mother was worried that we might be molested but we never were, I think the soldiers were just missing their own families. Mother cut my hair off and I had to wear boys' clothes as protection, though I didn't understand why.

Internment camp

My father was taken to an internment camp, then, some time later, it was our turn. A jeep rushed up the drive at six one morning, and we had half an hour to get ready. We could only take what we could carry. My mother had already given two rugs and some silver to an Indonesian doctor she knew for safe-keeping. I took two beautiful dolls and mother said we must take the wooden push-chair for them. I found out later that she had had a false bottom made for it and had hidden some jewellery and money. We had to leave our servants, they were almost like family, specially our amah who had looked after us children. A lot of Malays lost their jobs as servants, though some later worked for the Japanese We also had to leave our animals, my cat and my brother's dogs, we felt it really badly.

Our first camp was a big estate of tiny houses which had been built, I think, for policemen and they had put a huge fence around it. We had a little house, and were given a food ration which we had to cook ourselves. Mother had never cooked, so grandmother did that but my mother had to learn to clean, something she had never done before.

Clinic internment

We were to be sent to a bigger camp, but we didn't go because mother had terrible sciatica, so with eight other families who had someone sick, we were put in a disused clinic. This was fenced off, but only guarded on and off. Children were allowed out, but not the adults. Each family had one room and we shared the huge clinic kitchen. It was OK, we had quite a big room. We children all got malaria, we didn't have mosquito nets or medication you just put up with it, you were shivering and then you were boiling hot. My mother and grandmother didn't get it, but we children did, every few months.

We had to provide our own food. Traders would come into the camp and we would exchange a shirt for a bag of rice or a bunch of bananas depending on the quality of the shirt, or a table cloth for a skinny chicken or some eggs. Mother sold her hidden supply of jewellery and in the end we ran out of stuff to barter. There were a lot of people not interned because if you had any German or Javanese or Japanese blood you didn't have to be interned and these people would bring us food. My mother could have stayed out but she didn't want to; she said 'I'm married to a Dutchman and my children are Dutch.' She wanted to protect her children, so put her Austrian Jewish background behind her. We were sort of OK, though we did get a lot of sores from lack of vitamins, they just wouldn't heal and I had the scars for years.

My mother's sciatica got better, but the Japs didn't bother to get a convoy to send us away, so we stayed in the clinic. Mother would escape out of the camp at night dressed as a local woman, with a veil and go to the home of an Ambonese man who had a radio so she could hear what was going on in Europe. Radios were forbidden and there would have been quite serious punishment if they were found, like chopping an ear off a child. The day after her visit, she would write all the news down on a piece of paper, fold it up and put it in my shoe. I would then go round the people outside the camp, one family would read what she had written and then I went on to the next house. My brothers were never asked to do this, though I felt my older brother should have been. I didn't like it because I had to walk all round everywhere, but my mother wasn't the sort of person you could say 'No' to. Occasionally I would get a biscuit or something as reward.

There was a very sick man in the local hospital, the lover of one of Mother's friends, he was left in a back room and hardly cared for at all. Mother asked the head of police in the town if she or I could be allowed to take food to him. I still have the permit from the Kempetai, the Japanese Command. It was usually mung bean soup, very nutritious and very cheap, but even with the permit there were a lot of young male Javanese nurses who would push me around. Eventually I got through to this man, his arms and legs were terribly bent. He survived and came to see us after the war.

Prison camp

We were sent to another camp which was much worse in a disused barracks, you just had the width of a mattress on a platform and a little shelf above. We were given food, but it was very poor. I got very depressed and lethargic, cried a lot and got dysentery, there was no soap, no shoes, it wasn't cold so clothes didn't matter. But even grandmother survived. The sun was used as a weapon, people were punished by having to stand in the sun all day.

We got postcards from Father, maybe every three or four months, they were censored but we did at least know he was alive. In this camp mother couldn't get out to find news, so we didn't know the war had ended until the Japanese told us some ten days after. The Japanese guards remained to protect us from the freedom movement, but some were so ashamed of surrender they killed themselves. We couldn't go back to our house as it was too isolated, some people were murdered and the plantations around us had become very neglected.

Liberation and return to Holland

Eventually we were liberated by English and Gurkha soldiers. There was an English officer who had a great sword and he hacked into a wooden pillar and shouted at a Japanese officer 'I will do that to you if you won't obey my orders.' After a while we went to Batavia (Jakarta) and there were re-united with my father, he was very thin, aged and diminished. We had to wait five months till there was a boat to take us back to Holland

When we arrived at Suez we got off in little groups and went in a train to Ataka but they didn't tell us much about where we were going. The Canadian Red Cross had set up enormous tents and filled them with things we would need for the cold winter in Holland. The tents were manned by Dutch volunteers, it was just amazing as we didn't have anything of our own and here was all this marvellous new stuff. They had a list for men and a list for women, one for boys and one for girls and they took great trouble that we didn't all look the same. It was very good quality, coats and jumpers, shoes and stockings, everything you needed. I still find it emotional to talk about it, it was so wonderful. They gave us an enormous tea, which we weren't used to, and there was a playground where we were supervised by men with black diamonds sewn on the backs of their uniforms. They were German prisoners-of-war, left over from Rommel's Afrika Corps. Then it was back in the train and onto the boat, which was very overcrowded. Only the old and the sick got cabins, so mother got one because of her asthma and granny because she was old. The men and boys were in the hold at the front and the girls and women at the back, on mattresses and hammocks. I was on my own, aged 12, amongst all these strange women.

As soon as we entered the Mediterranean, all the children got measles. There was a tiny children's hospital on board but by the time I got it the hospital was full so I had to go back to my draughty hold. Then I got pneumonia and was very ill, so I was put into the hospital and they were all very nice to me. I was still ill when we got to Amsterdam, so I was taken off the boat on a stretcher, into an ambulance and straight to the house of my other Granny in Leyden. She had a big canal-side house, but she didn't like my mother and wouldn't have the wild children (us) in her house, she only had me because I was ill. It was cold and there were frost flowers on the window, I had never seen these before.

The government had prepared hotels for people with no relatives, so after I left Granny I went to the rest of the family in a hotel in Noordwyjk, a seaside resort. I still get excited when I go there, it was my first place of freedom. I went to the village school though I didn't understand much of what was going on. But with hard work and help from teachers, I got to secondary school and thence to Leyden University.

The picture of an Indonesian prison camp is taken from 'Kerels van de daad' by Willem Van de Poll published by Van Hoeve in The Hague in 1947. It is not the actual camp where Lola was kept, but is similar.

Jack Smethurst

I was born and bred in Manchester. My dad worked in a raincoat factory, so did my mum. I had an elder sister Pat, a brother Bill, and the twins who were younger. We lived in a very small back-to-back terraced house, with a bedroom for Mum and Dad, a box-room where Pat slept and the other room with two three-quarter sized beds for the four of us boys, so you had to climb over the others to get to bed. I have extremely happy memories of childhood. My grandmother Hester lived round the corner, she was a widow from the First World War.

Evacuation

There was a feeling of apprehension as war got near, but not fear. War was declared on a Sunday and that night a Black Maria drove up to the ice-cream parlour down our street. It was owned by an Italian family, and they took the old man away but left his sons who had been born in England. He was interned on the Isle of Man and they were conscripted into the army. Next day my brother Bill and I went to school, and then were taken to the station. We had labels with our names tied to our coats, it was chaotic but very exciting and I've never lost that feeling of anticipation at a station. When we heard we were going to Blackpool, we were so excited you couldn't have kept us off the train. It was such a holiday place, we'd been there on day trips by Ribble coach and you looked out for the tower.

Once there, we were put in trucks and taken round the houses, till we got to 99 Egerton Road and there was Mrs Moorcroft. She had two daughters, Eileen, and Gertie who was an usherette at the local cinema and used to sneak us in free on a Saturday. Mrs Moorcroft used to run a guest-house so she took about 12 of us evacuees, sometimes more. There was the phoney war at first, nothing happened and some children drifted back to Manchester. We didn't, but there were a couple of brothers from our school who decided they had had enough and wanted to go back, so they started back the only way they knew, walking along the railway line. Sadly, a train came along and they both were killed. Those were to me the first casualties of war.

My sister was evacuated to Accrington, goodness knows why, my mother and the twins came to Blackpool but only stayed a couple of months because nothing was happening and they went back to Manchester. Quite a lot did go back till there was only my brother Bill and me left with Mrs Moorcroft, so she replaced the evacuees with RAF men. That was great for us, there were a lot of Commonwealth airmen. I suppose there was some sort of racial feeling because there was one black  man and he ended up in the attic with Bill and me. We went to the local schools, they were overflowing with all of us, it must have been hard for them with this invasion of us from a foreign town.

The landladies were paid a small amount and ours was kind but firm. One day she was out and I was hungry, so I got some oats, mixed them with sugar and was eating them when she came back. I hid the newspaper with the oats under my chair. She came in and was talking to us, when the dog started scrabbling about under the chair and pulled out the newspaper and the oats. I was terribly embarrassed, but she was very good about it.

Manchester blitz

We didn't go home often, but once we did, for Christmas 1940. Which was the time Hitler decided to bomb Manchester to bits. The day we got home, the sirens went in the evening and we went to the shelter in the street. In the middle of the bombing we were told to go from our shelter to another one, so we were walking down the road with the bombers and the searchlights overhead and the ack-ack guns and bits of shrapnel, it was quite scary. When we got to the other shelter, there was a woman sitting by us who had in her hand a set of beads, saying her rosary over and over again. We stayed all night. Next morning as we turned into our street, we saw our house was just a wall and a heap of rubble. My Gran who lived round the corner had refused to come into the shelter, but she did get under her dining room table and though the whole house collapsed on top of her, she was all right and was pulled out by a sailor home on leave.

Blackpool

There was nowhere for us to stay, so Billy and I were sent back to Blackpool on the bus. We didn't realise quite how dirty we were, there had been no water to wash at home. Mrs Moorcroft threw up her hands in horror then took us into her house, cleaned us up and that night took us to the circus. There was a huge sawdust ring which they filled with water and they enacted the sea battle of the sinking of the *Graaf Spee*, with guns going off and puffs of smoke, So the day after we'd been in a real raid, there we were cheering at a mock battle. That was the only counselling we had!

I did have some sort of reaction during the night, and Mrs Moorcroft came and took me into bed with her and enveloped me in her great capacious comforting bosom. We stayed with her another couple of years. My parents were moved four miles to Blakeley, I suppose those houses were built in the thirties, the government must have been preparing. My mother stayed in that house till she died just a few years ago.

I have such happy memories of Blackpool. We would go down the Golden Mile and pay a penny to go and see 'the bones of Jesse James' – could have been any old bones. Then there was the 'moving hand', you all stood round in the dark, a hand would appear through the middle of a black cloth on the table and move, adopting a menacing pose and everyone gasped. Also the Fun House with the Laughing Policeman outside. I was always attracted to the theatre. Mrs Moorcroft would take us sometimes, we saw George Formby of course. Years later, appearing at Blackpool had a special resonance for me, to go to the Grand Theatre and see my name outside, that was great.

There was Percy, my brother called him Mrs Moorcroft's fancy man, he was such a kind chap, we'd dig for worms and then go and sit on the end of the pier fishing, never caught anything of course. Then there were her daughters, lovely young girls in their twenties, and the house full of RAF men. There was one with a magnificent body, who wore a tight fitting vest and trousers, he was a Physical Training Instructor, Eileen really fell for him, and in fact she married him and later became Lady Mayoress of Blackpool. Sometimes you'd see Eileen crying and it would be that one of the young men had lost his life.

My uncle Jacky Brown was fly-weight champion of the world in the 1930s and we were all immensely proud of him. There was this airman Len, came from Kent, really nice chap, he looked out for me. Another man, very unpleasant, started baiting me about Jacky Brown, saying he was a coward. Anyway, he went too far and I leapt on him and sunk my teeth into his arm and wouldn't let go. He just yelled and called me all the names under the sun, till Len intervened and said 'You've got what you deserved, now just leave the lad alone or you'll have me to contend with.'

New home

In about 1943 Bill and I went home to Blakeley, because after the blitz, they didn't hit Manchester much. I started at a new school, and many years later I met a man who had been there and remembered me arriving as a quiet, intense boy who had a penknife and was carving his name on the desk. We had a headmaster called William Froelich, he looked like the Kaiser and shouted like the Kaiser. Why didn't he get interned? I got on with him quite well because he played football and I played football, but my twin brothers were always in trouble. On one occasion he said to my mother 'Those lads will swing one of these days.' You couldn't say that nowadays. Then there was Father Pat who would walk through the playground with his soutane swinging, and he would swipe boys over the head as he walked. One boy asked 'What was that for, Father?' and he replied 'Just in case'. But we had a wonderful teacher, Miss Hewitt who would take us for PE, she rolled her skirt up and tucked it into her knickers, she taught us Gilbert and Sullivan songs and country dancing. Most kids had been bombed out from some very rough neighbourhoods, but she was terrific.

The war ended, I left school at 14 and went to work in a greengrocer's shop. You had to add up the sums quickly in your head, and I still do that. Then I worked in the raincoat factory for four years, it was utterly awful, until I was saved by National Service.

Julie Smethurst

I was four when the war started, living with my family in a modest semi-detached house in Sudbury. There was this fear of immediate bombing so I was evacuated to my grandparents' house in Hastings. I went straight to school there and the thing I remember was having to eat tapioca. We must have been there for Christmas because I remember a stocking my grandmother filled for me with her own things, a tiny dark blue bottle of scent and a little handkerchief.

Home to Sudbury

Fear of invasion then overtook the fear of bombing, so we went back home. My father was an Air Raid Warden and he built a magnificent shelter in the garden with bunks and a little rack above his bunk for my baby brother. He would settle us in there for the night, then put on his helmet and climb up the pear tree to look out for fires. One night we were all asleep, when my father woke with a most tremendous roar, but it was only that Peter had fallen out of his bunk and landed on Father's stomach.

Evacuation to Oxfordshire

After a while the bombing did start, and my brother and I were sent to an Oxfordshire village, to an uncle and aunt, who must have been newly married and had no children. We went to the local school. I remember being given a piece of canvas and my sewing being praised – that must have been the start of my interest in needlework. I got nits and impetigo, I had to take the scabs off, it was horrible. My brother also had nits, my aunt decided to shave all his hair off and she took him into the chicken house to do this. Being in the country, we had eggs and plenty of vegetables, and there were lovely plums in the Manor House garden. My aunt's father lived in part of it, and the elderly owner Mr Rose in the rest. One night there was a terrifying explosion, we couldn't turn lights on to see if we were all alright, but we never found out what it was.

Home and Doodlebug

By 1944, everything seemed quiet and we went back to London, till one night we heard the sound of a plane. We rushed to my bedroom window, and saw a plane, flying low and on fire. My mother cried 'Oh that poor pilot, he's going to lose his life' and the plane crashed into the hill a few hundred yards away. It was, of course, a doodlebug.

Oxfordshire Manor House

After that we were sent back to Stadhampton. My uncle and aunt by now had other relatives staying, so we went to the Manor House, to Mr Rose's part. He had a housekeeper Miss Churcher, who had a single crutch, padded to go under her arm. There was no water laid on, no electricity and the lavatory was a two-holer down the garden. No lavatory paper of course, you tore up newspaper and hung it on a piece of string. She was a wonderful cook, but poor Mr Rose, an elderly bachelor suddenly having these two children in his house. I had cousins in the village, and I was the oldest in the pack. We would wander round the old house, the fox hounds were kennelled nearby and there was a wonderful

freedom. I came to realise there was a social structure in the village, I got friendly with the policeman's daughter, she had a baby doll and so did I and I asked her to come up after school and play. I saw her standing at the gate and I asked Miss Churcher if she could come in, but she said 'No, better not.'

Mr Rose was a short man, with rather bandy legs and he wore leather gaiters. In the evenings he would take these off and polish them, then leave them standing, exact replicas of his legs. He had a greenhouse and grew grapes which always had pride of place at the Harvest Festival. The only time I had any was when I wasn't well. The other exotic fruit I encountered was when my brother and I had been put on a train in London to go to visit my grandparents. There was a woman in the carriage who produced from her bag a black object and told us it was a banana.

Our last evacuation was to Selsey, where we shared a bungalow. The beaches were all covered with concrete blocks and barbed wire. The thought of yet another new school (I went to seven different ones) really churned me up and I would be sick for a couple of days.

VE and VJ days

On VE-day we were at home in Harrow and my father organised a party with a bonfire in the middle of the road, dancing and singing. By VJ-day we were on holiday in Woolacombe, and there they arranged an impromptu celebration with fireworks. Only somehow the whole lot caught fire at once and there was a tremendous explosion and display!

Apart from that one night of the explosion in Oxfordshire, I always felt completely safe, I think that's a tribute to my family.

Mary St Leger-Harris

In the 1930s, I was at school and living at Long Stratton, in Norfok, where my father was the Rector. In September 1939, all the village was assessed for billeting of evacuees. The children had come by train and were gathered into the village hall where householders came to look at them and choose whom they would have. Because the Rectory was so large – we had 11 bedrooms in a beautiful Tudor building – we were able to have two women and their three small children. They had one end of the Rectory with their own stairs and bathroom, and would come and use the kitchen when my mother had finished. It all seemed to work quite well and most evacuees stayed for several years, the children going to the village school. We grew our own fruit and vegetables and I wasn't aware of food shortages. In 1941, I left school and did a secretarial course in Norwich, then my sister and I went to work in banks in Norwich, which were reserved occupations.

Norwich bombing

The night Norwich was bombed, we went out into garden to watch, it was horrendous. The next day walking through the streets of the city, everything was gone, the streets were full of rubble. The Germans went for cathedral cities, but they didn't get Norwich Cathedral.

All the young men were called up and my brother went into the Navy. There were RAF stations in East Anglia and later on the Americans came. I didn't drive, but petrol was rationed anyway. Around us were the county set, quite grand people in a way, who used to include the Rector's family in their tennis parties, but once the war had started there was very little social life. I wanted to join up, partly to help the country but partly to get away, even though I loved Norwich. My sister and I joined up the same day, 9 January 1943.

Auxiliary Territorial Service

I joined the ATS, preferring khaki to navy blue. We had our basic training at Harrogate in the requisitioned Queen Ethelburga's College. This was six weeks of jabs, and intensive drill. It was OK, but I was put on a charge because my hair was on my collar. As punishment, I had to scrub three square feet of the wooden chapel floor, with the sergeant standing, legs apart, staring down and telling me how to scrub, one square foot at a time. I was feeling awful with all the jabs. After six weeks, I was posted to St
Agnes in Cornwall, a gorgeous place. It was the 10th Light Ack-ack (Anti-Aircraft) practice training camp, training for D-day though we didn't know this. A plane would fly with a pennant about 100 yards behind and the artillery had to shoot it with the Bofors guns they later took to Normandy.

I went on courses to become a Physical Training Instructor, one in Newcastle and one in Dunblane. To get to Scotland, I left the St Agnes camp at 4am, going in a truck to Truro, then by train to London, across London lugging my kit-bag to Kings Cross and on to Dunblane. When we eventually arrived at the Hydro in Dunblane, we sat down at a long table. There was a bucket of tea from which we all helped ourselves and when the bucket was empty there was a dish cloth in the bottom. I said to the girls 'It's my 21st birthday today' and nobody moved a muscle. It didn't mean anything then, you couldn't buy cards, there was no celebration. I shall never forget that.

After the training and back at the camp, I was now a Corporal. As well as being a PT Instructor, I was also clerk to the adjutant. At 7.30am I took the girls for PT, outside if fine, inside if not, and most of the girls had never done anything like it. Next it was inspection of bed and kit, then breakfast and by nine o'clock I was in the adjutant's office.

Every month we had an FFI (Freedom from Infection) examination. There were 42 girls, all the rest were men. We had to line up with just our greatcoats on and a pair of khaki knickers. The woman sergeant at top of queue said 'Next' and you went in. The MO sat there and you had to open your coat, then he said 'Drop them' and you had to drop your knickers. It was meant to see you hadn't got nits, but he would have had a lovely time, looking at all those young girls. He didn't look closely at anything and we were never tested for sexual diseases nor given warnings. You just didn't do sex. If you went to a dance in the village you danced to Victor Sylvester records, then you could walk back with any stranger, they never tried anything on, it was marvellous really.

American arrival

Then the Americans came. I was in the mess with one of the girls and we heard this noise, and wondered what it was. As it got nearer we found it was the first Yanks, marching up from the station 'Hup, two, three, four, hup, two, three, four....' When they saw us girls, they whistled. The war all depended on them. They each had a little white tent which they pitched on the cliff edge and when it was stormy the tents blew away. They were only there three and a half weeks to train on the guns, then they would go; we had Canadians, Poles and Brits. When the Yanks came we had marvellous dances, they brought their own band and that was when I learnt the jitterbug. We danced in our awful uniform as we didn't have anything else, no civilian clothes, we were so envious of the few civilian girls who came in their frocks. The camp was fun and in such a lovely area on the cliff edge right by the sea, though you never got down to the beach. There was a tennis court in the village where we could play occasionally and mixed hockey with

194

the RAF, played in gym shoes. We went to dances in the RAF stations all along the north coast of Cornwall – Perranporth, Padstow, Polzeath and Newquay. We went in a truck, there were no drinks, maybe the odd beer. You could buy a cigarette ration in the NAAFI and get coffee and a doughnut if you were lucky.

What I did like was that you were mixed with all sorts of people, there was no class awareness. There was a hierarchy with officers though, you didn't mix on camp, but you could at dances, my boy friend was an officer.

We never knew where the men were going, it was all secret. Men came to train and then they were gone and another lot came. You lived in the present, not knowing if you were ever going to see anyone again. My ATS officer friend on the staff was a splendid person, she was married, with her husband in the navy, and would call us all 'child'. She had concerns of her own of course.

London and the Flying Bombs

I was told I was to get a commission, so was sent to the War Office Holding Unit in London to wait there to be called. I arrived in May, and the flying bombs started in June 1944. We spent the nights in a shelter, though we didn't know what these bombs were and I don't think the government knew either. We sometimes went outside at night when we heard them to see what was going on. One landed near and I got caught in the bomb blast. I didn't realise I was injured until a day or two later I woke and found there was something wrong with my vision. My sight wasn't right, then it altogether disappeared from one eye. It was awful.

Injury and hospitals

I went to the Army hospital on Millbank where I was diagnosed as having a detached retina. I was sent to the military eye unit at Shenley mental hospital where I had to lie still for days, no treatment, just seeing if it would get better. The grounds were beautiful, but I felt so sorry for the mental patients behind a high wire fence. My eye didn't improve so I was sent to Moorfields Eye Hospital, which had been evacuated to Mount Vernon. In trying to get the retina back the surgeon cut through the muscles of the eye, maybe they had to in those days so my eye was left with no vision, but staring up at the sky.

After the surgery I had to lie flat on my back, blindfold, for three and a half weeks, with my hands tied to the bed so I didn't brush against my eyes. I had to be fed lying down and I often vomited after the food. It was summer, there were wasps everywhere and I couldn't use my hands to wave them off, I just had to wait till an over-worked nurse came to clean me up. There were 52 people in the ward, including babies, and a radio loudspeaker high on the wall which all day every day blared out the Light Programme. It really was awful. I was just unlucky that I ended up in London, it would have been better had I stayed in Cornwall, but people were unlucky in those days

It was all to no avail, my sight got no better. Later another surgeon was able to repair some of the damage to the muscles. I had a dreadful year, most of it in hospital and always terrified the other eye would go. Nothing had worked and I had to be discharged on my 22nd birthday, as no longer fit for military service.

Medical Discharge

I came back to Long Stratton with no money and no job, the only thing I had been given was the railway warrant to get me home. One day I was sitting under a lovely copper beech when a German plane came hedge-hopping, so low I could see the man's face, luckily he didn't see me. After some months my father got me a job in UNRRA (United Nations Relief and Rehabilitation Association), in Portland Place and I enjoyed this enormously. My sister, a Wren, had a marvellous time in Egypt, didn't see any bombing or anything. My brother was on an aircraft carrier in the Pacific. I would have loved to have gone overseas, but felt that as the eldest sister my duty was to stay nearer home and look after the others. On VE-day, I went to London and stood outside Buckingham Palace. It seemed everyone was in uniform, and I was really sad to be in civvies.

I met my husband in 1946. He was a great authority on jazz, and as a broadcaster, author and critic did a tremendous amount to promote the post-war revival of jazz music. I had a very good life with him.

Audrey Stern

When I was young, the idea of nursing never crossed my mind. I am a Londoner, and didn't have a higher education because my mother feared that girls who were too educated never got married. It took me a time to get over that grievance. My father was a thermometer manufacturer with a small works in Hoxton, I was the younger of two daughters and we lived in Finchley. I took a secretarial course at Pitmans and worked in dreary offices.

Theatre company

Then in 1936 I got a job with a theatrical entrepreneur who sent out touring companies of shows from the West End. After a while I got to go out on the road with the company for two or three years, as stage manager and understudy.

This went on for the first year of the war and I was about to take over as Front of House manager at the Shanklin Theatre on the Isle of Wight when France fell. All the touring theatres closed, many of the venues were at the seaside and there was a real fear of invasion. My mother had sailed to America in 1939 to live with relatives but my father kept on with his work, travelling each day to Hoxton from Finchley. He was no good at looking after himself, so I took him on a train and evacuated him to a pub in Berkhamsted, from where he continued to travel to London to work. I then filled our house with Jewish refugees. Later in the war my mother came back, and brought my father home.

Jewish Refugees

The Jewish community in London ran clubs and social events for the Jewish refugees and invited them to their homes. I met my husband at a young people's club in Fitzroy Square, he had come over to this country in 1933. He had completed his law studies in Heidelburg and had a year at the Sorbonne but by then Hitler had come to power and Jews were no longer welcome. He had family connections in England, so he was able to make his way here and was naturalised as a British citizen before war broke out. He did not wish to take up law studies in England, seeing how powerless the law had proved in Germany.

A lot of refugees went into the Pioneer Corps, doing very basic work though many were highly skilled and qualified. Some were interned on the Isle of Man but my husband, having got his British nationality, was OK. He had an adopted brother who was not Jewish, and the British authorities wanted to send him back to Germany saying he was not in danger, but of course he was, having lived with a Jewish family.

Wedding

We were married in July 1940 in St Pancras Registry Office; not being religious I did not want to be married in a synagogue. My husband's call-up papers arrived the day of our wedding – when asked was he married he said 'No, but if you will give me a couple of hours, I will be.' Married men were not called up as early as unmarried. As my mother was still in America, I was able to do all the organising myself. We had a honeymoon at Stow-in-the-Wold but were a bit surprised when, shortly after our arrival, an army officer arrived asking to see us. Apparently a German parachutist was alleged to have landed in the area and the Army were out looking for him. When the officer discovered my husband was originally German, he got very excited and demanded to look through all our stuff, see our papers and our marriage certificate –

which of course we hadn't brought with us. The landlady protested that this had all been booked long before and in the end we were left alone.

London bombing

We had a room in Coram Street, Holborn where we slept in the cellar as the bombs dropped. My mother-in-law said we must get out of there as we were sure to be bombed, so we came to Highgate and the first night there we were bombed out. Our flat was in the semi-basement, so we weren't actually hurt. It was a landmine in the road, the blast blew the windows in and all the leaves from the trees on Hampstead Heath. Across the road was a residential home for elderly and demented people, I watched the firemen carrying all these poor people out from the shattered building.

My husband was by now secretary to a director of the Czech Trust, which had evacuated to Radlett. We were fortunate enough to get a flat in St Albans opposite the Abbey and we moved there with my mother-in-law. Father-in-law was in Halifax, organising his business. For a while I was still in the theatrical office, but it was difficult getting into London from St Albans. Also I felt I wanted to do something for the war effort, the Red Cross seemed obvious as it was just across the road, so I joined.

Red Cross nurse

I did a few sessions of 'dental day' at the local hospital. This entailed standing on one side of the dentist's chair holding a kidney dish. On the other side was the dentist and in front was a nurse with what I suppose was an ether mask, which she slapped over the patient's face. Once the patient was 'out', the dentist pulled the teeth and dropped them in my kidney dish. Several women patients came in with fetching hair-dos, and I was astonished to see that once the mask was over their faces, their hair stood on end and danced. Nurse was quite unfazed. 'It's the lice' she said. 'The women don't wash their hair because they don't want to lose the waves, so of course they get infested.'

Then I was moved to Cell Barnes Hospital, which had been for the demented, but Barts was evacuated there. I was at once sent to a ward packed with the seriously injured from the London blitz. There was a woman there who was delirious and my job was to watch her and stop her falling out of bed, but one look at her terribly injured face and I promptly fainted. Coming to I found Sister patting my cheek and saying 'Pull yourself together nurse, get up and get on with what you have been told to do.' So I did, but the experience had come as something of a shock after only six weeks in the Red Cross learning how to bandage a sprained wrist.

As so many of the trained nursing personnel were still holed up in France, I also worked in the operating theatre, fetching and carrying sterilised instruments and watching operations on the hands of badly burnt pilots. I really loved nursing and applied to do my SRN, but Matron would have none of it. 'I know you girls with husbands stationed in England, you always run off camp-following' which, of course, we did. My husband thought he  would be called into the RASC (Royal Army Service Corps) as he was educated and literate, but the letter S seems to have been dropped and instead he was called up into the Royal Armoured Corps, which was using tanks!

Auxiliary nursing

He went into the Army and I went into an auxiliary nursing home in Bishops Stortford; it was terribly dull after Barts, all skin diseases and undescended testicles. My husband was drafted to the Middle East and was actually removed from the ship when they realised he was a German Jewish refugee and it was considered unthinkable that he might fall into the hands of the Nazis. So because of this amazing compassion and understanding of the British High Command, two weeks after his departure he was back, and posted to Dorset as a wireless operator instructor.

I joined the Dorset Red Cross where we were sending parcels to prisoners-of-war. In 1944 my husband was moved to Intelligence, to a post near Amersham, and I became pregnant. We had digs there and he would go off each morning on his bicycle I didn't know where. In fact I didn't find out till 50 years later when I had come to live in Chorleywood. Talking to a taxi driver as he took me somewhere locally, I told him this story and he said 'Oh I know where he went. They brought all the captured German generals to Latimer House, no doubt he would have been a translator during their interrogation.'

As a private soldier's wife, I got ten shillings the first week and five shillings a week thereafter. Luckily my husband's family were able to help. After the war ended, my husband was selected for the War Crimes Commission and was at Nuremberg for the trials. By then my baby was born and we were back in the flat in St Albans. I had let out the sitting room and the main bedroom, retaining just the small bedroom, and often friends would come and sleep on the floor. It wasn't difficult getting things for the babies during the war, we would be allowed eggs, orange juice and cod liver oil. It was the old people who suffered, babies have never been healthier.

After he was demobbed, my husband went to the London School of Economics and got his degree. Following that he was offered a position on the staff where he stayed for the rest of his working life, and we returned to live in London.

Betty Stockwell

In 1939 we lived in Mill Hill, my father was a jeweller in London. In August when war was imminent, evacuation plans were put into action, and my sister and I were driven off to the country, in floods of tears. I was 15, my sister five. My father's business stopped during the war, he became the Chief ARP (Air Raid Precautions) Warden for Mill Hill.

Evacuation

My school, The Mount at Mill Hill, was evacuated to Amberley, in Gloucestershire. The head mistress of our school had a house there, and she took over the empty village school building. It was filthy. We lived in the school for some weeks, till the headmistress found Rose Cottage, and we moved there.

I had a dressing-room to sleep in and there were six little ones my sister's age I had to look after. If they were sick I had to clear up, if they woke in the night I had to go to them. If there was an air raid warning in the middle of the night I had to take them downstairs with a pillow each, I gathered them round me and told them stories, sometimes from the Bible, sometimes just ones I made up. Later on another girl of my age arrived, we were the only two older ones. We grew up fast, and I did my School Certificate there.

School holidays

When school holidays came, we couldn't go home, because Mill Hill was near Hendon aerodrome and there were air-raids. Instead, we went to the home of an Anglican minister, the Rev. Ernest Panter, in Brimscombe. He had been a missionary and with his pregnant wife and three children, they were a wonderful family, true Christians. Later I got holiday jobs locally, I learnt to milk cows, and worked as a chambermaid in a boarding house

London Secretary

I left school and came back to Mill Hill in 1941, whilst the bombing of London was going on. I went to Pitmans to do their secretarial course, then worked as a filing clerk for the Inland Revenue in Finchley Road. I was finding files for valuers to use when assessing bomb damage, these were called VOW (Victims of War) files. There had been so much bombing, it was essential to have material for the valuers to make their assessments so people could get some money. There was only one other girl, she was a telephonist and she taught me how to work a switchboard. The job kept me busy through a long day, and in my spare time I did VAD (Voluntary Aid Detachment) training; you had to get 100 hours experience to qualify.

At home, my father had strengthened the garage with a blast wall and reinforced the ceiling making it into a shelter where we all slept, including Granny who had moved to us from Harrow. My brothers were evacuated to Worcester and remained there another year. My father's business premises were bombed, he went up one day and found someone had tied a dog to a table leg in his bombed out office, Dad brought him home and he stayed with us for ever.

I left the Finchley job and went to work with W R Chambers, publishers, in Soho. There was a Lyons Corner House nearby where you could get lunch for half a crown, it even had a tablecloth. I met three really nice girls, and brought two of them home to Mill Hill, where my mother found out they were prostitutes and we got on fine.

WRNS and Station X

In 1942 I volunteered for the WRNS. I hadn't the faintest idea what I was letting myself in for, but it was the 'nicest' service to be in. I went first to New College, Finchley Road, for basic training, then to nearby Westfield College to be kitted out. We were given tests to see what our abilities were, whether we would be cook or steward or plotter or what. There was a wide range of jobs and I was told I would be suitable for Station X. When I asked 'What is it?' I was told 'You'll find out when you get there.' Once there I had to sign the Official Secrets Act, and I made such a good job of forgetting everything that I found it horrific when the first book about Bletchley came out about it 30 years later. At the time, nobody knew what we were doing, everything was pushed down so far that now it is quite hard to get it up again!

Bletchley Park

From New College we were taken by coach to Crawley Grange, a beautiful requisitioned house. We Wrens shared a ball room, with ten double-decker bunks and were bussed in to Bletchley Park, where we were shown the hut where we were to work. I was working on a Bombe, the electro-mechanical machines developed by Alan Turing and Harry Welchman to de-code German messages encrypted by their Enigma machines. Enigma had three revolving pre-wired drums, so if you pressed E it went through the first drum, maybe coming out as G, through the second to maybe S, and the third to maybe Z. There were different colours and variable settings, so there were many millions of possible combinations.

Each Bombe was eight foot wide, six foot high and three foot deep. Drums clipped onto spindles and connected with commutators working electro-magnetically. A menu was plugged up at the back of the machine, being a possible sequence of letters in the crib. There were 60 sets of rotors, and a whole run could take 30 hours, in which case the job was shared with several machines. The machine searched the drum orders and settings that might decode a short piece of message. If the machine found a possible 'stop' or key, it might be possible to break a coded message. Everything was intensely secret, you never discussed what you were doing with people from other huts even if you were great friends off duty.

Wrens operated the machines but I was curious and wanted to know more about how they actually worked. The machines were maintained by Air Force personnel, men who had been electricians in Civvy Street. We worked an eight-hour shift, changing each week, so we were divided into four watches. I found I could read blue-prints, which meant if something went wrong I could work on it. There was a 19-year old RAF technician called John and together we worked out how the machines ran. Then if there was a problem, it was always John or Betty who was called to put it right, because it had to be done quickly and we were young and enthusiastic.

Enigma technician

Because I had become a proficient technician, I was given a 'cabin', a room to myself and could work whatever hours I liked. This meant I could stay and get a problem worked out even if my shift had ended. I was promoted to Leading Wren and then to Petty Officer. I had tried to make a Christian witness initially and when I had a cabin to myself, I put up a notice on my door to say if anyone wanted a 'quiet time', they could come in here, bring a Bible and have some personal time. Rev Maurice Watts, minister at Mill Hill Union Church, suggested I should ask for a chapel. I got this, but no one used it, they continued to come to my room instead!

I was sent to Stoke Poges for Officer Training and came back with a commission. I became a Watch Officer, therefore had much more administrative work and found it very difficult to concentrate on the technical side. I was sent to Hollerith's in Letchworth, where they produced the machines; I watched them being made from scratch, and learned exactly how the wiring worked. Some of the RAF technicians came too, this was awkward because I was on officer and a woman, so I had to have different lodgings and could not mix socially.

Colussus

Tony Flowers lived in Mill Hill, attending the same church as we did. He made the very fast machine Colossus. He was a genius and worked night and day, using parts such as valves from the Post Office where he worked. Colossus was a faster machine than a Bombe and had a bit of memory, it was the fore-runner of today's computers.

Wrens did their training at Bletchley Park, then were sent out to stations dotted about. There were Bombes in huts around the area, at Wavendon, Woburn, Gayhurst, Adslock. Eventually they were all gathered into a purpose built place at Stanmore, now the orthopaedic hospital and another at Eastcote, now demolished. Fortunately there were no newspaper snoops wanting to know what you did, though one did get through and when he asked, was told, 'Oh it's very boring, we scrape barnacles off the bottoms of the ships.'

Sadly the dedication and skills of men like Tony Flowers, Alan Turing and others had no public mention until long after the war when the secrecy was lifted. Well deserved decorations were awarded, but for some too late.

After the German war ended, I was posted as EVT (Educational and Vocational Training) Officer to the Fleet Air Arm station at Arbroath. The job here was to help young men decide what they wanted to do and then find training for them. I was there till after the Japanese hostilities finished, when I was demobbed, came home, started a career in catering, and at a New Year's Eve church social met Derek playing 'Bigamy', and married him in 1948.

Derek Stockwell

Royal Army Medical Corps

After matriculation in the 1930s, I went for six months to France to learn the language, followed by six months in Switzerland to learn German before starting in business. In early 1939 war seemed inevitable, and on April Fools Day, I joined the Territorial Army, in the Royal Army Medical Corps. When war was declared in September we became full time soldiers, and our unit – the 168 (City of London) Field Ambulance – was billeted at a school near Finsbury Barracks, where I was cook to the sergeants' mess. Then we moved to Lincolnshire, and after a brief embarkation leave set out for Palestine in early 1940. We travelled by train across France, then by troop-ship from Marseilles to

Haifa. The country was fairly peaceful, and we spent just over a year there in different places including Nablus and Samaria. We were doing training and field exercises, I learnt a little Arabic and provided some medical help to an Arab village. I also visited a number of sites – Jerusalem, Mount Carmel and Tiberias, and imagined the people and incidents recorded in the Bible. At that time there was not much commercialisation, and the age-old feud between Jews and Arabs was more or less put aside.

Action in Crete

We went to Egypt for a short period, near Alexandria, then in March 1941 went into action in Greece as the Germans threatened that country from the north. We set up our First Aid station and had our first taste of bombing and machine gun firing from the air. Although our lorries were marked with red crosses, we lost by death one medical officer and one driver. The total British force was small, and the gesture rather futile, so we were soon retreating. I learnt years later that our CO wrote to my parents about my coolness under fire. We were evacuated to Crete, to a hospital in the north of the island, but after a week the Germans began to fly low over the area and spray the ground with machine gun fire from their Stuka dive bombers. We hastily dug slit trenches, but within a few days the Germans invaded Crete with 12,000 parachute troops landing on an airfield near our hospital.

The German losses were so heavy that they never tried such tactics again. We also suffered many casualties and soon had to evacuate the hospital and, along with other troops, began retreating towards the southern coast. We tramped by night, right across the island, through the mountains, hiding in ditches or woods during the days when the German planes were active and I narrowly missed bullets. We got to a small port on the south coast, where the Navy took off evacuees on several nights, but then had to stop as the dive-bombers were causing too many casualties. Despite its strategic importance, the island could not be held. The Allies had known that Germany was going to attack Crete, but they had insufficient arms and men to hold it, and could not get more there because of attacks on our convoys.

German capture

We woke one morning to find ourselves surrounded by German infantrymen. This was a great shock. I found it strange that their belt clasps bore the motto 'Gott mit uns' and to reflect that God was with them and with us. Our forces gave up Crete in June 1941 and these events gave me nightmares for years to come.

Trudging back to the north of Crete under escort, tired, hungry, thirsty and despondent, we encountered repeatedly the stench of rotting bodies, though one Aussie just in front managed to sing *Waltzing Matilda*. We walked all the way back to the former hospital, now turned into a temporary prison camp. As shipping became available, successive batches of men were taken away, and I worked as interpreter until my turn came to leave in September. After travelling in extremely primitive conditions (with no sanitary provisions on board) among the lovely Greek islands, we arrived at Salonika and stayed a week. Then into cattle trucks (again no provision for calls of nature) for the very uncomfortable journey to eastern Germany.

Prison camp

The base camp here, Stalag VIIIB at Lamsdorf became home for some 15,000 men. It was inhabited long-term by non-combatant personnel and non-commissioned officers, and short-term by soldiers returned from working parties on factories, farms or mines. Being protected by the Geneva Convention, I did not have to work for the Germans but it was important to have some occupation to avoid 'barbed wire sickness', so I worked as interpreter at the camp hospital.

Conditions in camp were often tough, but the treatment was reasonable and occasionally we had an inspection by an officer of a protecting power – Switzerland or Sweden. The huts were extremely cold in winter and hot in summer, the food was hardly enough to keep us healthy, though food parcels from the Red Cross made an enormous difference. The camp had a church, a school and a theatre, and I took part in the activities of all three. I was part of an active group of evangelical Christians, played the part of the leading lady in at least one camp show, and made good use of the school, both as a student and as a teacher of elementary Italian.

On one occasion I had the chance of returning home, under a scheme to exchange medical personnel and sick men, but I passed this up to allow married men to have preference. When a second exchange was planned, I prepared to go (after getting a cobbler to conceal some uncensored photographs in the sole of my boot), but the whole scheme fell through.

It was during my time in the camp that my call to the ministry became clearer, and when another interpreter came along, I began serious studies. The Red Cross obtained books and negotiated exam papers, so I was able to pass the intermediate and part of the final stage of the London University BA.

Evacuation march

In January 1945, with the Russians advancing, the Germans decided to evacuate the camp. Conditions on this march were really tough. I acted as interpreter to a chaplain in charge of a column of walking sick and wounded and the severity of cold and hunger caused many to drop out. At one point I was befriended by a farmer and his wife, had a bath in a zinc tub and realised how thin I was.

After nearly four months of walking and train travel we finished up in a temporary hospital near Munich, having crossed 600 miles of Germany from east to south-west, with very little food. We met men from the concentration camp at Dachau, and were struck by their gauntness and hatred of the Germans. Although our experience had been grim, theirs was far worse.

Release

We were released by the Americans in May 1945, and soon flown home. How good it was to see the English countryside again, with cow-parsley flowering along the roads. And better still to see the family after more than five years. After a long leave, during which Mother fed me up with all that could be found in that time of shortages, I rejoined the army and was transferred to the Royal Engineers.

Having been accepted for training as a minister, I was granted priority for demobilisation, and returned to civvy street in the autumn of 1945, when I entered New College, London.

I am grateful to Derek for permission to use material from his memoir "Looking Back Over Eighty Years"

Beatrice Strivens

Children's nurse

As a child I lived in Lancashire, where my family were involved in cotton manufacture. When I was 17 in 1937, I went to London to train as a Princess Alice Children's Nurse. Many of the babies went for adoption and part of the training was to work for a year in the adoptive home. I went with twin babies who were adopted by an older couple who did not have any children of their own. We started in their London flat, but when war was imminent they moved to Gloucestershire and I was there when war broke out. It was very lonely, though I had a bicycle, and could cycle into Cirencester.

WRNS

Once my year was finished, I joined the WRNS in 1940. While I was waiting to be called up I went to look after an elderly aunt who was dying from cancer, then I joined up along with a friend from school days. We went to Liverpool for an interview for the WRNS; I thought I might be a storeman but was put into Signals. I was sent to Silloth, a little place on the Cumbrian coast where there were only four of us Wrens, no officers and no uniforms as the depot had been bombed. The coastguards reported shipping as it passed and we had to pass the information on to the commander, a retired man, who then sent it further on. I was bored and fed up, so asked for a transfer and got sent to Holyhead. There were still no officers and I never did any initial training at all, but I did get a uniform. Later we got Wren officers but by this time we already knew the job, which was running the Signals Distribution Office. Signals came by Morse, teleprinter, telephone and wireless. There were trained men to translate the Morse and we then sent the signals on. I was there 18 months. There was constant shipping in and out, flotillas of MLs (Motor Launches) MTBs (Motor Torpedo Boats) MGBs (Motor Gun Boats), and a Dutch depot ship.

Holyhead

The only bomb that dropped in Holyhead landed one night when I was on duty. A message came in on the telephone exchange 'Miss, miss, there is a bomb dropped, outside the gentleman's lavatory.' Then another message 'Reporting one bomb dropped, no casualties, only one sitting case.'

We always had an officer on duty, but one time I couldn't find him when a signal came in reporting a damaged submarine. I knew what to do, so phoned the harbour master for a berth and they sent a signal to the ship. Next morning the officer said to me 'I hear you gave berth to a submarine last night, where have you put it?' He could have looked in the log-book.

Fleet Air Arm

We were in digs with a landlady who cooked for us; sometimes we would be invited to parties on board ship, just two or three of us. I asked to be moved, and was sent to Warrington, to a Fleet Air Arm camp for new recruits. These lads arrived with their long hair and their pointed shoes, and next day they would be there with hair shorn and in uniform, looking quite different. There was an American base nearby, and once 50 of us were invited to a dance there. We went on a bus, the dance was in a Nissen hut with a big stove in the centre and all round the walls these men, but no other girls. We were ushered into the middle, it was just like a cattle market. The Americans were standing around chewing gum, then they made a grab at us and started dancing cheek to cheek, they were very sweaty and it wasn't fun at all.

I was made Leading Wren and sent to another Fleet Air Arm base in Newcastle-under-Lyme, a camp for young entries, who were learning to be artificers. Someone formed a choir, they wanted girls so I joined and we sang Stainer's Crucifixion. I moved into a Wrenery, because it was more fun than being in digs

Great Yarmouth

In 1943, I was promoted to Petty Officer, and sent to Great Yarmouth. This was very demanding as there was fighting just out in the North Sea, our MTBs and MGBs, and German MTBs. I was in charge of a watch and had to see that incoming signals were passed on to the right places. Next I was sent to Burnham-on-Crouch, as I'd been recommended for a commission. They were building landing craft in the estuary, and training young men to use them. I was called to the OTC, which was no longer at Greenwich but Framwood Manor, near Fulmer in Buckinghamshire. (Recently I went to the Black Horse pub, and recognised it as the pub we used to walk two miles to get to.) There we

had to learn Officer Like Qualities and how to get troops to march in order. I'd never actually learnt marching before. I had to take my squad out on an inspection by the Chief Wren, Vera Lawton Matthews and I had somehow to get them back in the same order.

Invasion and doodlebugs

I was sent to Alton to train as a Cipher Officer, I was there for D-day and watched all the planes going over. It was all very secret, we weren't allowed anywhere outside the camp. Once I had passed out as an officer, I was sent to Dover, where there were masses of tunnels under the castle and I was billeted in a boys' school on the hill. One night on the hill outside the castle, we saw a great flight of doodlebugs coming

213

towards us in a straight line and our anti-aircraft guns shooting at them. A great cheer went up when one was shot down, but as they got near we had to go into the shelters. One weekend I went up to London for a bit of fun when one came over, stopped and dropped just close to where we were. I decided it was safer in Dover though by then, with our troops advancing through France, the Germans were sending their shells over to Dover. We would have to go into the shelter, then there would be a pause and just as we were coming out, they would start up again. Dover was badly damaged, all the shops and windows were boarded up.

Then there was a call for volunteers to go overseas. We assembled in Crosby Hall on Cheyne Walk, and were kitted out in tropical uniform by very high class London tailors. We didn't know where we were going when we were put on a train. It took us to Liverpool where we joined a boat, still not knowing to where we were going, but we went in a convoy right out into the Atlantic, then south round the Cape and eventually to Colombo.

Ceylon

I was sent on loan to Kandy, where Lord Louis Montbatten's HQ had been moved from Delhi. Our office was in the Botanical Gardens, and I was with the Secret Signals, in a Nissen hut. Next to us was the American Secret Signals in another Nissen hut, but they had guards outside and a maze of paths and sentries challenging everyone whereas in our hut were just two Wren officers. The signals had been decoded, were passed to us in plain language and we sent on these very secret messages about troop movements. It was quite demanding and I was only on loan. VE-day happened, but it didn't make much difference to us, then VJ-day, though even then we didn't celebrate particularly.

Released Prisoners-of-war

I was then asked to act as hostess to returning prisoners of war. They were in a terrible state, very weak and were first seen by the medical officers. They were then given a small amount of money and we took them to the shops. They couldn't believe the stuff that was there, one man got so excited at the bottle shop, another asked me what he should get for his mother. I showed him some handkerchiefs, and he bought one and gave it to me. We were the first white women they had seen in years.

I was then demobbed as I had been in the WRNS for five years, and was sent home on a ship which had spent the whole war in Trincomalee. The captain was furious when he found knitting needles in his ward-room, but we had to do something to pass the time. We got home just before Christmas and I went to look after my father who had a heart attack on Christmas Day. I got a job as a sound recordist, and later flew to South Africa in a little Skymaster plane which could only fly by day and stopped at Cairo, Khartoum, Nairobi and Johannesburg. There I got a job, met my husband and lived very happily for 50 years.

Gloria Thorp

Welsh childhood

I was born in Neath in South Wales in 1923 and I'd never been out of it till I joined the army. My Dad worked in the mines, at first he was down below and then he came up on top. I had a lovely childhood, my Dad did a lot for the church, he had a wonderful voice. Mum preferred to stay at home, she didn't want to go out anywhere. On my 12th birthday my Mum died. She'd had her appendix out, then she had to go back for another operation and she died in the hospital. Then when I was 14 my Dad died and I had to go and live with my auntie. It was dreadful. My elder sister was 16 by now, she got a job and moved out so it was only me. I think Auntie hated me, maybe was jealous of me. She had two boys younger than me, they were good brothers to me. One time my uncle was there when she was being really cruel and unfair to me, he really went to town on her, told her off; after that she was much nicer. He was lovely my uncle, he drove a crane in the steel works, he used to come in with his leather trousers all pitted with tiny splinters of steel.

Call up

I was working in an office, when the war came. I wanted to go into the Royal Army Medical Corps so I did three months hospital training at Neath, going in on Saturdays and Sundays and any days off, so that I'd done my 100 hours before I went into the Army. Auntie didn't like me doing that. When I was called up I was petrified. A letter came with a train ticket telling me to report to Aldershot. I wanted to leave home and I wanted to join the army, but I'd never been on a train before, never been out of Neath and now I had to get to the camp at Aldershot. Another girl got on at the next stop, she'd never been away either so we both stuck together.

There were lots of girls on that train going to Aldershot, so we just followed them. We sat at this big table, and there was so much food; of course I was brought up to hand plates round so then there wasn't any left for me. I learnt after that and always got my hand in first. We were in big dormitories. They wanted me to go into the police because I was tall, and strapping, but I stuck out and said I wanted to go to the RAMC. I learnt to stand up for myself in the Army.

RAMC nursing

I was at the Louis Margaret hospital in Aldershot for three months training, that was where I met Peter, he was working in the hospital next door. Then I was sent to a unit at Ottershaw, near Woking, where I was in charge of the sick bay and medical inspection room, and did sick parade every morning with the Medical Officer. I was the only nurse there. We were one side of the village and the men's camp was the other side, ours was a unit for drivers. It was lovely, we were in the park around a beautiful big house which had been commandeered. I had my own rooms in the sick bay, I was very lucky, had all my own stuff and was in charge. If there was anything serious the girls went off to the hospital and I would go with them in the ambulance, we had our own ambulance and driver, but I looked after them if they had bad period trouble, or flu, or had fallen down, that sort of thing. We had a very good dispenser and the doctor came in the mornings, evenings too if there was anyone who needed her. I loved it and they asked me if I would stay on. I would have done if I hadn't met Peter.

I'd been able to send letters and get them from Peter, when he was in France, that was very worrying as he was in a front line hospital. Then he went to India, and that wasn't so dangerous. He worked very hard, I worked hard too.

Nurse in Charge

There was very little social life, no dances or cinema that I remember. I didn't want to move away, or go abroad, I was very happy where I was. I had a uniform and ended up with three stripes, I'd been a corporal for three years. There was a canteen, but I had my own little kitchen. If there were patients in the ward, we had food sent up from the cookhouse, but often I'd do my own cooking, the patients much preferred it. I'd get eggs and bacon and all sorts, I was very friendly with the sergeant in the kitchen and she would see that I had plenty of food up in my sick bay.

When I had leave I would go home to Neath. None of my friends had joined up, they had gone into the factories. There was one factory where they made gunpowder and the girls' skin would go yellow; I wouldn't stand for that, I preferred the Army.

I was innocent as a babe when I joined up and I was horrified at what went on, horrified. I wasn't brought up that way. Girls with VD were sent to hospital and discharged as medically unfit. Then there were those who got pregnant, they were discharged too. There would be Sick Parade every Monday, I was there with the doctor and she would sort them out. Tough as old boots, that doctor. But when I came out of the army she rang up and asked would I go and work for her in Cardiff, but I said 'No, I'm married now.'

When I got married I had to get used to shopping for food, Peter gave me the housekeeping money each week. I knew he loved mushrooms and I saw these mushrooms in the shop, marked at so much per pound. I asked for a pound and it was so much money I nearly died. When Peter got back he said 'You should have asked for a quarter' but I didn't know, hadn't got a clue, never done any food shopping before. But he did enjoy those mushrooms.

218

Peter Thorp

In the 1930s I was living in South Harrow and my father was Clerk of Works to the Metropolitan Police. I was born in 1923 and left school when I was 14. I was in the Church Lads' Brigade and when someone asked was there anyone who wanted to take up an apprenticeship in a dental laboratory, they recommended me. My mother and father went to see this man, whilst I went to bed and when they came home they said 'You start work tomorrow.' It was a Thursday and in those days you worked Saturdays so I'd only done two days but I got a whole week's pay – I thought it was great and I did a four-year apprenticeship.

Joining up

In 1941 I was 18 and wanted to join up. I went with six of my friends to Acton to volunteer for the RAF, we all got the King's Shilling, were given a number and were sent home. They called us up at different times, all the others went to Canada to train as aircrew, six of them were killed. I wrote to the authorities because I hadn't been called, and they said 'Don't call us, we'll call you.' Then they formed the RAF Regiment and I got into that, did all the training at Whitley Bay, where we had 20 mile route marches.

Going into dinner one day, I was called out and told 'I don't know what you've done, but you're going to Civvy Street.' I said 'No way, I want to go to fight and kill Germans', but it was because I'd had the dental training and they wanted me to go into a hospital somewhere. The only way to get out of that was to volunteer for the paratroops, so I did.

Then one day I was told I was going on leave, but when I got down to the guard room they said 'You're not going on leave, you're going to Leeds' for a trade test. I didn't know what to do, whether to try to pass it or fail it, because if I passed they might send me to Civvy Street. After the first day, the Regimental Sergeant Major came along and said I'd passed. When I asked what did I do next, he said 'Stay here for a week', so I was billeted with some private people, I had wonderful food. My parents didn't know where I was, they thought I'd gone off with some girl or something as they had been expecting me home.

Anyway, I got sent to Aldershot to work in the hospital there. One day I was sitting there in my RAF uniform in the middle of a lot of men in civvies, when I became aware of an officer, all gold braid and everything and he said to me 'What are you doing here my man, are you in the ATC?' I said 'No, I'm in the Air Force', and he said 'What Grade are you?' and I said 'A1'. He said 'You don't want to be a non-combatant do you?' and I said 'No I don't' so he got me into the Royal Fusiliers. There I had to do all the basic training again, but the battalion was disbanded, they transferred me to the Army Dental Corps and I finished my service in that.

Normandy Invasion

I went to Europe on D-day+4, to Arromanches where the Mulberry harbour was. Then up through Caen, there were so many bomb craters, crater in crater in crater, the place was obliterated. We were in the front line hospital, dealing with mouth and facial injuries. We were in Dieppe for a while, then finished up in Belgium, at a place called Renaix where we had our unit in the 113 British General Hospital which had 1,000 beds. This was in what used to be a nunnery with a general hospital attached, it had a great big red cross on the roof. The nuns had half and we had the other half, they made us most welcome. Some of the men with burns and facial injuries we could make splints for and treat there, the worst ones we had to send back to England.

India

We stayed in Europe till that war was ending, then they brought us back home, formed us into a unit and flew us out to India with a view of going to Burma. We stopped to refuel in Egypt at Castel Bonito, then Iraq. We were in Liberators, there were four of us down below in what used to be the bomb deck. But as we were taxi-ing for take off, two of the engines caught fire and we finished up in the barbed wire fence. We all got out, the pilot and co-pilot were shaking. This was only a transit aerodrome and all the planes coming in were full, so we were taken out in ones and twos.

When the last two of us got to Bombay, nobody was expecting us and nobody knew what to do with us. There was a boat there going back to England and they said we'd better get on that. I thought, can't do that, so we were stuck in a camp, no mosquito nets and the bugs many sizes bigger than what they are here, I didn't like that part of it. Then our RSM came and gave us a right rollicking, asking what were we doing there? We said we'd just been landed and didn't know where he was. When he calmed down a bit he gave us a ticket to go on the train to Calcutta, this took three days and three nights, on wooden seats. The food we had were K-rations – army packs – the only things that were any good were the three cigarettes, some toilet paper and four toffees. There were a lot of Indian troops and they had a carriage set out for their meals, basically curry, so I used to go along with my mess tin and have some beans and curry and thoroughly enjoyed it.

We were in India when VE-day came, and the chaps who had been in Burma were very angry at all the celebrations because, as far as they were concerned, the war was still on.

We got to Calcutta and were there when they dropped the atom bomb and the war ended. The unit moved out to Dum Dum and we were held in transit whilst they broke us up and sent us to different places for demob. I was sent to Poona. I'd heard of Poona, I'd always though "When I was in Poona..." was a stage skit, but I had a good time there, it was the Number One dental lab in India. The food was terrible, we had corned beef for breakfast, corned beef for dinner and corned beef for supper done all different ways – fried, boiled, mashed up, never nice cold slices.

Demob

When my number came up for discharge, we sailed from Bombay to Liverpool and went to a discharge camp. Here you got your civilian suit, I think you had the choice of one out of two, and choice whether you kept your greatcoat or not, also you had shoes and socks and underwear. Then they gave you a travel warrant and you simply went home. During the war, my parents had moved three times and I had to find the new house each time I went home on leave. By the time I was demobbed they were in Finchley and I didn't know a soul there. When you get back you miss the comradeship and I was a bit concerned about a job because there had been so many changes in the technology; we used to use vulcanite for dentures, now it was all plastic and lots of other advances. I got three months pay, but that didn't last long.

I went into the war as a boy and came out a man. I lost all my youth because we were moving around all the time. Lots of my school chums had been killed, some of the others had got married. But by then I knew Gloria, and all I wanted to do was get married.

Vera Thurtell

In 1936 I was 17 and left school to start work in the Civil Service. I worked as a clerk in the Ministry of Health in Acton. My parents were divorced and I lived with my father, grandmother and two aunts in Hendon. In 1938 we all expected war to happen, preparations were made for evacuation, blackout, and gas masks.

European holidays

In 1936, my father had taken my brother and myself on holiday to Germany. There were swastikas hanging from the roof of every house, great notices saying 'Guns before Butter', ersatz foods, tanks and brown-shirts everywhere, yet in France three years later it was very different. At the beginning of August 1939, my boy-friend and I and four others decided to go on a holiday to France. Looking back now I'm astonished that all our parents let us go. One of the girls I met on that French holiday remained a very good friend throughout the war, and still is. We went by boat from Dover, everyone was scrambling to get away from France and we were going there. I spoke schoolgirl French and there was no sign of war or panic. We went to Brittany, where they were in their traditional clothing. We hitch-hiked all round with no difficulty, we didn't go to Paris, maybe there would have been more preparations there. We came back on the boat from Calais; by now most people had already come to England and the boat wasn't crowded. We had been a bit concerned that we might have been interned in France and were quite glad to be back in England.

Wartime London

We came back to blackout and sandbags everywhere. I was moved from the Ministry of Health to Pensions, in the same building. Some departments were being evacuated to the North but I wanted to stay in London. It's terrible to say this, but I found London very exciting during the war. I was used to going places and independence and I can't say I was ever frightened, a bit apprehensive maybe but never frightened.

223

I was moved again, to the War Office in Whitehall where we had to learn First Aid and fire watching. I had been upgraded from Clerical to Executive and was moved to the Ministry of Supply, which had just been formed. I was dealing with contracts for supplies and equipment for the Army. First it was boots and clothing, and then components.

I belonged to the Youth Hostels and on a Saturday, if I thought I can't face this weekend, even if the rain was lashing and the wind was howling, I packed some food and got on my bike and cycled off to a hostel somewhere. I do love wild weather. I've always gone off on my own, it seemed quite normal to me, though I don't think many girls had so much freedom.

Air-raids

The bombing started at Easter 1940. I was at the Ministry of Supply in Westminster, next to the hospital. It was much better to be working in London rather than Acton, despite the bombing. It wasn't too severe at first, then there was a month of bombing every night. Going in to work each day, whole streets would have disappeared. Our home in Hendon was quite close to the military aerodrome at Colindale. There was a big air-raid shelter nearby, my grandmother and aunts used to go there, but it was so horrible I decided I'd rather take the chance of a bomb and slept in my bed. Travelling to work in the tube, everyone was from the same area, had been through the same experience and we'd exchange anecdotes. The atmosphere was incredible.

I travelled with my father who was manager of a wholesale merchant firm in Regent Street. He sometimes got hold of a bolt of cloth and would send it to one of the Saville Row tailors to make a suit for me. I would have to endure the fittings which I hated because I was a bit chubby, but they were beautiful suits by such a skilled tailor. I'd love to have one now, though at the time I didn't appreciate them. The only thing I liked was a rusty coloured Harris tweed suit. My father knew a milliner who made me this marvellous boat shaped hat with an emerald green feather in it. I loved that. My father hoped I'd get married after the war and he knew cloth would be in short supply. So when a traveller brought in three lengths of flannel, one in turquoise, one in pink and one in dove grey, Father put a length of the pink away ready for my wedding. I wish he had chosen the turquoise.

I had met my husband before the war. My first job in the Civil Service was in a post office; he was an accountant for the Church Army round the corner, and he used to come in and buy a penny stamp just to speak to me. He was called up into the Army in 1940 and went to Italy. After the Italian surrender he had a lovely time where his job was to exercise the Cossack horses. We got engaged on my 21st birthday, then about a year later I broke it off, and he went abroad. We wrote, but he was four years without getting any leave.

London bombing

We had some very heavy Roneo machinery in the office building, the air-raid shelters were in the basement and the thought of this machine coming down and landing on me was too awful, so I would spend my time on a higher floor. We knew how to use stirrup pumps and had trained for Gold Medals in First Aid. We also learnt to recognise the smell of gas by going through a room where there was gas, it smelt like burnt straw. Afterwards we rushed outside to a milk bar, where our instructor had glasses of milk lined up for us, which was said to be the antidote. It took us a long time to get over it. We had to carry gas masks everywhere, it didn't do much for your appearance, those big boxes and after a while we just didn't bother. The worst bombing was in the East End, they used to send the incendiary bombs first, so the fires would light the way for the heavy bombers. One time when I was in the War Office, I saw Churchill up on the roof in his siren suit with his cigar. I believe someone told him to put it out because it glowed, but I can imagine what Churchill said to him.

One night I was in the theatre in Piccadilly to see a play called *Outward Bound.* In the middle of the play the curtain came down and the manager came out and said 'Ladies and gentlemen, I have to tell you that there is a red flag showing' (which means the bombers are actually overhead.) The sirens had gone long before, but you didn't take much notice of them. The curtain came down to enable the people who wanted to leave to do so, but nobody did, so the curtain went up again and the play went on. It was a good thing we didn't go out, because that

225

night a bomb landed on the Café Royal, just across the road, and 60 people were killed.

Bromsgrove

The blitz finished, and my section of the Ministry was evacuated to Bromsgrove. I developed eye trouble with headaches, continuous lights in front of my eyes and deteriorating vision. I went to Moorfields and they said my vision was that of a woman of 60, but they couldn't make any diagnosis. I was told I must not do close clerical work, so I had six months on full pay and three months on half. I stayed in Bromsgrove because my friend was still there and did voluntary farm work for a while. For a change I cycled up to Scotland and worked on a farm there for two months, then cycled all round Scotland. I used to cycle by night and sleep on the beach during the day, the only company I had were curlews. It was rather lovely. One night in Stornaway, it was terribly wet and I wanted somewhere to stay. I went to a little police station and they let me stay the night there, I'm not sure if it was actually in a cell.

Land Army

I wanted to join the Land Army. It was difficult because Civil Servants could not be released into the forces and the Land Army counted as a force. I had a very good boss who fought for me and in the end they said I could join, but I wouldn't get any pay. Luckily I had a very good father who looked after me. I don't know how the Land Army girls were meant to live on their pay of a guinea a week, they would have had to give that much to their landladies.

Anyway, I got my uniform, with its tiny pinched in waist, and went to a farm outside Worcester, then to Malvern. We did everything.

The first job was to unload a lorry full of hundred-weight sacks of potatoes and I couldn't even lift one. I was in a hostel with other Land Army girls, a lorry would come and pick us up in the morning and take us round the various farms. I used to milk the cows, drive the tractor, work on the harvester, and stook the corn in stacks of three, that was rather lovely. In fact I had a wonderful time, absolutely loved it. In Malvern we had three American Army camps right by us, we used to have them to our parties and go to theirs, we would butter them up because they had such lovely rations and we'd come back with tins of spam and sweets. We behaved ourselves, though, didn't have to do anything! It may have been a promiscuous age, but certainly in my circle, that wasn't done.

On the farm we had big shire horses. You're going round with a plough and this big shire horse and you have to allow enough room for it to turn round. At first I didn't and this great horse turned and did the light fantastic on my foot, nearly broke it.

Wedding

We were billeted in private homes in Bromsgrove. Some people didn't really want us and could be horrible, but there was this dear old couple who were lovely to us. One day, after I had moved to Barnet, I got a telegram from my friend saying she was getting married at eight o'clock the following morning and would I be her bridesmaid. I had to drop everything, get leave for the next day and go across in the evening to the place where we had been billeted. The bridegroom was already there, he had got leave from the navy. So, early in the morning, off we went in his car, the bride, the bridegroom, me the bridesmaid and this lovely couple who were to be the witnesses. We drove five miles to a little village church, there was nobody else there and we had to get the gravedigger to come in and witness the signing of the register. That impressed me more than any other wedding I've ever been to because you heard every word and could take it all in. I only had my ordinary summer dress and so did my friend. Afterwards we came back and this lovely couple had made us a wedding breakfast. By nine o'clock she was back at work and nobody knew she had gone and got married.

Hospital treatment

I kept getting bladder trouble and went to the local doctor who thought I was malingering. I knew I wasn't and went home to my own doctor who referred me straightaway to a specialist in Kings College Hospital. They diagnosed a papilloma of the bladder which they would remove. The hospital was terribly crowded with casualties from the bombing on extra mattresses between the beds and there was a great shortage of staff. I was on the operating table and the surgeon was preparing to inject anaesthetic into my spine when the needle broke. As they were finding another one, we got talking and he said 'You are young to be losing a kidney' and I said 'There's nothing wrong with my kidneys.' He asked was I Mrs Harris and I said no I was not – they had got the notes of the wrong patient! So I was very lucky not to have lost a kidney. I went back to the ward and had my dinner of steak and kidney pudding and plum duff, expecting my operation would be postponed till the next day, but later that afternoon they came, I had my operation and it all went well. Years later when I had to have my eye removed for the malignant melanoma which had been growing behind it for all that time, I said to the nurse, 'Do be sure you take out the right eye.' So they drew lots of arrows on my cheek and my forehead, and some daisies and the words 'This One' just to make sure.

I went back to the Land Army for the rest of the war, and then managed to get back into the Civil Service. My boss, who had done so much for me, got me an *ex gratia* payment of £468 – an awful lot of money in those days.

Marriage

I had kept in correspondence with my future husband and we decided we would get married when he had leave. It was like marrying a stranger. When I went to meet him off the train I thought 'Who is this man, I'm going to marry him in four days', we were so awkward with each other. Anyway, on 25 September 1945, we were married.

For my wedding dress, I went to Petticoat Lane where you could get material without coupons and bought seven yards of most beautiful cream satin with flowers painted on it. One of my aunties was a court dressmaker and she made it for me, it was absolutely beautiful.

Afterwards I put on the new pink suit made from the material my father had saved, said goodbye to Dad, and my brother-in-law took us to Maidenhead. As soon as I got to the hotel, I went upstairs and changed into my lovely Harris tweed and put the pink suit into a box which my brother-in-law and a friend smuggled back, my father never knew. If only it had been the turquoise fabric, not the pink.

Ian Tibbs

I was born in 1918, when my father was still away in the First World War. We lived in Wallington, in Surrey. At school I had to hold my left hand behind my back to try to cure this illness of being left-handed and that made me rather bellicose. I left school and became an office boy, then went to Pitmans and learnt some commercial subjects and by 1937 was articled to a solicitor in London. My grandfather had been a solicitor so it was easy for me to get a post. I became restless with the war threatening, and joined the Territorial Army in April 1939. Then I was summoned back from a holiday in Scotland to become embodied as a soldier on 1 September 1939.

Call-up

We were billeted in the basement of the Army and Navy Stores. There weren't enough uniforms, so we wore busmen's overcoats. We were the Queen's Westminster Rifles, which was made up of people who worked in London, and were guarding important place like bridges to see nobody attacked them. We had actors and opera singers amongst us and it was all something of a giggle. That finished when in April 1940 I was sent off to Shorncliffe for training as an Officer Cadet. Trains full of soldiers were coming back from France and we expected German troops to follow very soon. They already had a long-range gun on the

French coast which had landed one shell on the cricket pitch and another on the kitchen.

At the end of the four months training, all but one of us passed. We used to go into Folkestone which was a ghost town, we really thought the Germans might come at any time. In July as we were training on the cliffs above Shorncliffe, we would watch German and English planes in the sky above us, sometimes crashing to land around us. Once I saw a little cargo ship sailing in the Channel, then suddenly there was just its funnel showing, that was the first ship I saw sink, it was so immediate.

Northern Ireland

I was posted to Northern Ireland, to the Leicestershire Regiment. There was talk of invading Southern Ireland, and we practised driving along the narrow lanes. We were at Carrickfergus, 10 miles east of Belfast, which was where incoming bombers turned towards the city. They flew so low you see these giant German crosses painted on the planes, it felt very personal. At that time we had no anti-aircraft guns there.

The Leicestershire Regiment was very good. They had been chased through Norway by the Germans, were hopelessly overwhelmed up north and only escaped with the help of the Navy. They were sent to train people like us, because they had had the experience of warfare. I was in Northern Ireland for a year and a half, there was no rationing at that time and we led the life of Riley, going home every three months for a couple of days leave. There was just a simmering quarrel between Protestants and Catholics.

Voyage to India

In April 1942 I was sent by boat to India, a seven-week journey to Bombay on a former Canadian luxury boat. Officers were trained to go onto the sun deck to fire at enemy planes should we be hit and sinking. We were in a convoy with immense naval protection until well out into the Atlantic, then the battleships turned back and we had just a cruiser and a destroyer accompanying the 30 vessels. We had to go at the pace of the slowest boat which was very steady as you go. We came into Freetown, but were not allowed ashore because it was said to be disease ridden. Then we went south to Durban for a few days, where we had a very pleasant time ashore.

Meanwhile the news was bad. The desert war was going against us, we were losing ships and we didn't know whether we would be going to Bombay, or North Africa, or Singapore. In the end we got to Bombay and I went by train to my first station at Lucknow. We had been sent to build up the Indian Army to go and fight the Japanese. I ended up in the Royal Indian Army Service Corps, concerned with supplying the army.

Training in India

I was sent to Berali which was a vast training camp, where my job was supervising training of people from Southern India to drive the three- and six-ton lorries. We went up into the hills, it was good to get into the cool mountains for a day or two. I was there for three months, training troops in everything from butchery to motor mechanics, all very basic.

Then I was posted to a company using American jeeps, to be ready for use in Burma. We had started to learn Urdu on the boat, but now every day I had an Indian teacher so I could speak Urdu with the troops. I was then sent to the North West Frontier. There we met the warring tribes, the place names are those which we hear on the news now. We used to take them into the Army as recruits. The Japs were continuing to press, and the Europeans were getting uncomfortable, the Indians were quite restless and there was fear of an uprising. The Japanese were in the mountains of Assam and threatening to enter India.

I was sent to join the 6th Battalion of the South Wales Borderers who were in Poona, and there we trained with boats, practising a sea landing to get behind the Japs on the coast of Burma. But they wanted more boats in Europe to invade Sicily, so our boats were sent there and instead we went by train from Poona to Calcutta, then three days by boat to Chittagong. I had had fever, and brought up some men from Poona. The Colonel said we were about to have our first battle, and I was to take supplies on mules up to the men on the nearby Mayu hills.

Action in Burma

Through these hills there were two tunnels, built originally for a railway but used by the Japanese as a road and for storage and gun emplacements. I was with B Company, three platoons, going for three pimples along a narrow ridge top. The first platoon took the first pimple with virtually no opposition, but the Japanese remained in the tunnel. On the second pimple the Japanese were there and had killed the platoon commander, so Tibbs was able to get his platoon. I went to

the top of the hill, and got into a Japanese foxhole, just two yards from the flapping cheeks of a dead Japanese who had no face left. I ordered a section to come up, one man was Archie Jones, and he had a Bren gun. I called him to get into the foxhole, but he was a big man and couldn't get in. I took the Bren gun, but by now it had got some soil on it so it wouldn't fire. Meanwhile the Japs were tossing grenades, using their dead companion as a mark.

Then I popped my head up at the wrong time and I got my first wound. I lost most of my hearing and my head was pouring with blood. I wasn't frightened, I wanted close fighting having always been bellicose. Archie pulled me out of the foxhole and rolled me down the hill to where there was a first aid post, and a wonderful chap called Sergeant Mills wrapped some bandage round my head. It was Archie who did the painting of the battle. He got the Military Medal.

The third platoon took the third hill successfully which relieved the pressure on the hill I was on; the company commander got the Military Cross for that. A Sherman tank was brought up to fire into the tunnel, which enabled its capture. I was wandering about with this white bandage round my head, then I got back to an American medical team who said there wasn't much they could do except pick the bits out. I was sent by boat to India to recover, I think at first they sent too many men back who could have been managed nearer the front.

A month later the battalion came back to the same area. We were near the coast, and through the fighting you could see the sea. I joined the North West Combat Command, in Michena, well behind the Japs and we started to roll them down to the south, We flew into a clearing, and the Japanese were still firing into it. There I met Vinegar Joe Stillwell, an American general with fluent Chinese and considerable experience of China. We were just a few miles from the Chinese border and fought alongside two Chinese armies and American units.

We were in this area of teak forests and paddy fields. We were to pass through the Japanese lines, then hold them up as they tried to get away. That was the theory. We were a battalion of 800 men, but the Japanese held up our company, my company commander was killed, my fellow platoon commanders were killed, other ranks too killed and wounded. So I became the leading platoon commander. I saw Japanese throwing grenades and excitedly talking to one another. I ordered one section of eight men, to charge and get them. Then I had a guilty conscience, here was I in command and I was sending these men without knowing what was there, so I called them back. I wasn't getting any information from headquarters, there was just me.

Daylight came and I decided we had to get to our objective, so I got the men to crawl through the three-foot high grass to the copse where the Japs were. We heard Japanese voices but you couldn't fire because you might have hit your own men, so I decided on a bayonet charge. I told my men to fix bayonets and led the section down a path to the clearing where the Japs were. And there I was confronted by a

Japanese man dancing, just dancing like mad, wonderful looking chap. Out of the corner of my eye I saw another Jap with a rifle pointing at me, the idea was that one danced as a diversion while the other man shot me. The man behind me quickly polished off with his bayonet the chap who was aiming at me, then I had to kill this wretched Japanese who was without any weapon. This upset me terribly but I had to do it as I was going to be killed by the others. We over-ran the group, it was a team effort, but I was very very upset, the first man I had killed close to. I had some minor injuries from grenades.

Wounded

We won that second battle decisively, we had broken their defences as we were meant to, enabling our troops to go forward. I was awarded the Military Cross for this episode. We should have caught more. I was ferried out by light aircraft, it was the second time I was wounded, but it wasn't the wounds so much as my guilt at having killed an unarmed man which so troubled me.

I was sent to hospital in Bangalore, and there met a fellow officer who had completely lost his mind. He had been taken prisoner and been threatened that he would be used as bayonet practice if he didn't tell all he knew. I had no hatred of the Japanese, in fact I really liked them having had Japanese friends before the war.

Back to the battlefront

I returned to Burma, where my battalion was approaching the Shweli River. The Japs were the other side and they could see us crossing. We were five battalions, it was really quite well organised. You always fought in circles, never in a line so you didn't get over-run. But to cross a river it had to be a line, and on the other side the Japanese made half circles round us. We had to break these from our foothold, whilst they were trying to push us back into the river. I was by then for a time a company commander and I had this idea you had to encourage your men to be brave. We had some very well trained young officers, including one who was superb at taking camouflage advantage, using the jungle against the Japanese thereby not exposing his men to danger.

We were in a half circle around the place where we had landed, I crawled to a place at the side of the cart-track, and then I nonchalantly kneeled up and became a perfect target for the Japs. I must have started getting up, as the first shot caught me in the thigh and the hand, just where my heart would have been if I had still been kneeling, then there was another shot and another wound.

Our batallion were ex-farmers, ex-unemployed miners, ex-steel workers, exceptional men, highly responsible, extremely intelligent these south Welsh. I used to wonder what they had to fight for, to go back to – unemployment? We had a very fatherly colonel, the son of a Welsh doctor, and he was very tolerant of people. There was a time when the Japs had scarpered and one of my sections had left their Bren gun unattended, which was absolutely criminal, so the colonel told his batman to take it back to his headquarters. That night at dusk I crept out of my company circle, went half a mile down the road, got into the battalion headquarters and pinched the commanding officer's Tommy gun. He'd got my Bren gun and I'd got his Tommy gun. Eventually the adjutant negotiated so we each got our guns back.

By now I had been in India and Burma three years, and had had three wounds and this enabled me to apply for return home. I was in Bombay, waiting for a ship when they celebrated VE-day, with marches and the fleet in the harbour. I came back to England and was stationed in the Midlands, training Dutch officers and helping equip them to recover in their colonies in the East Indies. I then came to London, to Knightsbridge and to the army legal department until I was able to leave the army and finish training as a solicitor.

Gerd Treuhaft

I started journalism when I was 14 and living in Berlin. My birth mother was Austrian and Jewish but not married, so she could not support me. She took me to an orphanage in Berlin from which I was fostered by Mr and Mrs Siegfried Levy who lived in a comfortable part of the city. I kept my name and my Austrian citizenship, and this meant that for a while I was fairly safe from the Nazis. In 1934 I travelled with my brand new Austrian passport to Prague where I visited the offices of newspapers printed in German, who employed German refugees. I really wanted to be a journalist and I could write about what was happening in Berlin. I met the editor of a long-established German language daily, *The Bohemia*, and he said he would consider anything I sent from Berlin. I was delighted when the first report I sent after my return to Berlin was printed and that started me on my career.

Berlin job and journalism

I didn't earn money through my writing at first and I had to get a job. My foster parents' marriage broke up so my mother reverted to her

237

maiden name of Koopman – she needed to get state assistance to live on, and she would never have got it with the name Levy. I got a job with a kindly man who ran a small wholesale business supplying ladies' coats to retail outlets. My job was to deliver items to shops around Berlin so I was able to get about a lot and keep up with international news through the foreign papers sold in the kiosks. I also contacted the Austrian and Czech embassies, got to know the Press Attachés, and heard about reports banned by the Nazis. I could then warn the anti-Nazi newsagents what the Gestapo would be looking for and they could then sell the papers discretely.

Arrest by Gestapo

On 11 March 1938 Hitler occupied Austria and I realized I should think about emigrating, but my mother was shocked and didn't want to be left on her own. That afternoon at work I went out to get some stamps and when I came back, the lift-boy warned me that there were two men upstairs waiting for me. I wondered whether I should try to contact men I knew in the Czech embassy, but decided I would be followed anyway and went up to meet the men. They showed me their Gestapo credentials and then drove me to my home to look through my books and correspondence. I had already destroyed anything anti-Nazi, so there was little they could pick on. But they took me anyway, for questioning. They told my mother I might be some time and she made me some egg sandwiches. I felt the Gestapo had nothing on me as all my contributions had been published when Austria was an independent state so I had broken no laws.

I was interrogated about my journalistic activities. My fingerprints were taken and I was bundled into a cell with other prisoners. One remarked 'Now they are arresting children' and another asked if I had anything to smoke. I didn't, but we shared my mother's egg sandwiches. I was kept in that prison for weeks. My mother came to visit me, she said she was doing everything she could to get me out but it was no good. I was issued with a document from the Gestapo that I was to be taken into protective custody as I had offended the state and the Hitler Youth.

Dachau

On 30 May 1938 I was taken into a large hall in the cellar of the police station which was packed with prisoners of many nationalities, and nobody knew what was going to happen. At three in the morning I was hand-cuffed, pushed into a crowded police wagon and driven to the vast Brandenberg prison. A few hours later I was taken on to Halle, then to Leipzig, then to Nuremberg where our legs were cuffed as well, then on to Munich. On 11 June 1938, a hot summer's day, we eventually arrived at Dachau. Our clothes were taken, we were pushed under a cold shower and then given a camp uniform. We had to sit with knees bent and arms outstretched from 11am till 6pm in blazing sun. They gave me a number, 15642, and told me I would be there for ten years. I was determined to survive.

There were so many new prisoners coming to Dachau that some of the older criminal or political prisoners were put in charge of the working parties. My boss was a man who had murdered his daughter and he could be brutal to us. Among my fellow-prisoners were the two sons of the Archduke Franz Ferdinand whose murder at Sarajevo had started the First World War. Later I had another foreman who was much fairer and never shouted at us, his name was Kurt Schumacher, later the leader of the Social Democratic Party.

After four months 150 of us were herded into railway trucks where we lad to lie on the floor, hands behind our heads, guarded by two SS men. Once, when the train stopped, a man leapt up and jumped through the window. There was a single shot, and he was hauled back into the carriage and thrown to bleed to death next to his brother. In October 1938 we arrived at the wooden barracks of Buchenwald.

Buchenwald

In November came Kristallnacht, which marked the increase of the campaign against Jews. Hundreds of civilians were arrested and lorry loads arrived at the camp where five more emergency huts were hastily erected by working parties. New prisoners were taken to a compound where wallets, watches and rings were removed, and gold teeth extracted. Prisoners were taken at random to be kicked and beaten. In December I was attached to a 'First Aid' working party, where our job was to pick up the bodies of Jews who had died from their beatings, carry them to a hut, wash them in disinfectant, put them into a coffin onto which we had already chalked their name and number and arrange them in alphabetical order to be taken by a lorry for cremation. Winter came, with snow and bitter cold.

Through 1939 some Jewish and political prisoners were released if they could show they would leave Germany within two days. Names were read out at roll call, but day after day not mine. Then one day it was my name. I were given back the civilian clothes I had arrived in and any money I had earned. I had enough to get a train to Leipzig and then on to Berlin. At midnight I phoned my mother from the station to say I was home and free.

England

We both knew I would have to get out of Germany. We contacted a cousin who had emigrated to Florida, my mother negotiated a visa to a transit camp in England, at Richborough in Kent, and within a month I bade her a sad goodbye as I boarded a train. With a dozen others I went through Belgium and France, boarded a ship for England and then to Richborough. This had been a First World War Army base, the huts looked horribly like those I had left in Buchenwald but there was

no barbed wire. There were, however, strict limitations on our movements. We couldn't get a job or even travel without special permission, though I was able to visit old friends. We were given sixpence a week and a tuppence-ha'penny stamp to write home. Then my cousin in Florida died, and with him my hopes for emigration to America. On 3 September 1939 England declared war on Germany, and I became an 'enemy alien'.

Pioneer Corps

I wanted to join the Forces, but to do so I had first to join the newly formed

240

Pioneer Corps made up of 'aliens'. We had a uniform and were paid 14 shillings a week to do manual labour towards the war effort. The first two weeks of 1940 we were drilled and marched, but with no weapons. On 20 January we were told to pack our kit and be ready to leave the next day but we didn't know where to. I was thrilled to find we were going to France, crossing from Southampton to Cherbourg, then by train to Rennes. Here we were billeted in a run-down warehouse, sleeping on straw and working to build roads and a railway station. Off duty I went into Rennes and met some French soldiers. They were very friendly but we had to disguise the fact that we were German, not English. The war was going badly for us; we heard of the German invasion of Norway and then the surrender of Belgium and the unopposed entry of German troops into Paris. Then came Dunkirk. Following that, the Royal Engineers blew up the railway crossing for the new station we had spent so long building. We were ordered onto a train which took us to St Malo and, leaving behind all personal belongings, we boarded small boats. Next morning we arrived in Weymouth and were told France had capitulated.

London blitz

We went first to London, and then by train to Devon to a holiday camp at Bideford where we worked putting up tents for the Army. It was not hard work and the weather was fine, but we were forbidden to speak German even amongst ourselves. We could only leave camp on alternate Sundays, and then only to go to the cinema. Then came the Battle of Britain, and the London blitz. Our company was moved to Bexleyheath and our job was to clear the bomb damage in London each morning after the raids. One evening I met friends for tea in a Lyons Corner House before returning to camp and stayed on after they had left, listening to the band. As I came out of the cafe a firebomb landed just down the street. There was great confusion and the raid continued, so I could not get back to camp and spent the night with a family I had just met. Next day I learnt that the bomb had landed on the bus carrying eight of my friends and they had all been killed.

Yorkshire

I kept trying to get into the RAF but without success because my reading of left wing papers had caused me to be labelled as a Communist. I had written articles on life in the Pioneer Corps for *Die Zeitung*, but had had to submit them to the Major for approval. I later learnt he had never passed them on. Early in 1942 the War Office issued orders allowing members of the Pioneer Corps to volunteer for fighting units. When I found that, even if I did so, I would still be classified as an enemy alien I decided against this. Our company had moved to Darlington and I was allowed to write short features for the Darlington journal *The Wheatsheaf*. I also wrote to *The Spectator* about the negative attitude of anti-Nazi propaganda in the BBC and that it would be more effective if directed against specific Nazi groups such as the Hitler Youth and not at the German people in general. I was invited to the BBC in London to explain my views (having had to get a special pass to travel) and was very pleased that within a month they had adopted my suggestion. But I never received any acknowledgement or fee.

I continued to press the case for permission to speak German, went on writing letters and articles, and worked laying cables in the Yorkshire countryside. Then in February 1942 I was moved to another company stationed near Cheltenham. I think the Major knew my reputation for being outspoken and he set me to cleaning out lavatory buckets. After two weeks I reported sick and was admitted to hospital. There I was seen by an army psychologist who realised what I had been through in Dachau and Buchenwald and said he would speak to the Colonel about my discharge. Things became easier, and I was given work in the kitchen. Then I was transferred to Liverpool, as Company Clerk to the Major and this gave me the opportunity to do more free-lance writing.

I was summoned to an Officer Cadet Training Unit – some of the politicians to whom I had been writing thought this might be appropriate for me, but I was not selected. Instead, in the spring of 1944, my company moved to Surrey and in August I was told I was to be released on technical grounds – though what these were I never found out.

Journalism & washing up

I had eight weeks before I would once more be an alien without a British passport. I tried my journalist contacts, but there were no jobs, and nothing at the Labour Exchange. My army pay had almost run out when I met an old friend from Germany who suggested I join him washing up at Lyons in Piccadilly. It was long hard work to earn enough to live on, but I did at least get my meals. So it was that on 8 May 1945, as everyone was celebrating VE-Day in London I spent the whole day washing dishes!

Later I was able to get journalistic work, including covering the inaugural session of the United Nations for *World Review*. I met and married my wife, Joan, and have made a career of writing, which I continue to this day.

I am grateful to Gerd Treuhaft for permission to use material from his book "Goodbye Yesterday" published in 2006 by Book Guild Publishing, available from Chorleywood Bookshop

Ann Turner

I was born in 1919 in Southsea where my father was a bandsman in the Royal Marines; he also spent time as Band Sergeant on the Royal Yacht. By the thirties he had left the service and we were living in Kenton, Middlesex. He played the bassoon in an orchestra in the pit of West End cinemas during silent movies but with the coming of the talkies this work dried up.

Thirties Schoolgirl

To keep his family (there were six of us children by then) Father joined the Office of Works. He had something to do with carpets and our house was full of samples which Mother would stitch together. He continued his music, playing with the BBC Empire Orchestra.

I won a scholarship to Harrow County Girls' School, which was fee-paying, and my mother had to buy all the expensive uniform, gym-slips and little white blouses with pin tucks. I'm afraid I was a very naughty girl, shooting water pistols and throwing marbles at the teachers' legs. I used to get good marks for music, which came easily, but I really didn't work at the other subjects. When I was 15 my mother got a letter to say if I didn't work harder my scholarship would be given to someone else and it was decided I'd be better off leaving school and getting a job.

The lady next door, who was a Church Visitor, said I spoke well enough to work on the telephones and arranged for me to go for an interview. All I had to do was listen to a gramophone record playing numbers and then repeat what I had heard. It was very easy. I got the job, and began working at the Pinner exchange which I thoroughly enjoyed

Post Office

One day the supervisor said I was far too intelligent to be working there and I should try the Civil Service entry exams. I asked a teacher friend if she would give me lessons, which she agreed to do if I would sit for her to paint me as I worked. I took the exam, but just failed to make the grade. However, a fortnight later, I got a letter telling me to report to the Radio branch of the Post Office Research station at Dollis Hill. There was only one other girl there, but loads of research engineers, mathematicians and boys in the YIT (Youth in Training). I was in my seventh heaven. I fell in love straight away and had a very happy time. My work was mainly clerical, but there was a lot of highly secret stuff. When my boyfriend heard my name was Emily Harding, he said I looked like the film star Ann Harding, and I've been called Ann ever since. But as war loomed, my engagement fell through and I decided to join up.

Joining the WRNS

Getting into the WRNS wasn't easy. The only vacancies were for stewards, which I didn't want, so I told them all my family had been in the Royal Marines and the Navy and they ought to give me a proper job. When they asked me what could I do, I said I'd learned Morse code in the Guides and I could see they were starting to take more interest. They gave me some tests and said I could join the newly formed Visual Signals section where I would have to know Morse and semaphore, and learn to recognise ships' flags. After a medical examination and an intelligence test, in which I was the only woman (and beat all the men bar one), I was enlisted into the new category of Visual Signaller. I went to Mill Hill for initial training; this was very hard, and included getting up at half past five in the morning to scrub

245

floors, doing PE on the roof and going on route marches. When they were deciding who was to go where some of the girls were told they were going to Station X; we didn't know what this was, but much later I found it was for the de-coding place at Bletchley. But I wasn't called for that, they needed girls with very good brains!

Visual Signals

In the Visual Signals section there were no officers to start with, We were sent to HMS *Cabbala*, a great big shore station near Warrington.

My father was past retirement age but had volunteered to be a Railway Transport Officer, working at the London mainline stations seeing that troops got onto the right trains and so on. When he saw us girls with no proper uniform and lugging great big kit-bags he cried, but then he got us sandwiches and cups of tea before we got on the train.

Warrington was a strange place. Early each morning someone would go clattering round the cobbled streets in clogs calling the factory workers to get up and go to work. We had to study very hard; there were constant examinations and if you failed you were out. You had to get 90% to pass, which we all did. Whilst I was there the *Daily Herald* photographer came to take a picture of the Wrens in training. There was great excitement as to whom he would choose and when it was me the others were so envious. Next day my sister Cynthia was in the tube in London and seeing this picture in someone else's paper she cried out 'That's my sister!'

Milford Haven

I was posted to Milford Haven, to HMS *Skirmisher*. This was a degaussing base, which provided a system for protection against magnetic mines by neutralising the ship's magnetic field. We were at Dale Fort, 15 miles out of Milford Haven, right on the point at the entrance to the harbour. In the spring the headland was covered with great banks of primroses. I used to send my mother boxes of them wrapped in cotton wool. It was marvelous, very peaceful. Nowadays it's the place from which people sail to get to the nature reserve island of Skomer.

Milford Haven harbour had a boom across the entrance to protect against enemy ships. The bigger ships were run over the underwater degaussing range and the smaller ships had their bottoms wiped with an anti-magnetic preparation. We really didn't know much about the procedure – our job was to look out for ships coming in, make out the name, the draft and the nationality, see what signal flags they were flying and send any messages. We had signal books telling what the various flags meant. One was called the Yellow Peril, and it was impressed on us that should we ever be torpedoed at sea the first thing we had to do was to sink our Yellow Peril book so the codes could not be picked up by the enemy. Luckily I never had to do that. We kept naval watches of four hours, though we had to be on call to go out to incoming ships at any time.

One night there was a Force Nine gale, some of the ships pulled their anchors and were drifting in the storm. With the rain lashing we couldn't see the signals from inside the fort, so we went outside and found we couldn't even stand up in the wind. We called the Petty Officer and he sent sailors up to hold us upright, so we could send messages by the Aldis lamp which we had to hold on its stand against the force of the wind. It was a terrible, terrible gale. Next morning some of the ships were in a bad state.

It could take quite a long time for the ships to go over the degausser and if the engineers were not satisfied they would have to do it again. The shipping was of all kinds, oil tankers and merchantmen as well as the naval vessels. Later we were moved to South Hook Fort, still part of Milford Haven, and there again we looked out for shipping, sending and receiving messages. Battleships would come in for re-victualling, hospital ships came in and out; if we saw the hospital ship go out we would know something big was happening. We saw huge sections of the Mulberry Harbour being brought in ready for assembly and landing-craft, including the big ones for tanks. We went to bed one night in June with the harbour crammed full of ships. Next morning they had all gone. That was D-day.

The drifters – the fishing boats – were moored side by side in the harbour and we would use these if we needed to get out to a ship. If the drifters were required by the Navy, the crew got a shilling an hour danger money. Convoys to and from America would signal their expected time of arrival and the Third Officer would have to go out to the ship in a drifter, go aboard, give the captain his sailing instructions and stay with him till he had read and understood them. Sometimes I had to go as well if they needed to send a signal, because with the wireless silence they would have to rely on visual signals. To get aboard, we would have to climb a rope ladder, which could be 30 foot long, up the side of the ship, carrying the Aldis lamp and its heavy battery. You had to make sure a sailor had his foot on the ladder at the top, and he'd say 'Come on Blondie'.

The worst part was getting off the ladder coming back down again. The drifter would be rocking, the big ship would be rolling, the rope ladder would be swaying, you would have the lamp and battery, and you had to time your jump back onto the drifter. We were told if ever a sailor held out a hand to help you, you must take it. There was a story that one Third Officer was snooty and would not and she fell in and broke her neck. As we left, sometimes the sailors would give us gifts, tins of fruit and cigarettes. Once it was a 26 pound tin of pineapple, which came down in a bucket! We didn't smoke the rough Woodbine cigarettes though, we liked Balkan Sobranie or Pink Cloud and we had little cigarette holders with a gilt trim. We did think we were smart.

It was really quite exciting. We could be going out in the middle of the night, down the slippery steps of the quay, then onto the drifter, out into the open sea and standing by till the ship came. We would deliver the messages, then going back we would have to jump over the line of moored drifters to get back to shore. Sometimes there would be a lot of drunken sailors going the other way back to their ships after an evening ashore and they would call out at us. I really didn't like that. One time, after a group of American Liberty Boats had been in port, their signallers were allowed ashore to meet the Wrens who had been sending the signals; it was a lovely day and we had a picnic.

The signaller on one battleship was so quick and clever. If I wanted to signal to a little ship, a destroyer or corvette the other side of him, he would pick it up and I got so cross that I signalled 'Not you'. A newspaper reporter came to see the work we were doing and he wrote that the signals were 'operated by a fluffy-haired 18-year old Wren in a hilltop look-out. Her wisecracks in Morse are building her quite an international reputation.' I can still talk in Morse.

There was no rank higher than Leading Wren in that part of the service when I was there. Our uniform consisted of bell-bottom trousers and sailors' flannels (like a T-shirt) with crossed flags on our sleeves. When I became Leading Wren I had an anchor on my sleeve as well, this was called 'getting the hook'. We had 'blackouts' – thick black knickers – but we never wore them, preferring pretty underwear. You could cut a hole in the blackout and turn it into a jumper, though I never did.

We lived in Dale Fort. It belonged to a Mrs Leigh Roberts and right in the very depths there lived her caretaker, who seemed to us an ancient lady; she would climb out of her window and pick nettles to cook and eat. She became a good friend to me and dyed some wool for me to knit, using berries to make a beautiful blue. She showed us some of Mrs Leigh Roberts' valuables, chests of drawers stuffed with wonderful fabrics, white satins for her daughters' weddings, lots of lovely stuff. And, of course, we couldn't get any material at all.

Marriage

I had met Ron at Dollis Hill and when my engagement broke off he was waiting in the wings. Ron was a very quiet man and we stayed in touch by letter; I still have a pile of them. He was working with the RAF on radar and sometimes he would be sent to Wales. He took his bicycle on the train so he could come and see me after the job was done and we got engaged. We married in June 1944. I arrived at Paddington at half past five in the morning for my wedding at Kenton, it was the day after the first flying bomb and they were all talking about it. I was provisionally allowed a fortnight's leave for my honeymoon, but I had to be ready to come back at once if called. But I wasn't and we had our two weeks in the Cotswolds.

That morning at Paddington was the first time I was aware of prostitutes. I thought the women waiting for the troops coming off the trains were all wives, but of course they weren't. I was very innocent, you wouldn't believe it. Once I was receiving signals from a ship which was being revictualled, and there was one word I really couldn't understand. I kept asking them to repeat the word, but I still didn't know it. The Chief Petty Officer asked if I was having trouble and I said 'Yes there's this word I cannot get – C-O-N-D-O-M'. I'd never heard it. So he took over the signal.

HMS *Ganges*

When we were married I applied for a transfer and was posted to HMS *Ganges* at Ipswich in October 1944. We called it Bloody Point it was so awful, miles from anywhere. We could see the American bombers coming back to their bases in East Anglia. I was working in a Martello tower, counting the flying bombs going overhead. It was bitterly cold up in this tower, I would be wearing a storm coat which covered me from head to toe with a wide collar you could turn up, and they would bring me hot ship's cocoa. I was pregnant and being sick every morning. Once I asked for a weekend leave to go and see my husband and was told if I had that, one of the sailors would have to do extra. So before I went I had to do a 24-hour watch, which was four hours on, four hours off for 24 hours. I believe this was only done in the Navy when there was a real emergency and I'd just asked for a weekend leave.

Commendation

One day the First Officer sent for me and said 'Leading Wren Turner, I have in my hand a commendation from the Flag-Officer-in-Charge Western Approaches to the Flag-Officer The Nore that you have a commendation for your devotion to duty' – that was on that terrible stormy night at Milford Haven. I was to go three steps up onto the platform, salute the Flag Officer and then take the salute at the march past. I had to stand whilst 4000 men marched past. At the order 'Eyes right' they all turned and saluted me. At the moment he handed me the commendation on a piece of paper the heavens opened, it poured with rain, the bit of paper got soaked and he said "I can't give you this, I'll get another one', but he never did. At my golden wedding, another Wren who had had the same letter got me a copy done.

I left the WRNS when I was five months pregnant. When I first thought I was pregnant, I went to the naval doctor and he said 'We can't tell if you are, but only if you are not.' They did some sort of test on rabbits, I believe, and he said he could only say I was not 'not pregnant'. Ron got a top floor flat in Dollis Hill and I had my first baby there in 1945, just after the end of the war. Then in 1947 when I was expecting my second baby I developed polio. I heard the nurses say they had measured me for my coffin – I didn't realise that was their name for an iron lung. I did get better slowly, though it took me ages to get up the stairs and we were advised to find somewhere on the level. I had been to Chorleywood in the Guides before the war and liked it, so we came and had a look, bought a building plot and I have been here ever since.

Sheila Vischer

Schoolgirl

At the start of the war I was living in Middlesborough with my family. The ICI works were a frequent target for bomber raids and we spent many nights in the cellar, but our house was not affected. My father was a GP and my mother ran a First Aid post for the Red Cross, so they were often called out at night. I was at boarding school in Sussex and I remember sitting the School Certificate exams, listening to the guns in France, and watching dog-fights in the sky between the RAF and the Luftwaffe as we were playing lacrosse. The school was evacuated to Somerset, but when they found the place was on top of one of the biggest ammunition dumps in the country, we returned to Haywards Heath though with the classrooms upstairs and dormitories down.

WRNS

I left school in 1941, and went to secretarial college. I had wanted to join the WRNS, but my father insisted I got a qualification first, and a secretarial course was the quickest way to do this. I joined the WRNS in July 1942. You were a 'pro-wren' for the first couple of weeks, paid one shilling and ninepence a day, then once enrolled you were kitted out with a uniform and the pay went up to two shillings (10p today). First I was sent to Dunfermline for T/P (teleprinter) training. I was to have been sent to Shetland, but there was a smallpox epidemic in Scotland and they wouldn't have us. Once trained I was sent to Liverpool, where I worked in the Signals Department, underground in Derby House, Headquarters of the Commander in Chief Western Approaches.

It was so vast I didn't much like it and a few months later, I was sent to the Roseneath Combined Operations camp on the Gare Loch, where I was the only T/P operator. We lived in Nissen huts which were knee deep in mud. After three weeks the camp closed down and I was drafted to Greenock where I stayed nearly three years.

Greenock

This was a bigger base and there would be four or five T/P operators on each watch. We usually worked four watches; these were rotated so that every few days you would get a day and a half off before going on night duty again. This was long enough to go to Glasgow for shopping or to the theatre. There were good hostels in Glasgow run by the Church of Scotland which cost only a shilling for a bed in a cubicle. We had to be in uniform, of course, carry our gas-masks everywhere and salute every Naval or Wren Officer we saw. Sometimes we were invited on board ships whilst they were at anchor in the Clyde. We had to get permission for this and produce a pass at the docks. It was quite hazardous in rough weather if the ship was anchored far out and we had to climb up a rope ladder from the launch on to the deck, particularly wearing Wren skirts!

We lived in uniform most of the time, obtained from Naval stores, and were given chits instead of coupons to buy our own underwear and so on. You could buy 'dusters' (no coupons required) which were made of old parachute silk and could be used as scarves. Some of these were from Army Surplus Stores, squares of silk printed with maps of Europe originally intended for issue to parachute troops as they could be folded very small to fit into a battle dress pocket.

The work was interesting though sometimes monotonous. The teleprinters were connected to shore stations round the UK and to warships when anchored at buoys. We sent and received signals, many in code, and passed them to the appropriate authorities. On night watch we were sometimes busy all night through, but if it slackened off we might drop asleep with our head on the teleprinter only to be woken up when it whirred into activity with another signal. As Head of Watch I had to make sure the 'Top Secret' and 'Immediate' messages got quickly to their destinations for action or de-coding. I was on duty when peace in Europe was declared and still have the signal which came through on all our machines at once, addressed to all ships and shore stations in the Western Approaches saying 'Splice the Mainbrace!'

Australia

I applied to go abroad as soon as I was 21 but didn't get posted till after VE-day when I was sent to Australia, arriving in Sydney in July 1945. We were billeted in converted hotels on Bondi beach, so a lot of our free time was spent surfing. Once the atom bomb was dropped and VJ-day came, Wrens were given the opportunity to go home. Having been only a few weeks in Australia, several of us volunteered to stay on. We continued to work in the Signal Station in Sydney, side by side with Australian Wrens (WRANS) and sailors. We had more time off and were able to go – in uniform – to the airport and hitch a lift in any internal service plane that had spare seats. This way we saw quite a bit of Australia and had some adventures. The planes were usually troop carriers with bucket canvas seats down each side. Once the escape hatch flew open beside me and I lost some of my belongings before one of the crew managed to pull it shut. Another time a fire broke out in the tail and the cabin filled with smoke. The crew rushed through with fire extinguishers and put it out.

In 1946 I came home on a troop ship, the *Athlone Castle*, the most uncomfortable trip imaginable. We were well below deck in bunks four deep. Lots of people were sea-sick and there was only a heavy curtain between us and the main troop deck. It was stifling hot, so quite a lot of the time we took our bedding and went to sleep on deck. We stopped at Singapore to pick up more troops and some ex-prisoners-of-war and then home.

On return I had two weeks' disembarkation leave and was then sent to Portsmouth for demob. This took a fortnight, so we scrubbed floors and polished and re-polished everything in sight. Finally we were given £30 to kit ourselves out for Civvy Street and said good-bye to the Navy. I had four years in the Wrens and rose to the dizzy height of Leading Wren. This was called 'getting your hook', the anchor badge on your sleeve, and I wouldn't have missed it for anything.

I worked for a while as a secretary in London, then in 1948 I took a job with the Colonial Service in Nigeria where I met my husband and where two of my three children were born.

Patricia Watson

In the 1930s we lived in Loudwater, and my father was a cardiologist at University College Hospital. When I left school I took a General Domestic Science course but when war seemed imminent, my father sent my young sister and me to relatives in South Wales. My uncles jeered at me and as nothing seemed to be happening, we came back.

Land Army

My sister was sent to America and I joined the Land Army. I had a month's training at a dairy and pig farm at Bishops Stortford where I learnt how to milk a cow, drive a tractor, clean out pigs and poultry and prepare animal feed. After this I was meant to be able to do anything, but the farmers weren't interested in mere girls because at that time they still had their men.

So I came back to Chorleywood and helped my mother with the evacuees. The ones that nobody wanted were sent to Warwick House in Shire Lane. One boy was called the Impetigo Boy and he had to sleep on the landing. Another refused to take his trousers off to be bathed, though eventually he had to. I took them some toys from home, but they got broken and my mother scolded me.

Wiltshire

Then I got a Land Army job with a Methodist dairy farmer, six miles out of Swindon. We had about 30 cows and I was carting feed, carting muck and milking by hand. I would get up at six to fetch the cows in, tie them up, wash them and start milking. I quite liked this, you got comfortable and it was warm, with just a hurricane lamp for light. I lived in the farmhouse and had my meals there. I made friends with a neighbouring farmer but there wasn't much social life so I was on my own most of the time. I would go into Swindon on my bicycle but it was a boring town and there was nothing to buy. I read a bit, but the farmer considered that to be a waste of time. We had church twice on Sundays and religious class during the week.

It was an all grass farm but it had been arable so the buildings were not all that suitable. In the winter the cows were kept in the old stable where the cobbled floor was difficult to clean. The old cart shed was converted to calf pens using bales and these you had to climb over with hay and water. We lost a number of calves because they were fed on linseed gruel which seldom got cooked properly, because the oil stove only had two burners and was wanted for other things. Washing was difficult because there was only cold water in the bathroom, you had to take a kettle of hot if you wanted warmth. There was a well from which we could get water, but Mrs Hill decided this was not fit for drinking. Instead I had to carry water – two and a half gallons a day – up the hill from the spring.

Between milkings I worked with the horses, carting manure to the fields and spreading it. Once a week in the winter we went to fetch hay, cutting it out of ricks belonging to racing stables. I would go with the horse and wagon, riding the five miles there and walking back. I had no lights on the wagon and no brakes, to check it I had to run it into the verge. Hay-making time I enjoyed, though the hours were long; with double summertime we could work till 11pm. You couldn't start till the dew was off the grass, could be 12 noon. I used to sit on the back of the old horse mower, now pulled by a Dennis lorry, and I had to lift the knife as we turned.

In the summer we would drive the cows along the road to another piece of land through a neighbouring village. We did the milking in the field, fastening them to a rail with a block and tackle; you'd have to round them up and they were always escaping. We did get a milking machine towards the end, but I could never get on with it. One weekend the farmer and his wife went away to relatives and I was left on my own. I let the milk churns overflow and lost about six gallons of milk. Was he angry! We put the churns in the lane and the milk lorry collected them once a day, thankfully not too early. Then I developed an abscess in my armpit but went on working till I could only use one arm, my temperature rose to 104° and then I went home. My father said I wasn't to go back, but I had to because all my belongings were there and I stayed another month. We parted on good terms.

Chorleywood Farming

In 1944, I came back home to farm for Tom Dickens at Green Street Farm. He had 500 acres of farmland and two dairies, one at the farm

and one at Chorleywood House, and arable as well. There I just did relief milking, afternoons and weekends, so I didn't have to get up at six in the morning. There was quite a large staff and three of us Land Girls. I spent a lot of time doing field work and market gardening – brussels, cabbages, turnips, swedes, carrots. Some of the work was done with tractors, some with horses. One man in his eighties used to take a horse and wagon up to London to the early morning market.

I enjoyed harvest work. The sheaves were shocked, stood up in sixes or eights as they came off the binder. Round the edges they used a scythe, and we tied the sheaves by hand. The sheaves had to stand in the fields for a while, and if the weather brought them down we had to re-shock – stand them up again. One year we had to go and help out on a farm near Sarratt where a gang of landgirls were in difficulty re-shocking because they were wearing short shorts, the wheat sheaves were tall and scratchy and you were supposed to slide them down your legs to stand them up. This was the time of the doodlebugs. One came over and we hid behind the shocks but thankfully it didn't stop. With the sheep I had to hold them whilst someone else dealt with the maggots, cut their tails or removed their testicles, which Mr Dickens did with his teeth.

In 1945, girls who had been in the Land Army five years were summoned to London to assemble in Parliament Square. We marched to the Guildhall where we were briefed, then marched on with an Army band to the Mansion House where Queen Elizabeth was waiting to see us. I was one of the 14 chosen to be presented to her and I felt very proud, only sad that my father had recently died and could not be there to see me.

After the war, I took a course in horticulture. My mother bred chinchilla rabbits for fur, my father had already got a goat and we ended up with eight nannies and a billy, as well as pigs and chickens.

Sinclair Watson

At the start of the war I had just left school and was hoping to train as an architect. I thought I would like to fly, but a friend in the RAF told me the war would be over in six months and advised me just to do what I had to and then get on with my life.

Army enlistment

Early in 1941 I joined the Royal Armoured Corps and went for initial training to Bovington in Dorset, but after a couple of days there was an enormous panic. During the hours of darkness, some German U-boats had come into the bay and found a massive fleet of our ships. It was too small a unit to attack but they radioed the information back, a whole lot of German bombers came over and there was all hell to pay. Because we were all such raw recruits we were a drain rather than a resource for the army, so they sent thousands of us up to Catterick.

The Royal Armoured Corps was made up of various different units, including some branches of the Hussars who had to abandon their horses for tanks. I once came across some regular officers behind the lines grooming their tanks, blowing on their flanks and rubbing them down as if they were horses.

Western Desert

After initial training we were sent to Birkenhead to go by ship to Palestine. This meant going via New York and Miami because the Atlantic was rife with German ships and U-boats. We had duties on board; I volunteered for the ack-ack (anti-aircraft), but there were real gunners there so I ended up skivvying. We doubled back and came through Gibraltar where U-boats were sitting on the bottom waiting for ships to come along. We got through, ending up in Palestine. Then we had to catch up with our army across the Western Desert, aiming to get to Tobruk before the Germans left. The heat was tremendous – you could put a frying pan on the metal of the tank and cook an egg. When we got up in the morning, we would take one of the big metal containers from the tank, empty the sump oil into the sand, fill the container with water, put it on the oily sand, throw a match onto it and brew up a gallon of tea which would last us all day.

Alexander was our general. We thought a great deal of him, he only had to appear for the whole crowd to break into cheers. When we got to Tobruk we found the Germans had sailed the day before, and the North African campaign was virtually finished. We were simply guarding the southern approaches to make sure no more Germans got through. The Italians had to surrender, they sent an emissary to our general applying for honourable surrender. They had, after all, been let down by the Germans who just left them behind. They would surrender all their ammunition, but would be allowed to march in order with their weapons. We agreed, and they marched past and saluted us, it was quite moving.

Italy

We went up through Italy as a rearguard and defence for the Indians and the Gurkhas. I was by now chiefly involved in communications, including laying telephone wires. There was an occasion when I was ordered to lay a wire and place a telephone right up at the German front line in order to listen to their movements. This meant carrying heavy drums of cable across dangerous ground. I didn't really expect to get back, but they insisted I should take a rifle and ammunition. How this would help I didn't know because if the Germans saw me, they'd shoot me before I could get the rifle off my back, my hands being full of telephone equipment. Anyway, I got there, set up the line and the telephone and got back. I don't know if it was ever used, but I did get 'mentioned in dispatches'. Afterwards I was talking to an Italian civilian and was surprised he knew exactly what I had done. It turned out that he was a member of the Resistance and his job was to shadow me and see I came to no harm.

There was one old soldier, he'd been a regular since the First World War. We'd been on a night pass into the nearest town where a lorry would collect the men and bring them back to camp, often the worse for wear. Now the Cook Sergeant always made a meal for everyone who had been out, to eat on his return. If the meal hadn't been eaten they would be in trouble. One night this chap was so drunk he didn't want his food and we kept telling him he had to eat it. He said he wasn't hungry and went on and on refusing to eat. In the end he took out his false teeth, plonked them on the counter and said to them 'You're hungry, you eat it!'

We got to the River Po, and there we stopped. Other divisions of Infantry and Artillery went across and into Austria, but we had to guard the land between two mountain ranges of Northern Italy to stop the Russians who wanted to get through to France, also maintain the supply lines for food and ammunition. Later we did cross and in Vienna the Russians had their quarter and we had ours.

Austria

In Austria we had a Colonel who was very keen on sports – inter-regimental competitions, all done on a very grand scale. A downhill ski race was organised and I had to climb up the hill with my cables and set up telephones at various positions down the course. I'd never been on skis before. You put bear skins on the bottoms of the skis to get a grip in the snow as you climbed, then you were meant to take them off at the top to ski down. I kept mine on as brakes. Anyway, I came down, setting my telephones, did a test to see everything was working and joined the crowd to watch. The skiers set off at one minute intervals, unless there was a phone call to say there'd been an accident. We were watching them appear out of the woods onto the plain at the bottom of the hill when something caught my eye over to the left. There were two figures walking up the valley towards the ski track making to cross it. I recognised one as my colonel. Now there's no way a skier coming down at 60 miles an hour could have stopped. I was absolutely furious and yelled at them using the most foul language, despite having the Brigadier's wife beside me. They did hear me and stopped, and I never heard a word from the colonel.

We were in Austria as an army of occupation for a while and then were demobbed. I didn't really know what I was going to do, the army had been my whole adult life; there were a lot of us like that. I went to Cable and Wireless for a while as I had been Regimental Signals Sergeant and knew a bit about it. Then I went into farming.

Sinclair Watson died in 2008

Jo Whelan, Helen Forrest and Patsy Tyden

Three sisters

In the 1930s our family lived in Shanghai, a bustling cosmopolitan city where my father had a job in the civil administration. We were the twins Jo and Patsy, born in 1932, and Helen, three years older. In 1937 the Japanese war started and Shanghai was bombed. We were living in a flat which was not damaged, but my aunt's extended family were bombed out of their home and took refuge with us. The sleeping arrangements were chaotic, but it was great fun for us children. Along with many British families we were then evacuated to Hong Kong, travelling by ship, blacked out at night. We were excited, but worried about Daddy still in Shanghai. We stayed in Hong Kong for six months, going to a strict convent school and surviving typhoons, and were then glad to return to Shanghai.

Shanghai life

Daddy was highly respected by his staff, he was honest and incorruptible and had learnt to speak Mandarin, which helped him in his work as Chief Inspector of Taxes. In 1938 we came home on leave, by ship through Suez to Venice, and then by train to England. There we stayed in Preston with Grandma Forrest and went to the local school. She was a stern, unsmiling martinet who had brought up her ten children on very little money, and was now caring for her widowed son and his three children.

There was talk of imminent war. Daddy wanted to leave Helen in boarding-school, but she and Mummy protested so hard the plan was dropped and we all returned to Shanghai. We went to live in an apartment block overlooking the Foochow creek. This was home to sampan dwellers who used the creek water for everything and in the summer the smell was awful. The block had a swimming pool, where Daddy taught us all to swim, and a servants' wing where our amah and cook lived. The flats were mainly occupied by middle-class Europeans and Eurasians like ourselves and for us kids it was great. There were always parties and dances and clubs to visit, and it was exciting to see Mummy and Daddy dressed up to go out for the evening. Shanghai was in its heyday, and the outbreak of the European war in 1939 passed almost unnoticed, though Daddy listened on his short-wave radio to the news from London.

As far as we remember, Mummy led a leisurely life. She would meet her friends in town, often at the chocolate shop, go to the cinema, play mah-jong, or go to the Canadrome where they had greyhound racing. She was a fabulous needlewoman and spent a lot of time on embroidery.

Japanese war

Many of the men returned to England or Australia to join the forces, but employees of the Shanghai Municipal Council like Daddy were advised to stay on. Then on 8 December 1941, the Japanese attacked Pearl Harbor and everything changed. We were at school that day and we knew something was wrong because we all had to wait for our parents to collect us. Barricades were put up on the roads and we moved into the heart of the international settlement, to a ground-floor flat. We heard that two British battleships had been sunk in Singapore harbour. All British and American citizens over the age of 13 had to wear a red arm-band, and anyone with a red arm-band was not allowed into cinemas or other places of entertainment. The Japanese hoped the local population would shun us, but they didn't because they hated the

Japanese. All wages were confiscated and proclamations were slapped on the front doors forbidding the removal of any belongings. We only missed this because the man who lived in the flat above us collaborated with the Japanese.

We continued with our normal schooling, were close to all our cousins and spent happy times playing in the streets or at mah-jong. We could not keep our servants who left us to set up small businesses. Mother had to learn to shop and to cook. Camps were being established for internment, but nobody thought the war would last long. Municipal workers were being held back so the Japanese could learn how to run the city.

Internment

On 1 April 1943 our turn came for internment. We were told to take a few possessions, like a bed, table and chairs, and one suitcase each. We assembled outside Ash Camp, which had been built as army barracks, and were herded into a large hall. The Japanese commandant and his guard had their offices in a magnificent white house with a pillared verandah, whilst the internees were in wooden huts, 40 foot long by 16 foot wide, divided by plasterboard into smaller spaces so families had some degree of privacy. The huts were raised about two foot to avoid flooding, toilet facilities were a row of commodes in another hut which were emptied nightly. There was a football field, and a small building we commandeered as a chapel. We had a priest from Sheffield who stayed with us for the duration, and he always volunteered for the most menial jobs.

One large hut was for the cook-house, and a hall was the communal eating area, dance-hall, theatre and games place. The Japanese left us to organise ourselves apart from a twice daily roll-call, and the camp settled into a routine. One boy even learnt the bugle to summon us for meals, roll-call and lights out. Everyone had a job to do, teachers taught, a woodworker made cots and wooden toys. One man became the camp barber, another ran a changey-changey shop, no one had any money so we used a barter system. Daddy, who had had a duodenal ulcer operation and wasn't really well, ran the quartermaster's stores.

265

There were so many children around, it was like a large commune. We had school first and play afterwards and I think it was our parents who suffered more because they couldn't give us what they thought we needed. What they did give us was love and a feeling of security. The Japanese were kind to us children, even showing the younger boys how to do martial arts with long poles. The one fear I had  was that as our rulers, they could do anything they liked and might pick on one of us and hurt us. There had been an incident when the Japanese dragged in an old Chinese man and were beating him and seeming to be enjoying it whilst we watched from a distance, terrified.

We gave the guards nicknames according to how they looked or behaved. There was Forty-five Degrees, because he always insisted that was how we should have our feet at roll-call, Poison Ivy, Napoleon, and Felix who was such a gentle person. These guards were servicemen who had been given light duties before returning to the front. They didn't harass us because we were civilians, not soldiers who had surrendered.

Camp life

Our room was at the end of the hut, with three windows and electric lighting, but no water. Mummy curtained off part for we three girls to have camp-beds, she and Daddy had brought in their large brass bedstead. Every household had a chatty, a primitive sort of cooking-stove made from tin cans. Each family was allocated a ration of coal and coal-dust, and this the children made into briquettes. We also scrounged cinders thrown out from the cook-house.

We collected the food from the cook-house and learnt to use a grindstone, cracking wheat to make flour, and if we were very lucky,

266

peanuts for peanut butter. We got water from a stand-pipe nearby, and Helen did the heavy washing in cold water in the wash-house.

We were given breakfast and one meal a day in the dining-room. It was mostly gruel made from cracked wheat or rice. Lunch was SOS – Same Old Stew. As an invalid Daddy was entitled to a small portion of vegetables and one pint of milk a day and Mummy would use this to make milk pudding for us all. Once there was some pork, it was rancid, but Mummy took the fat and rendered it down to dripping, which we had on bread or used for cooking. Food was short and very monotonous, but I think our stomachs must have shrunk because we didn't feel pangs of hunger. Daddy, at the quartermaster's stores, could sometimes filch a bit of fish or meat from the guards' rations. People tried growing vegetables, but not very successfully, and occasionally we would get Red Cross parcels, mostly from the Americans. There was only one death in the camp.

Ash Camp was small, with 450 inmates, (including seven pairs of twins) compared with some camps of 2,000. We had the majority of the teachers and not very many able-bodied men, so with true British spirit, volunteers were requested to go to other camps, and we got a number of stronger American men. We children were divided by age for teaching. In the mornings, the seven of us older ones were taught specific subjects and took examinations which eventually were recognised by Cambridge – Helen got her matriculation there. Afternoons there were voluntary activities, anyone could learn Latin or Greek, country-dancing, sport, there were Scouts and Guides where we worked for badges. There was a keen astronomer who taught us the stars at night.

Camp pastimes

Saturday night was the highlight, we put on performances of four Gilbert and Sullivan operas, but were too young to take part in *The Beggars Opera*. We did straight plays too, including some we had written ourselves, and revues where anyone could do a turn, tap-dancing, acrobatics, or singing. The Japanese attended all our shows, taking the front seats. If there were no production, we would have a dance to the music of a piano. One man had a guitar, another a ukulele and would do George Formby songs. A lending library was formed from books brought in by other internees, and Helen spent a lot of time reading, and walking round and round the football ground talking with one or two other girls.

We the twins never remembered being lonely, there were always other children around. Someone managed to get roller-skates into the camp and we spent hours on the concrete parade ground, or doing acrobatics on the grass, getting up to tricks like knocking on doors of people we didn't like and running away. We had a maypole, and learnt to dance round it. Auntie May had two babies whilst we were in camp, and we were delighted to look after them. We soon outgrew our clothes, so Mummy would unpick bodices from skirts, and we started the fashion for bare midriffs. One Christmas Mummy gave us cardigans, made from wool unpicked from other garments. We adopted a cat called Mimi who had kittens and we were allowed to keep one black one. We never saw a rat or mouse in the camp, I remember it as being very clean, very British and for us children totally secure and happy.

Escape

Two men did escape from the camp. There was a great to-do when this was discovered, and all adults had to congregate on the lawn outside the White House for interminable roll-calls on that cold and miserable night. When at last they were satisfied that only two were missing, we were allowed back to bed. We heard later that both had been recaptured. One was killed in the process, the other had to spend several months in prison, and was desperately thin and covered in lice when he returned to camp. Two American men were caught trading through the fence with the Chinese, they were interrogated and beaten to be almost unrecognisable.

There was only one time when we were really frightened. Daddy and some others were playing bridge after lights out. They were arguing about the last hand, when suddenly the door was kicked open and Japanese guards came in. We children cowered out of sight, but Daddy was taken away. Hours later he came back. He told us he had managed to get the guards to take him to the room of the English interpreter where he was interrogated for hours, standing to attention. Daddy had grown a beard, and looked much older than his 45 years. The guard Felix, who had always been friendly, saw through the window what was going on, and he went in to persuade them to be lenient to the old man, and they let him go.

I was very frightened about how the war was going to end, and what would we do outside the barbed wire, how would we manage. We heard a bomb had been dropped on Japan, and then one morning during breakfast someone came in shouting 'The war is over!' We didn't know what to do next, but were advised to stay in the camp for fear of violence outside. Then visitors were allowed into the camp and the first person to come and see us was our old cook-boy, who cooked us the most delicious meal on our chatty, though he was very embarrassed when we insisted he sit down to eat it with us.

Afterwards

We had been interned for two and a half years. The Americans appeared within a day or two and were welcomed with open arms, then the British warships came into the harbour and arranged medical and dental checks. Oddly enough, there was nothing wrong with our teeth. The crew of the HMS *Belfast* organised a dance on board, and we had food we had not tasted for years.

We went back to our flat in Shanghai, and found it exactly as we had left it. A Korean family had commandeered it, but someone had committed suicide, and after that no one would enter it. We cleaned it up and moved back in September 1945. We came to realise that people outside had suffered more than we had from the food shortage. The Shanghai Municipal Council no longer existed, and though Daddy was only two years off retirement with a reasonable pension, there was nothing for him and we were destitute. He got a menial job with American commercial ships, waiting for repatriation, the twins went back to school and Helen helped Mummy at home.

On 2 February 1946, we boarded the SS *Highland Chieftain*, and waved a tearful farewell to our cousins on the quayside and our happy carefree Shanghai childhood

Jean Williams

Secretarial Training

When war was declared in 1939 I was still at school, approaching my 15th birthday. In the summer of 1941 I took my school certificate but the question of staying on in the sixth form did not arise. My father, who had a drapery business in Halifax where I was born, had been paying school fees for my brother and me, and could not afford to consider university. I left school, learnt a little shorthand and typing, and found a job with a transport company. I soon realised it was a reserved occupation, and if I didn't leave before my 18th birthday, I would be there till the end of the war. I'd always admired the Royal Navy so I decided to volunteer for the WRNS.

Joining the WRNS

I managed to overcome my parents' initial opposition and in October 1942, two months before my 18th birthday, I arrived at the WRNS Training and Drafting Depot at Mill Hill. Our first week was spent on lectures and Naval procedure, the second on house duties. This was pretty horrendous, cleaning windows and floors and washing up, so we would know what the stewards and cooks had to do. We were given our uniform and were enrolled, then a group of us were sent to the Royal Navy barracks at Plymouth to be told the category for which we would be suitable. I was told I could be a gardener at Plymouth or a messenger on a Fleet Air Arm station. I was horrified to think I had joined the WRNS to become a gardener so I took the other option. On a dark November afternoon I found myself on a train, on my own with all my kit, heading for Padstow. I was met by a sailor in a truck who asked if I was for the *Vulture*. This was HMS *Vulture*, a Fleet Air Arm station at St Merryn. We didn't sleep on the camp but in requisitioned hotels, first at Treglos in Constantine Bay and later at the Metropole in Padstow.

WRNS Messenger

I enjoyed the messenger job at first. Dispatch riders brought the signals to a central office, and we had bicycles to take them round the base. It was a large station and when it was wet, we wore oilskins and sou'westers. I was promoted to Confidential Bag messenger, carrying bags which had to be unlocked at their destination.

One of the jobs for messengers was to raise and lower the colour at the beginning and end of the day. This was quite a ceremony and I was proud to do it. You had to anchor the flag to the halyard without it touching the ground and raise it in time to the bugle call whilst the duty officer saluted. One very windy Sunday disaster struck. The Sunday flag was the size of a large table-cloth, I lost control and saw it sail to the top of the mast, only half anchored on. I was horrified. The young officer and bugler stopped in their tracks and a sailor was sent to climb to the top of the mast to retrieve it. I thought I would be court-martialled but heard no more about it.

271

Signals Section

I didn't want to be a messenger for the duration and with a like-minded friend Aline, asked to be transferred to the Signals section where we became Radio/Telephonists. Our job was to communicate with the Swordfish aircraft on training flights. The sailors came in groups of 40 to be trained as Telegraphist/Air Gunners in Swordfish and they stayed for two months before being drafted for operational duties.

North Cornwall was a good place to be stationed. We had lovely walks by the sea in our off-duty times. Sometimes we walked the five miles into Padstow and enjoyed egg and chips at May's Café before catching the bus back to camp.

Aline and I were sent with one of our squadrons to an RAF Coastal Command station at Chivenor in North Devon. We were flown there and had a very interesting and enjoyable four months at this operational station. After this experience we were sent on a course at HMS *Heron* at Yeovilton. It was quite demanding, learning about Radar and Direction Finding. We both passed and were then entitled to wear a signallers badge and, more importantly, received an increase in pay.

Fleet Air Arm

In the spring of 1944, we were drafted to a Fleet Air Arm Station, HMS *Nightjar* near Blackpool, and I was there till the end of the war. Here we had the experience of flying in a Swordfish – the remarkable bi-plane that was flown from ships – so that we would know what it was like for the men to whom we were sending messages. The pilot was in front and the telegraphist behind, it had an open cockpit with no protection. The Swordfish performed some amazing feats in the early part of the war, and though it was in theory obsolete, it was still being used in operations and for training right up to the end of the war.

There was a high proportion of men to girls on the station, many of the girls were engaged or married and some had husbands who were prisoners of war. I was young and unattached and loved the life. There were buses to Blackpool and Preston; we cycled a lot and walked for miles. I liked the traditions of the RN shore stations which were exactly as if you were on a ship. You soon got used to 'going ashore' when you went into town. I became a Leading Wren.

272

At HMS *Nightjar* we slept in Nissen huts, quite a come-down after the comfort of luxury hotels. We had coke stoves to keep us warm, with a small ration of coal to get them started. There was never enough coal, so we used to go on raiding parties when it was dark – there was quite a pile at the sick bay. We had counterpanes for our bunks and I was amused after the war when I was having my first baby in hospital to find naval counterpanes on our beds!

My general memories are of a fun time and growing up. There was tremendous excitement when the war was over but I missed the life very much when I was demobbed in January 1946 and went home. I was glad that I had been involved.

Robert Williams

At the beginning of the war, I was in the Sixth Form at grammar school in Bristol. During Higher School Certificate exams in 1940 there were air-raids, and we had to go to the shelters where we had useful discussions about the papers before returning to the examination room. In October 1940, when I was 17, I went to Bristol University to read economics. I did fire-watching once a week during term time and nightly during the vacations, for which I was paid three pounds five shillings a week. We did one two-hour watch each night in the Tower, a solid building in which we felt relatively safe although there was a lot of glass about.

Air-raids on Bristol

That summer, there were daylight raids, particularly around the aeroplane works at Filton. I watched a dog-fight when two or three German bombers were brought down and I saw four German airmen parachuting to earth. One night when the siren went, I cycled out into the country to get away from the bombing, but was nearly killed by shrapnel from our own anti-aircraft guns falling all round me. In the city, though the sound of anti-aircraft fire was more or less continuous, you could look to see when shell bursts were immediately overhead and duck into a doorway. Once the noise of falling shrapnel had stopped, you could venture out and continue on your way.

At home during air-raids, we all crowded into a small Anderson shelter in the garden. The bombs usually came down in 'sticks' of six, and it was particularly unnerving when each bomb in a stick seemed closer than the previous one. The last bomb of one such stick landed on our garden wall and killed two of our neighbours. They were in a shelter but the brick walls were reduced to rubble and the concrete roof came down on top of them. We could hear them calling for help but there was nothing we could do. That same bomb blew in our windows and doors, and took tiles off the roof. We had friends who had vacated their house on the other side of the city to escape the bombing and we lived there for several weeks while our house was being repaired.

The night of the first heavy raid on Bristol the sky was a fierce angry red from the light of the fires, and my father and I watched from a hill. Next morning as I cycled across the city to the University there was an acrid smell of burnt material, the rubble of collapsed buildings lay in heaps across the streets and fire hoses snaked everywhere. During the day, rubble was cleared from the streets, hoses were removed and any remaining fires extinguished. We were then ready for the next raid, which might be that night or the next week.

Call up to Army

My call-up was deferred for one year because I was in the University OTC/STC (Officer/Senior Training Corps), where after a year's infantry training I specialised in signals. This enabled me to complete two years of my three-year degree before I was called up in August 1942. I went straight to pre-OCTU (pre-Officer Cadet Training Unit) at West Malling in Kent. Even then I was slightly delayed because the evening before my scheduled departure, I was cycling down a hill when the siren went and two ladies dashing in front to me to get to the shelter, knocked me off my bike and I cut my head.

My first two weeks in the Army were spent doing infantry training with the Royal Berkshires. They did everything at the double, on a major escarpment on the south side of the North Downs, carrying anti-tank rifles and other heavy equipment. Then I went to 152 Signals OCTU at Catterick, where training was from seven in the morning till six at night every day. I was having difficulty getting to the required ten words of Morse per minute, and had to put in extra time. I spent a lot of evenings doing Morse. There were exams in technical subjects including line transmission and wireless theory, I didn't find these difficult because I was used to doing exams. We did a week at Battle School in the Lake District in early in March 1943, going to Penrith by train and then marching 12 miles to Deepdale at the far end of Ullswater, where we camped by the stream. We marched right round Ullswater sleeping in the open and fighting mock battles as we went. We climbed Helvellyn in full kit including rifle then ran down. We learnt how to throw hand grenades and fire mortars and had live ammunition fired over our heads.

Signals Officer

At the end of the course we were all posted to Lines of Communication Signals (L of C) because that was the need at the time. L of C dealt with communications between the Area Headquarters and the armies, and is about as far from the front line as it is possible to get. I was commissioned in 1943, and posted to 13th L of C Signals.

So before I was 20, I found myself in command of a Line Construction Section, which consisted of 80 men, including two sergeants, two lance sergeants, six corporals, six lance corporals and some 65 other ranks. Some of these men were in their early forties, so as a young and inexperienced officer, I found my situation quite daunting. Our task was to provide communications using cable or wires as opposed to wireless.

Journey to North Africa

In December 1943 my section was posted to North Africa. We were not told where we were going but we knew it would be warm because we had been getting tropical kit and termite resistant metal uniform boxes. We went by train to Liverpool where we boarded the P&O liner, SS *Majola*. That evening we sailed to Belfast Lough, where a mighty convoy of troop ships assembled, complete with escort destroyers. To avoid the German submarines, we sailed north, nearly to Iceland, then west towards Canada, then south. In the North Atlantic we encountered a fierce storm with waves so high the destroyers disappeared in the troughs and the propellers of the liners came right out of the water as they crested the waves. I found it quite exciting with the sea crashing over the decks and the spray streaming past the superstructures, and was one of the few passengers not to be seasick. The men were all accommodated in the holds of the ship whereas officers had shared cabins with access to daylight.

The *Majola* was wanted back in England urgently, so with just one destroyer for escort we left the convoy, and headed east to Gibraltar. Each ship each put out paravanes, fish shaped devices with fins that could be towed from the bow of a vessel to deflect mines and sever their moorings. As far as I know we encountered no mines.

We sighted the Atlas Mountains early one morning. It was magical, this exotic land peopled by Arabs with donkeys and camels, bazaars and minarets, just as in the 'Tales of the Arabian Nights'. We arrived in Algiers on Christmas Day 1943, where the houses on the hills around the bay were white and gleaming in the sunshine.

As a Line Construction Section we had brought a lot of stores such as poles, cable, motor-cycles, trucks and so on. Such was the haste to get the *Majola* back that she sailed the next day before we had completely unloaded. It had not occurred to me that the ship would leave without discharging all its cargo, but I was interviewed by a Colonel who made it very clear that I should have made greater efforts to get the stores off the ship, as they would now have to make up my stock deficiencies from their own limited supplies.

Algeria

By now the war in North Africa was over, and our troops were fighting in Southern Italy. Eisenhower still had his Headquarters in Algiers. He insisted that the British, American and French had to work together, so in every office there would be Americans and their British counterparts. It seemed to work well.

Algeria was part of Metropolitan France, so there were many French people, an Opera House and a large central Post Office. The Arab City, the Casbah, was out of bounds to British troops. It was a place of narrow streets and many smells, there were metal and leather workers, storytellers and places where visitors could smoke the hookah.

We were billeted in schools, but education somehow continued and the troops mingled happily with the local population.

Communication construction

I was ordered to take 80 Construction Section to Bone, a town on the coast about 300 miles to the east, almost in Tunisia. The convoy of 12 trucks and six of us on motorbikes had to climb 200 miles up into the Atlas Mountains to Setif. I made two mistakes early on. First the sergeants had wanted to put the motor-cycles on the lorries, to which I said 'No' because I liked riding a motor-bike. Second, seeing on a map what I thought was a shortcut, I took the whole convoy down this road, (also against the advice of my sergeants) which turned out to be narrow, heavily potholed and almost impassable. I ate humble pie and we had to turn the whole convoy round.

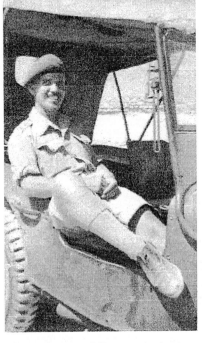

It was dark before we got to Setif and it was snowing. We were cold and hungry, and were greeted by two rather blasé Signals Officers to whom it was quite clear, we were a bit of a nuisance. Next morning we continued on the plateau to Constantine, a town on an impressive gorge looking over a plain to the sea, some 50 miles away. It was a very tortuous road down to the plain, but I delivered my section to 4 Company HQ in mid afternoon – where I met an officer who had been at my school! We were to maintain many miles of 'airline', like telegraph wires but of lighter construction, high in the Atlas mountains, part of the main communications link between Algiers and Tunis.

Nothing was said to me, but during the next few days it was decided I was not experienced enough to have such a remote command. A captain arrived from Algiers and took the Section over. It was a blow to my pride, but quite the right decision.

I went back to doing telephone and line repairs all round Algiers. I had a motor bike and a Personal Utility Vehicle with a canvas cover. I once got caught in a plague of locusts whilst I was on my bike, most uncomfortable. If you were in a car they piled up over the windscreen, and the windscreen wipers couldn't clear them. I lived in the officers' mess in a suburb of Algiers, first in a school, and then in a camp in a vineyard at Ben Messous, just outside Algiers. We were among the fruit trees in tents at first, then I had a room in the house, adjacent to a building which held large vats for the wine they made.

Duff Cooper came to Algeria to represent the British Government, and I had to install a telephone at his villa at Chréa, in the Atlas mountains. I went on my motor-bike, 100 miles south and 5000 feet above Algiers, and found it a cool and refreshing ski resort!

Perugia

With the end of the war approaching, the Army worried about what to do with the troops. They created Education Officers, to teach men and fill their time until demob. I was sent to the University of Perugia to train for this in January 1945, and there was a lot of snow. Teaching was given by British Army officers, and we used the university building. In the main hall there was an enormous mural of Mussolini, discreetly covered by curtains. I was there for two weeks, and met chaps fighting in the Gothic line, where they were having a hard time. We were nearing the end of the war, and men didn't want to get killed.

Tunis

I was posted to Constantine, back to telephone repairs for six weeks, then on to Tunis, where there were troops but no officers. When I got there fighting had finished, and being the only British officer, I used to be invited to cocktail parties and got to know all the top brass of the French Army. I knew the language from school and learnt quickly so became fluent in French, and still am. I had to return material lent by French residents, and give communications equipment back to the French Post Office. I went to Bizerta and Bone, and an oasis 200 miles south in order to pay the troops. Quite a lot of it was enjoyable, I got on well with the troops and they were very loyal to me. Some French navy officers didn't like us much because we had sunk their ships in Dakar and elsewhere, but I used to lunch with them. I had a large French Delage car. The day the European war ended the local population went mad, and I went round the celebrations with a visiting officer from Algiers.

Home

As I was eligible for service in the Far East, I was posted to the 10th Indian Divisional Signals at Klagenfurt, in Austria. I got as far as a transit camp at Casserta, near Naples, when I learnt my university had asked for my immediate release. I travelled by train, over several days, fitting in visits to the opera in Rome and Milan, and was eventually demobbed in December 1945. Then it was home to Bristol, and back to university. Having been an officer, I found it difficult to settle back into undergraduate life. I took my honours final in June and worked for some weeks until I got a job in London.

War matured me, and in retrospect I wouldn't have missed it. I wasn't really suitable to be in charge, having always been a renegade, and I nearly didn't get my second pip. If you passed university exams after two years, you got a pass degree after being in the Army one further year. When I got my honours degree after the war, I was not formally awarded it at a degree ceremony as I was already a graduate, and I felt cheated.

Dorothy Wood

When the war started I was 25 and a shorthand typist at Apsley Mill, in the department making paper bags for shops where I was secretary to the boss. The making of paper was so important that it was a reserved occupation, and though some of my friends were called up, I was not. I didn't like the factory and the journey from Oxhey to Apsley was awful. There was a man in the RAF I was rather keen on, and when he was killed, I wondered about joining up but my father wasn't in good health, and as the only child I felt I needed to be around.

Home Guard

A friend of mine who worked at The Grove at Watford suggested I might join her there. The London Midland and Scottish Railway's headquarters had been evacuated there from St Pancras and they had put up a lot of huts, shops and a canteen. They offered me a job and I could get the firm's bus from Watford. One day the boss of the typing pool asked if there was anyone who would go and work for the Company Commander of the Home Guard. My father was against it, asking what would I do when the war finished? I met the company commander at home, and he told me the Home Guard would pay ten shillings a week more than I was getting and I would be working in the Company office. So I agreed and started early in 1941.

The Company Commander, Major Campbell, was proud to have served in the Argyll and Sutherland Regiment in the First War. He was now ran the bridges section of the LMS Railway and in addition was in charge of C Company, 8th Battalion Hertfordshire Home Guard. This also included workers from the asbestos factory in Tolpits Lane, and the paper mills in Croxley. Each of these had their own captain and training schedule. It was easier for them because the men lived locally, whereas many workers at The Grove, being LMS employees, lived some distance away. Sometimes we did weekend training all together.

The Company office was a brick hut in the grounds, and a man with an injured arm came and lit the stove every morning. My first job was to check the addresses and next of kin of all the Home Guard members. They didn't know who I was, and I didn't know them and it was quite awkward. The bosses were in the main buildings, one of them was polite but others were quite nasty. As time went on they got used to me, I became part of the Company and they asked if I could take part in a forthcoming exercise. Major Campbell said I couldn't be there on my own, and brought his daughter along to share my sleeping quarters, curtained off from the canteen. I went to the firing range and learnt how to fire – I have targets to prove it. They tried unsuccessfully to get a uniform for me, but I had a Home Guard arm-band and a badge. We had a sergeant-major, a really tall man who took me under his wing, and if I had so much as a cough he would get me medicine.

I would have to type out training programmes and take notes of the officers' monthly meetings. When Major Campbell was promoted to command Watford Home Guard, the intelligence officer, Mr Dunkley became C Company Commander, and the sergeant became the Intelligence Officer. Nearly all the men had been in the First World War, and they worked hard. The Home Guard was voluntary and they got no pay for the training and work they did in the evenings and weekends. Most of the LMS workforce consisted of older men, as the rest had been conscripted. Major Campbell got all the Scots into the Home Guard, and they really looked good marching down the road.

Bombed out

Each night I went home to Oxhey, where I did fire watching. One night in October 1940, my father said 'That plane sounds low', and then there was a huge bang and a bomb had dropped in a field across the road. All our windows were blown out, and we spent the rest of that night with friends. The only accommodation we could find to rent was over a butcher's shop in Watford. One night after we'd gone to bed we found there was smoke coming from the shop freezer. Father went out to look for a telephone, the first one wasn't working but eventually he found one, called the fire brigade and they came and dealt with the fire. It was a terrible place that flat, it smelt, the only heat was a fire in the corner and it was winter and very cold. The bath had an antique geyser, and I was afraid to get into it. We spent several months there, including Christmas 1940. We used to go out in the dark without any worries, sometimes we went to Watford Theatre.

Meanwhile, we stored our furniture in an empty garage. My father did the books for a builder who was able to get windows and doors for our house, and we got permission to put these in. We went back to live there, even though the ceilings were down.

At the end of the war the Battalion Commander asked me to come and help him clear up the Home Guard things from Croxley House. He then asked me to join his firm of merchant bankers, Balfour Williamson in the City, where I became the boss' secretary. The Home Guard was disbanded and at the final parade they all turned to me, and I had tears in my eyes.

Peggy Wood

When war broke out in September 1939, I was preparing to work for a Diploma of Education, having graduated BA from Manchester University earlier in the year. Immediately things changed. There was the blackout to be coped with, curtains to be put up so not a chink of light could be seen from outside. My father was Clerk of Works on Lord Vernon's estate in Poynton, a village outside Manchester, one of his jobs was to confirm the whereabouts of water and gas mains in the village in case of bombing.

Manchester student

The University hall of residence, Ellis Llywd James Hall where I had been a student, closed down because it was close to Trafford Park, a huge industrial estate and therefore at risk of bombing. The Warden, Miss Buckmaster, took over a high position in the WRNS, and we students were transferred to another hall of residence at the other side of Manchester, much to our disgust.

Once lectures re-started, many of the men students had already gone into the forces. I had become friendly with a small group of which two were conscientious objectors, one went into the mines and the other worked on the land. Another, who was a Quaker, was James

Lovelock, now well known as an environmentalist. The head of the group Father Fish, Professor of Oriental Studies, wrote to the then Pope begging him to do something about Germany's policy towards the Jews, but without any response

By this time my fiancé Gerry was working at Metropolitan Vickers, having taken a BSc with honours in Physics. There he was put in charge of building radar, which was in its infancy. Every piece of equipment built had a code number or name. One in particular was marked SFO – Something For Oliphant, Sir Mark Oliphant, who was working on radar in Cambridge. In 1975, when he was Governor of South Australia we met him, and talked of this. He asked my husband if it had worked, remarking 'I didn't know if it would work, I just designed the bugger.'

School teaching

My own war work was neither glamorous nor particularly dangerous. I was teaching small children in Stockport, 40 in the class, all having to keep their hats, coats and gas masks with them in the classroom in case we had to evacuate the school to the air raid shelter. The government allowed children to start school at the age of four, to free their mothers for war work. Imagine 50 to 60 little boys and girls all crowded into one room, at least until the older ones – all of five years old – could be moved along to a class higher up. I know that teachers nowadays feel they have too much administration, but even then there was quite a lot. Children were encouraged to buy National Savings stamps at sixpence each, so every Monday morning, after the register had been taken, we sold stamps. Then the free milk had to be dealt with, warmed up on the heating pipes during the winter months. School dinners were started, and we had to take turns in serving and keeping order. School holidays were a no-no. With fathers either working or in the forces, and often mothers working too, the children had to be entertained during the holidays, and teachers were the ones to do this. It was in many ways harder work than normal teaching.

Manchester blitz

Fire-watching was another chore. Once a week, each member of staff spent the night on a camp bed in the staff room. Most of the time nights were uneventful – the mice were more bothersome than the enemy – until the blitz arrived at Christmas 1940. Gerry and I had visited an aunt of his in Staleybridge, about ten miles out of Manchester. We caught a train back for Manchester as dusk was falling and the bombers began their attack. We spent the night in the sidings at Staleybridge and when morning came we arrived in a bombed out city. We went in search of Gerry's father, not knowing how he had fared. I remember walking through the streets of Manchester, crunching through glass and debris, with ravaged buildings on every side. Fire-fighters were still hosing the ruins, and everyone looked black. Stupidly, I said to Gerry 'I never knew there were so many black people in Manchester'. 'Don't be silly' he replied 'they're not black, just filthy from the smoke and fires.'

We found Gerry's father safely in the house of a friend, then off we went with him, back to the railway station to take him to relations in Stockport. The station was crowded with men, women and children, but there was no panic. Standing next to me was an elderly woman with a parrot in a cage! We had just got out of Manchester when the bombers started to arrive again. Having left Gerry's father in Stockport, we set off to walk the six miles back home to Poynton. We could hear the bombers flying overhead, and the bombs falling on Manchester.

Gerry's father moved away, and Gerry came to live with us. His work on radar took on a pattern. He would leave home at 6am to be at work for 7.30, arriving back home sometimes as late as 10pm. In winter he hardly saw the light of day and might not come home from Monday to Friday. I began to realise there was something important afoot. Once it was the Dam-busters raid, then the imminent invasion. Of course not a word was ever said. I joined the St John Ambulance Brigade (which gave me a warm winter coat) and learnt to drive the ambulance. This was not easy because it was a big American vehicle and I am quite small. I passed the test, but I never had to drive it.

The Home Front

Mother managed our rationed food very well, though she often queued for hours. Occasionally there would be a treat, but she would have no truck with the Black Market. Yet I never remember feeling hungry. As far as clothes were concerned, make-do-and-mend was the order of the day. A dress that had worn under the arms would be cut into two, and either given a new top or made into a skirt. Coupons both for clothes and food were saved for special occasions, when friends and relations contributed for sugar for a cake as happened for my wedding in 1943. The village dressmaker made me a fashionable dress in 'crushed raspberry' colour, my bridesmaid was in 'powder blue', outfits we could wear on other occasions. When my son was born, I did a lot of knitting, and got a Utility pram. It was good stuff, Utility, I still have two of their Parker-Knoll chairs and a little chest of drawers. My father built our bed, he was an extremely good carpenter.

The Hallé Orchestra kept going – Barbirolli came back from America, Beecham, Malcolm Sargeant, Solomon, Moseiwitch and Myra Hess all appeared. After the Free Trade Hall was bombed, the orchestra moved to Belle Vue Zoo

Then the Americans arrived! There were three camps in and around our village, and on the whole they were welcomed, especially by the young women. They brought candy and nylons – all far too big for my size two feet. But we did not like the segregation of the black soldiers, who were not allowed in the pubs where the white soldiers drank – their rules, not ours.

You learnt to make do and I still tend to do that. I very rarely buy something just because I see it, only if I need it.

Bob Woodward

Naval background

Generations of my family had served in the Royal Navy, and I spent my childhood on board the Training Ship *Cornwall*, moored off Purfleet on the River Thames. My father had been appointed Captain Superintendent when he retired from the Navy in 1922 and accommodation was provided for his wife and family to live on board.

I passed into the Royal Navy from the Nautical College, Pangbourne in September 1932 at the age of 17. By September 1939, I was a Lieutenant serving in the destroyer HMS *Fury* in the Sixth Destroyer Flotilla of the Home Fleet. I was the Navigator, the Torpedo Control Officer and the Anti-submarine Control Officer, all duties centred on the bridge of the ship.

First Naval attack

By 2 September 1939, many ships of the Home Fleet had taken up strategic positions at sea in anticipation of war being declared, and *Fury* was part of a two destroyer anti-submarine screen ahead of HMS *Ark Royal*, the Navy's only modern aircraft carrier. Our position was about 100 miles south of Iceland, with *Fury* about two miles ahead of *Ark Royal* on the starboard bow, and our sister ship HMS *Firedrake* in a similar position on the port bow.

At 11am on 3 September, there was a deathly hush in *Fury* whilst the Prime Minister was making his broadcast ending with the words '…consequently our country is now at war with Germany.' At 2pm that same day, *Fury*'s ASDIC (Anti-Submarine Detection Investigation Committee) set obtained an underwater echo of a

submarine in an ideal position to attack the *Ark Royal* with torpedoes, but too far away for accuracy. We signalled the information to *Ark Royal* who immediately turned away whilst we increased speed, turned towards the submarine, and when over her estimated position dropped five depth charges. I remember thinking 'I'm glad I'm up here and not down there.'

Shortly after, we picked up the echo again, astern of us, and were preparing for another attack when *Ark Royal* told us to rejoin her. *Firedrake* had come across to help with the hunt for the submarine, leaving *Ark Royal* wide open to anything that might now be ahead on her new course. Now that the submarine was no longer a threat to *Ark Royal*, we rejoined her, and continued our patrol.

On 14 September, *Fury* and two other destroyers were steaming through The Minches, the channel between the north-west coast of Scotland and the Outer Hebrides, when at midnight we sighted a stationary submarine on the surface. We fired and it dived, but we must have hit it because a short while later it surfaced. Being trapped between us and the land, it had no option but to surrender, they opened the sea-cocks and let the water in so it sank, and we picked up the crew. They told us that on the day war had been declared, one of our destroyers had dropped a whole lot of depth charges and then ran away! We asked where and when was this incident, and found it was indeed the one we had attacked on 3 September, the *U39*.

Norwegian Campaign

During the winter and spring of 1939-40 there was constant naval activity in the North Sea, Arctic waters, North Atlantic and as far south as the approaches to Gibraltar. Germany had invaded Norway, and support was required with troop and equipment convoys. Although the invasion was a military campaign, the occupation of Norway by Germany had an enormous effect on the war at sea. The German Navy's only access to the oceans of the world was from Heligoland Bay into the confined waters of the North Sea, over which the Royal Navy and Royal Air Force had reasonable control. But now the enemy could use the long and sheltered fjords of the Norwegian coast as bases for their ships and submarines to attack Britain's life-blood of merchant shipping in the Atlantic.

Our battleships and heavy cruisers were now constantly at sea guarding these routes, but they could not operate without a destroyer screen for anti-submarine protection and reconnaissance. This put an enormous burden on the limited number of Fleet Destroyers, and in May 1940 the Admiralty estimated from destroyers' 'reports of proceedings', that the Home Fleet destroyers were averaging 25 days and nights at sea in each month. The weather that winter in Northern Waters was terrible, and we often wondered if we were fighting the storms more than the enemy.

But the enemy was there all right, especially in the two battles which took place right up in the Narvik Fjord on 11 and 14 April 1940 when a total of 12 enemy destroyers and one submarine were destroyed. Fury was present at the second battle, but by now my time on her was coming to an end.

North Sea attack

Germany had also invaded Holland, and on 7 May 1940 I was appointed as First Lieutenant (second in command) to the destroyer HMS *Versatile*, an old destroyer now on convoy duties. On 10 May we were ordered to the Hook of Holland where Queen Wilhelmina of the Netherlands was to be evacuated by our destroyer HMS *Hereward* to a place of safety. On 11 May, we were moored at a jetty in the Hook of Holland, when four low flying German aircraft attacked us with bombs and machine gun fire. I was on the bridge and saw a bomb coming towards us and it landed on the deck above the engine room. Both engines were put out of action, and there was a lot of damage on the upper deck as well. We lost a third of the ship's company killed (ten men) and wounded. Our rudder had also been damaged so we could neither steam nor steer. Another destroyer moored alongside us and was able to manoeuvre the two ships side by side out of the harbour and across the North Sea, rather slowly, at not more than five knots. It was a fine sunny day, and the medical attendants had the injured lying along the deck. Half way across the North Sea, the engineer officer reported that they'd got one engine working, and a bit later they were able to straighten the rudder. We couldn't use it, but it was fixed so that we could go forwards in a straight line under our own power at about 12 knots, and we got to Invergordon where a tug came out and towed us the rest of the way in. I had only been in the ship three days, and hardly knew any of the ship's company at all. Consequently I could not do much to keep the morale of the men up to scratch in these difficult circumstances. However, having finally got the ship back to Invergordon, I think they began to realise that their new First Lieutenant did know what he was doing. And Queen Wilhelmina got safely away in the *Hereward*.

Meanwhile at home…

At that time, my future wife Pamela was working at the Admiralty, and it was she who received the signal that *Versatile* had been hit. I don't know how and when she found out that I was all right. My parents were living in Tonbridge where my father was Chief Air Raid Warden and my mother worked with the WVS and as a duty Air Raid Warden in the HQ at Tonbridge Castle. There was a lot of action in the skies over them, and it so happened that a German bomber returning from London had one bomb left, saw a town and released his bomb. A Spitfire nearby saw the bomb falling, flew beneath it and caught it on the tip of his wing, went on till he could see a green patch below and tilted his plane so the bomb dropped off – on our tennis court! But it did no damage to the town

Coastal Waters convoys

The refit of the *Versatile* took about six weeks, our casualties were replaced and then we were back on convoy duty. We were based at

Harwich, so a lot of our work was in the South East Coastal Waters. The waters here are very shallow, with natural deep-water channels through which the convoys had to pass. Of course the enemy knew this as well as we did, so we were attacked from the air in daylight, and at night by E-boats, fast shallow draught motor boats armed with torpedoes, which could attack over the shallow waters. The enemy also laid mines in the deep water, and our minesweepers did a great job clearing these. The Royal Air Force was wonderful with the air escort they were able to offer in daylight. Gradually our destroyers were fitted with a double-barrelled pom-pom gun which fired two-pounder shells at 45 rounds per minute from each barrel, 90 per minute overall. This was all controlled by the ship's radar, which detected the position of the E-boats at night, and swung the gun round to the firing position. Despite this, casualties among the slow merchant ships were frequent. The wrecks did not sink deep in these shallow waters, and we used them as navigational aids. Convoys had with them small vessels known as rescue ships that served a wonderful purpose in saving the crews from the sunken ships.

By this time, the summer and autumn of 1940, the Germans had occupied France and installed heavy guns along the French coast of the English Channel. This made  convoy work hazardous, particularly in the narrow waters of the Straits of Dover. Once when we were escorting merchantmen, a German shell just missed us as we steamed ahead as fast as we could. The next day, my Captain and I went to the cinema in Dover, and saw a newsreel of this dramatic encounter, and the following day a photograph appeared in the local paper.

In October 1940 Pamela and I were married in Tonbridge church. It was not a big occasion, there were about ten of us, and after the ceremony we went for lunch in a pub. That Christmas we made our own cards, by folding some stiff paper, putting the rubber stamp of the ship's crest on the cover, a photograph of the ship inside and typing the usual Christmas message followed by 'It is regretted that owing to enemy action, our supply of Christmas cards has become a total loss.'

Atlantic convoys

Although our official base was at Harwich, ships required convoy all round the coast of England to the port where they could find a convoy sailing to their final destination. We also had our fair share of Atlantic Convoy work with several escorts for a large convoy. There was always a shortage of Escort Vessels, and occasionally we would take a convoy far out into the Atlantic and then disperse it for ships to continue to their final destination alone.

Ocean rescue

On one occasion when we were returning alone, we sighted something on the horizon. We steamed towards it and found it was a life raft from

 a sunken merchant ship, about ten foot square, with ten men on it. They had been on it six days and nights since their ship had been sunk. The sea was fairly calm, and we managed to manoeuvre our ship alongside and take the men aboard. They had been extremely well organised. They had tinned biscuits which they rationed and still had enough water in a barrel to last a bit longer. In fact one or two got a bit angry with us when we said we didn't need to take their water on board – they knew what had saved them! I had the highest regard for the men of our merchant fleets. They had tremendous losses and went through hell, always returning for more. They had little or no weaponry to defend themselves, and received few awards for bravery and never the recognition they so fully deserved.

Training post

After 18 months in *Versatile*, I was given a six month shore job in Portsmouth training a class of 'Upper Yardmen'. This term goes back to the old sailing ship days of Nelson and before, when the ships had three square sails suspended from yards attached to the mast, a Lower Yard, a Middle Yard and an Upper Yard. The upper yard was right at the top of the mast and the men managing the sails there were always the best seamen in the ship. The term is now used to describe the best men in the Navy, who were now being trained as officers. I had a class of 14 men from the Lower Deck, who I am proud to say all passed their exams and obtained commissions as officers in the Royal Navy.

My next appointment was as First Lieutenant to one of our latest destroyers, HMS *Kimberly*. I cannot remember very much about this ship, I have a photograph, but no other records, not even a report from my Captain when I left the ship. It was employed on the East Indies Station and after a few months it was the victim of an accident and went into dock. I can't even remember what the accident was, but it obviously was not anything to do with enemy action, or I would have remembered it.

Indian Ocean Command

However, a new Captain was required for an old First World War destroyer, HMS *Scout*, and I was selected. On 4 January 1943 I joined the *Scout* at Colombo, my first destroyer command. She was a small ship, only 900 tons but very fast, and part of the Arabian Bengal Ceylon Escort Force. It was a very relaxing period with long hot days at sea in the calm waters of the Indian Ocean. We were the only destroyer in the force, and were mostly engaged escorting fast ships whose speed made them difficult targets for attack, so one fast escort was considered adequate. Our most frequent journeys were to Bombay, Aden and the Red Sea to the north-west, and the Calcutta area to the north-east. The Japanese war was now under way, and we provided support for our army in Burma. From time to time we would join the escort of a convoy which had rounded the Cape of Good Hope, destined for the Far East, and which we would in due course hand over to the Royal Australian Navy for escort to it final destination.

Home Waters

In August 1944 I was back to the coastal and Atlantic convoys in command of HMS *Whitshed*. By now things were very much quieter, though we were still using the wrecks as navigational aids. On 8 May 1945, the day the European war ended, I was the Commanding Officer of the escort of a convoy of merchant ships steaming up the East Coast of England. So I started the war at sea, and I ended it at sea, with very little respite between, a situation shared by many regular Naval officers and men of my generation.

Within a week of VE-day, *Whitshed*, which had been built during World War I, was ordered to de-store and pay off to be reduced to scrap iron. It is a custom in the Royal Navy that when a ship pays off for good, the last White Ensign it flew is presented to the Captain. So when we dispersed our final convoy, one dirty, tattered, smoke-encrusted ensign was lowered, and a new ensign hoisted in its place. I am still the proud owner of that flag, and I fly it from the balcony outside my bedroom window on national – and sometime on private – occasions.

After a month's 'end of war' leave, I was appointed to command a new Hunt Class destroyer, HMS *Wheatland*. We had a new crew, and after working up to fighting pitch we were to sail to the Far East to finish off the war with Japan. A week before we were due to sail, the Japanese war ended, so our departure was cancelled. My dear wife always used to say that VJ night was the only time she ever saw me really sloshed – but that was on shore of course!

Postscript

In 1926, the Training Ship *Cornwall* on which I had spent my childhood, had been moved to a new berth off Gravesend. In April 1941, she was sunk by a German bomber. The only person on board at the time was the night watchman, who rowed ashore in the jolly-boat. But even in death the old lady had the last laugh. After 126 years of exceptional service, her wreck was bought by one of London's major furnishing stores for the value of her timber. She was built of Malabar teak, considered superior to the Burma teak mostly used in 1815, and now she is part of someone's dining room table, but I know not where.

Christopher Wrigley

Evacuation plans

In 1939 I was 18, in my last year at Merchant Taylors school, and living with my parents, brother and sister in Chorleywood. My father John Wrigley was a senior civil servant in the Department of Health, in charge of the housing programme, so he was familiar with local government, which really was local then. The government decided that in the event of war, they would evacuate children from cities at risk of bombing, and my father was put in charge. In September 1938, he was called back from a family holiday in Cornwall and given a fortnight to plan the immediate evacuation of London. This would have been a shambles as no preparation had been done, but when the Munich pact meant war didn't come at once, he had a further year to develop the scheme.

The country was divided into evacuation areas and reception areas, with some neutral areas where the danger was not great. Every local authority appointed a billeting officer, usually a retired man, to the reception areas. They went round each house assessing how many children each could take, so when the evacuation came, they knew how many children were to be decanted at each station. It was not compulsory to take in children, but there were not many refusals. As The Times obituary of my father stated in 1977 'It was inconceivable to

Wrigley that British people would not open their homes to children in danger.' There was a maintenance allowance, but not enough to make it profitable.

Schools were instructed that when the signal came, they were to take all children aged five to fourteen to the nearest rail terminus and put them on the first train. Nobody knew where they were going. People were encouraged to go, but didn't have to and during the phoney war a number came back. The idea was driven by the Air Ministry, who exaggerated the effects of bombing, and thought Londoners would only be able to bear it if they knew their children were safe. It was traumatic for the children, though.

Chorleywood 1939

That September morning, as soon as Chamberlain stopped speaking, the sirens went and we huddled in the porch. It was of course a false alarm, and after that we didn't bother. Neighbours had a shelter in the garden, but we didn't use it. A few bombs did fall in Chorleywood, and through the summer of 1940 I was a messenger for the ARP. One Sunday lunchtime a bomb fell in the field behind The Gate pub, but no harm was done. Another late at night struck the side of house in Park Avenue but it didn't explode. In the winter of 1940, a string of small bombs fell across Chorleywood House grounds and the Common. One crater is still there, the clay it threw up took 40 years to grass over. I joined the Local Defence Volunteers (precursor of the Home Guard), and walked round Chorleywood in the dawn looking for parachutists. I also went back to school for a week with the Cadet Corps to defend the playing fields against the expected paratroops.

The 51st Highlands Regiment was billeted in Chenies. There were troop manoeuvres on Chorleywood Common, a few cows grazed there, and Lark Field was ploughed. Chorleywood House was scheduled to be a back up hospital for bombing casualties, and in September 1939 teenagers were summoned to fill sandbags to protect it. In August 1940, I went with the school camp to North Bucks to get in the harvest. We also dug a slit trench as the last ditch against an invading army. It was very hard work, we schoolboys flaked out by afternoon but there was one real labourer who carried on all day.

My father had made Chorleywood part of the reception area, so although my mother already had three teenage children and a husband, on 2 September she also became responsible for three little Jewish children from Whitechapel. Families were kept together as far as possible. One evacuee, Miriam came back to see us later, she had married a GI, and became an all-American Mom. Their mother came once to visit whilst they were there, their father was 'away'. In May 1940, my mother developed pneumonia and they had to be found somewhere else to go, though later she had three more evacuees. I remember clearly one summer afternoon, playing a desultory game of cricket whilst disaster loomed in France, mother lay seriously ill at home, and father was attending high level government meetings to discuss plans for the expected invasion. But the evacuation from Dunkirk proceeded, our doctor was aware of the new sulphonamide drug, which saved my mother's life, and so both crises passed.

My father was keen on our kitchen garden, we had chickens for eggs and for meat, and we became home for stressed out Londoners. These included an aunt who was a physiotherapist at St Thomas' and had been bombed out, and a South African bomber pilot who came to us on his leave. He actually was to be married from our house, his bride was staying with us, but on the day before, a V2 landed on Finchley Road station and there was such travel chaos that he didn't get to us till five in the morning. We brushed him up and got him to the church on time.

Mother had a very hard war, before it she had been thinking of getting a job, but by the end was too exhausted. Some of the privations were exaggerated, people didn't go hungry, in fact many ate better because what food there was, was good.

Call up

I started at Oxford, reading classics, but I knew I was going to be called up. Some classicists were set to learning Japanese, and some mathematicians went to Bletchley. I was called up in March 1941, and put into Signals. I trained in Barmouth, Hounslow, Brentwood and then Catterick. In April 1942, I was posted to India, and sailed from

Liverpool. We stopped in Freetown where the convoys gathered, then on to Capetown, where we were well entertained by the English residents. It was cold and wet, not what we had imagined South Africa to be like. The voyage was very boring.

India, the Forgotten Army

We arrived in Bombay, then on to Mhow, then Meerut in Uttah Pradesh. I didn't see much of the real India, I did go to Agra but the Taj Mahal was under scaffolding. The purpose of the army was to defend India against the Japanese who had conquered Burma, and to suppress the revolt by the Congress party. I spent a year in Ranchi Bihar, doing nothing much, the British were marking time. I then went on a long train journey to Madras, by ship to Chittagong (now Bangladesh), and camped on a peninsula. This was the last bit of India, half the peninsula was in Burma, and the Japs were there. Early in 1944, the Japs launched a big offensive, but they were held off, and retreated. My job was in signals, and most of them were in cipher so we didn't know what they were saying. We camped in a nullah, which seemed dry till the winter monsoon arrived when it became a swamp. I experienced some discomfort, boredom, and home-sickness, but no direct harm

We were in the 14th Army, commanded by General Slim, he was the best commander we had, but we were called the Forgotten Army. Signals was a mixed British and Indian unit; under the Raj, any British man was superior to any Indian, except for the very few officers. Many of my comrades had heard about the gorgeous East, and were very disappointed to find the poverty and squalor. We had radios so we knew about the war elsewhere, and I heard Lillibolero for the first time after el Alamein. I got early release, to go back to Oxford in October 1945, but changed to read Philosophy, Politics and Economics because I wanted to change the world. The dons liked the ex-service men because we wanted to work, and I slipped back into my former life.

I was lucky. Several of my school-friends were not.